I
MARCHED
WITH
PATTON

★ ★ ★

I
MARCHED
WITH
PATTON

★ ★ ★

A FIRSTHAND ACCOUNT OF WORLD WAR II ALONGSIDE
ONE OF THE U.S. ARMY'S GREATEST GENERALS

★ ★ ★

FRANK SISSON

WITH ROBERT L. WISE

wm

WILLIAM MORROW

An Imprint of HarperCollinsPublishers

HarperCollins books may be purchased for educational, business, or sales promotional use. For information, please email the Special Markets Department at SPsales@harpercollins.com.

A hardcover edition of this book was published in 2020 by William Morrow, an imprint of HarperCollins Publishers.

FIRST WILLIAM MORROW PAPERBACK EDITION PUBLISHED 2021.

Designed by Nancy Singer

Library of Congress Cataloging-in-Publication Data has been applied for.

ISBN 978-0-06-301948-5

21 22 23 24 25 LSC 10 9 8 7 6 5 4 3 2 1

CONTENTS

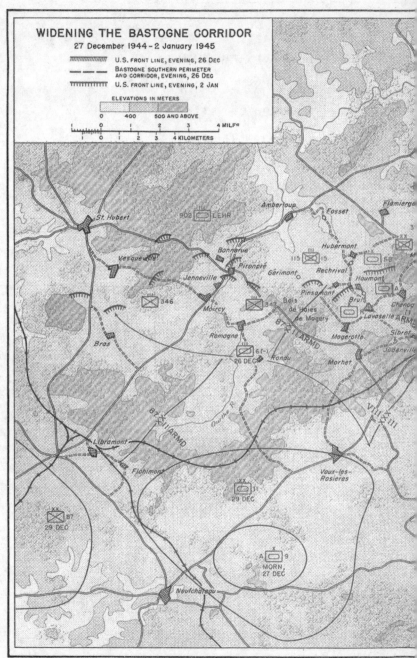

WIDENING THE BASTOGNE CORRIDOR
27 December 1944–2 January 1945

U.S. FRONT LINE, EVENING, 26 DEC
BASTOGNE SOUTHERN PERIMETER AND CORRIDOR, EVENING, 26 DEC
U.S. FRONT LINE, EVENING, 2 JAN

ELEVATIONS IN METERS

0   400   500 AND ABOVE

0   1   2   3   4 MILES
0   1   2   3   4 KILOMETERS

St. Hubert

902 LEHR

Amberloup   Fosset   Flamierge

Hubermont

Vesqueville   Bonnerue   115 115   56   Houmont   Rechrival

Pironpré   Gérimont

Jenneville   Pinsamont

346   Moircy   347   Bois de Haies de Magery   Brul   Lavaselle ARM   Chenog

Bras   Remagne   Magerotte   Sibret

87 II ARMD   Morhet   Jodenville

6(-1)
26 DEC   Rondu

Ourthe R.   VIII XIII

87 II ARMD

Libramont   11
29 DEC   Vaux-les-Rosieres

Flohimont

87   A   9
29 DEC   MORN,
27 DEC

Neufchâteau

D. Holmes, Jr.

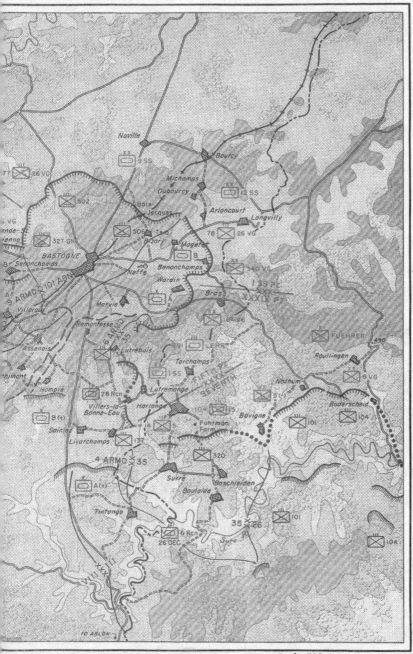

Credit: U.S. Army   *MAP X*

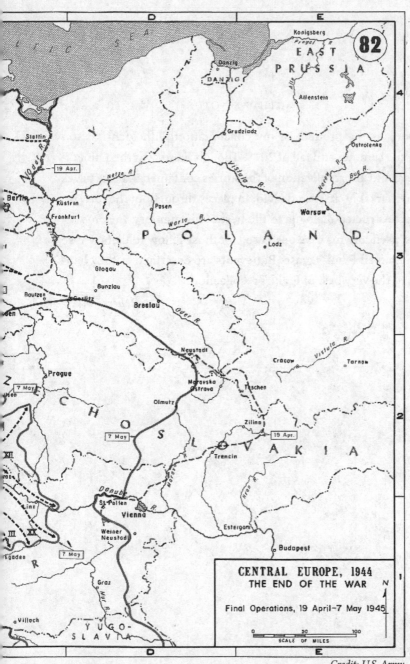

CENTRAL EUROPE, 1944
THE END OF THE WAR

Final Operations, 19 April–7 May 1945

SCALE OF MILES
0   50   100

Credit: U.S. Army

COAUTHOR'S NOTE

This book is the product of my collaboration with Frank Sisson during the summer and fall of 2019. Though Frank was then ninety-four years old, his recollection of the stories contained in these pages is still remarkably sharp and vivid. In places throughout the text, we have reconstructed dialogue to the best of his memory. In some instances, pseudonyms have been used for those fellow soldiers whose names escaped Frank's grasp. But events are described as they happened, to the very best of Frank's recollection.

—*Robert L. Wise*

I
MARCHED
WITH
PATTON

★ ★ ★

1

★ ★ ★

MEET THE MAN

Clouds of dust rolled across the dirt road, adding to the confusion of a traffic jam. A line of Sherman tanks blocked a military convoy bringing truckloads of American troops to the front in France. The vehicles and equipment looked like they were backed up clear to Texas. This particular crossing was a vital connection that had become a piled-up main road because of the heavy transportation needed to serve the outposts. The bitter wind made for short tempers. The two soldiers watched the traffic jam. Both men shook their heads.

The sergeant turned to me and said, "Corporal Sisson, you know how to make things work. Go out there in the midst of that mess and show them how the Six-Sixty-Seventh Field Artillery Battalion, Third Army, Tenth Armored Division does things."

"Yes, sir," I said and trotted out to the center of the snarl just as a tank commander popped up out of the turret to scream at a truck driver.

"Okay, boys!" I yelled like I owned the road. "I've been appointed the coordinator of this junction, and I'm telling both of you to move back. We got business with the Germans, and you're holding up the action. Now, move back *now!*"

The tank started to rumble backward, and the truck shifted into reverse. Once I got the vehicles rolling, I allowed a truckload of infantry headed for the front line to plow through. The boys waved a friendly salute as the truck turned to the north. Nobody had to tell me that the truck would probably come back empty or with bodies piled in the back.

While I didn't get there as early as some of the men who landed on Normandy, I knew what we were facing. The generals had nicknamed the breakout from the Normandy beachhead Operation Cobra. Air-support bombing had taken a heavy toll on the Panzer Lehr Division tanks working the area and knocked the Nazis on their butts. The Cobra assault bit the Nazis with a deadly venom.

Hitler's nefarious battle plan had relied heavily on the Panzer Lehr Division to spearhead shutting down the Allies' D-Day invasion. A general named Fritz Bayerlein headed the German tank assault and was known for his hard-driving command under General Erwin Rommel. Nobody had to lecture us that we had to stop this son of a bitch from killing our men.

"Come on!" I screamed at a jeep trying to fudge its way ahead of one of our Sherman tanks. "Stop right there!" I rammed my fist at the jeep. "Stay in line."

The driver halted.

The sergeant joked to me that they might promote me to head traffic cop, but I wasn't listening. Keeping the company rolling demanded my full attention. I wasn't trained for any of this troop movement stuff. I had to watch the drivers carefully, or I'd get run over.

The brisk wind blew snow in my face, and the temperature had to be way, way below 32 degrees. I had experienced cold weather back home in Oklahoma, but nothing like this. I thought my nose might fall off. Heavy engines propelled warm steam that helped protect my face, but the putrid smell nearly turned my stomach.

"Okay!" I shouted. "Keep it moving! No slowing down!" Truckloads of soldiers kept rumbling by.

I looked up the road and saw a jeep barreling toward me with flags attached to the fenders. Only one such vehicle was ever dressed out with those kinds of ensigns. This had to be the "big boys." I threw up my arms to stop all traffic.

As the jeep got closer, I recognized General Dwight D. Eisenhower, the supreme Allied commander of the multinational forces in Europe, coming straight at me. I looked again. With him were General Omar Bradley, and, sure enough, there was General George Patton.

Patton was taller than I expected, six foot two, and both sat and stood with straight posture. As they approached the traffic, the general stood up as if to get a better view of the traffic jam. He had the bearing of an athlete, and wearing that steel helmet over his white hair added to the sense of authority that he bore. Patton's face carried a stern, no-nonsense look. I could see his eyes surveying the entire scene with an intensity that wouldn't stand for any monkey business. To say the general was impressive, is to say the least.

With all the propriety they taught me in boot camp, I snapped to attention with the classiest salute I had ever given in my entire life. My backbone stiffened like a cedar board.

The jeep swerved by, with all three generals returning the salute. General Patton looked me straight in the eye, smiling like he appreciated the way I was directing traffic. I stood there in rigid attention until they were long gone down the road. Finally, I relaxed. I couldn't believe my eyes. I had just ushered along the top brass, and General George Patton had grinned at me. I could see that he approved of what I was doing. His slight smile struck me with an affirmation I'd remember all my life.

By this time, the traffic jam had cleared, and my job directing traffic was virtually over. I started back for the other side of the road when I heard a whistling noise far above my head. My reflexes sent me diving into the bar ditch. An explosion hurled dirt and debris in every direction. Another artillery blast suddenly took out three trees not a hundred feet away. The Nazis must have picked up on General Eisenhower's trail and started shelling the crossroads with everything they had.

I couldn't stay in the ditch, or I'd be dead for certain. I looked up and saw our infantry running in every direction. Twenty feet away was a panzer tank that had been knocked out earlier and was sticking halfway out of the ditch on the side of the road. If I could get under that hunk of steel, I might survive. I ran and took a dive.

Another artillery shell exploded in the middle of the field far enough away that I was still safe. I scooted under the panzer. To my surprise, I found another soldier with the same idea lying a few feet away from me.

"You all right?" I asked.

"I think so," he muttered. "Hell, who can tell?"

I stared. "A-Are you . . . Greg Cain?"

"What?" The soldier rolled over. His jaw dropped. "Frank? Frank Sisson?"

Another explosion shook the ground.

We grabbed each other. I had gone to high school with Greg, in Weleetka, Oklahoma. Now we had been reunited nearly five thousand miles from home. We hugged each other, and tears came to our eyes.

"Out here in this godforsaken French field, we run into each other!" Greg Cain kept shaking his head.

I just couldn't believe my eyes. What a deal! I had left England on Christmas Day 1944 and crossed the English Channel to land in

Saint-Lô, France. Of course, D-Day had already occurred on June 6, when General Omar Bradley's First Army landed. General Patton had flown into the battle on July 6 in a C-47 transport airplane accompanied by P-47 Thunderbolt fighter planes. He landed on an airstrip close to Omaha Beach. The general wasted no time in moving the Third Army forward and kicking the Germans in the pants. The Nazis still didn't know he was in front of them and assumed he would show up in the Pas de Calais area of France. By the time I got to Saint-Lô, I was sure the Germans had figured that they'd made a couple of horrendous mistakes, including trying to guess where General Patton was. So, here I was out in the middle of a crossroads, talking to an old buddy from high school while Patton's Third Army surged forward.

Another thunderous blast rocked the tank, and we hung on for dear life.

"How long you been here, Greg?"

"I came ashore on Omaha Beach on D-Day. Been sluggin' it out ever since."

"Got here later than you," I said. "Just came up from Saint-Lô."

"Listen," Greg said. "Sounds like the Germans quit shooting at us."

We both lay there, listening intently. No sound.

"Yeah," I said. "Guess they figured they'd done all the damage they could do on this corner. I think we can crawl out."

We scooted out and looked around. One of the shells had nearly smashed into the crossroads and left a crater that vehicles would have to drive around. The field was probably for milk cows, but the pasture had been fairly well trashed.

"I guess I better get on down the road," Greg said. "I'll never forget finding you out here under that tank. God bless you, Frank. God keep you safe." He started walking back up the road that led to the front. "I'll never forget you," he repeated.

"Keep your head down!" I shouted. "Bless you, brother!"

I watched Greg Cain disappear. I never saw him again.

My unit had run for cover when the barrage started. I knew I had to find them before they got too far away. I started walking and thinking. While trying to unravel a traffic jam, I had seen the top command roll by and give me a salute. I had eyeballed General George Patton! And then in the middle of nowhere, I run into an old high school friend. Who would believe it?

I started wondering how I ever got into this war.

2

★ ★ ★

EVER HEAR OF WELEETKA?

I was fifteen and a half years old and living the good times in Weleetka, Oklahoma. The town always seemed typical of the eastern part of the state, with lots of trees and rolling hills. Of course, Weleetka was a small town of maybe eight hundred to nine hundred people on a good day. The railroad ran through Okfuskee County and kept the town in business. We were just like all those sleepy little towns with a city jail and almost more churches than people.

Like every other kid in town, I lived a carefree life, milking each day for all it was worth. We'd go out to the railroad tracks that wound a hundred or so miles east to Fort Smith, Arkansas, and walk across the thousand-foot-long train trestle, hoping no freights were coming. One day I got halfway across when a big locomotive came steaming toward me from the other end. The best I could do was jump to the side, crawl under, grab a timber, and hang on for dear life until the train went rumbling by. Each day had some sort of adventure—until everything changed one spring afternoon. Stillness had settled over every room. Nothing stirred or moved. Mother stood by the window, looking out and saying nothing. A gnawing hunch that I refused to recognize churned inside me. My father had come down with appendicitis, and they took him to the makeshift hospital over the hill. I knew he was going to be all right, so I hadn't paid much attention, only going up there to visit him once, because my mother made me.

Mother turned around with tears running down her cheeks. "They waited too long," she said. "The doctor simply didn't act fast enough."

I sank down in a stiff-backed chair. "What do you mean?"

She slowly sat down across from me in the old overstuffed chair that dominated the living room. I could tell she didn't want to talk about this in front of the other children right then.

My father's appendix had burst, she explained to me, and peritonitis had set in. The infection spread throughout his body. There was nothing the doctors could do. No one had heard of antibiotics to combat infection at that time. My father had died two hours earlier, she finally said.

I bolted forward in my chair and felt like the room was whirling around me. "God help us."

I started to cry. For a long time, my mother and I sat there sobbing.

I knew that times were hard. The Great Depression had finally begun to abate somewhat around the country, but not where we lived. No one had any money, and jobs were scarce. Banks were going belly-up every day. My father was a hardworking man out there in the oil field. He was what they called a "pusher": a foreman of the drilling crew who oversaw various aspects of swinging pipes and cutting below the surface. He went drilling for petroleum every day of the week, but all we could do in this time of depression was survive. Now we were up against the wall. I knew that I was going to have to start making a living if we were to survive.

I suggested my getting a job at McAbee's Funeral Home, where I had helped out a few times, but my mother said we'd need something more substantial. She was too overwhelmed by my father's death, however, to know what that something might be.

"Mom, don't worry," I said. "I'll take care of everything."

"You're a good boy, Frank. A good son. Bless you."

I waited until my brothers came home. There had been seven of us, but my three oldest sisters had married and were gone. My sister Fern was two years older than I was, but I knew she'd depend on me just like the two younger boys would. They all came in the back door and sat down at the kitchen table. Nobody said anything. Finally, I broke the silence.

"I guess you know what's happened."

"The word's all over town," ten-year-old Buck said. "I heard two women talking on the street. That's how I found out."

Fern had found out at school.

"I don't know what we'll do," said Bob, who was twelve, sobbing. "We're already strapped. With Dad gone, nothing's certain anymore. Buck's wearing my old shoes that I outgrew, and we haven't bought new overalls in a long, long time." He kept crying. "I'm scared."

"I'm going to work," I said. "At least I can keep food on the table. I don't want any of you worrying about how we'll survive. I'm going to take care of everything."

"Frank, you're only fifteen and a half," my sister said. "Can you get an adequate job?"

"Well, I might have to lie about my age, but I'll find something. I know the WPA has positions of some kind. I'll just have to make some inquiries. Got to get out there and hit the streets. I just don't know." The WPA, or Works Progress Administration, was the government's way of putting people back to work.

"I heard the WPA pays thirty dollars a month for their workers," Fern said. "May Ann Smith's father went to work for them cementing rock to make a structure of some kind over there in Dripping Springs Park."

"Sure. I'll look into all the possibilities."

"How's Mother doing?" Bob asked.

"Not good," I replied bluntly.

Buck looked at me with fear in his eyes. "Are we going to have to go down to the funeral home to take a look?"

"You don't want to go?" I asked.

"I don't think so. Scares me to think about it."

"Don't worry," I said. "We'll cover for you in some way. Maybe none of us will have to go."

"Okay," Buck said.

"Mother's already gone down to the funeral parlor," I said. "As soon as she gets back, we all need to tell her not to worry. Everybody gather around her and tell her we support her with our whole hearts."

My sister nodded her head. "Certainly. Now, I think I'd better go see if there's any food in the icebox. Of course, I imagine people will be bringing food by. They always do at times like this. You know, those god-awful casseroles and all."

"I guess we ought to go sit in the living room and wait for her to come back," I said. "We can sit there quietly. I'm sure seeing us not fighting over something or other will be a shock to her."

We all giggled. We sure needed that laugh.

All seven of us children gathered around my mother as we walked down the aisle of the Pentecostal church. The old lady playing the piano pounded out the hymn "Abide with Me." My oldest sister, Ruby, had her arm around Mom's shoulders. Mildred and Faye walked behind them. The rest of us trailed at the rear. I could feel people staring at us. We slid into the front pew. They had already rolled the casket down to the front. Some of the oil field workers had chipped in to buy flowers that stood beside that odd-looking wooden coffin.

The church wasn't so old. It just looked worn. The unadorned white walls had taken on a touch of yellow, and the carpet was made of that cheap gray stuff that looked used even on a good day. With one pulpit in the middle at the front, the rest of the building appeared functional at best. The preacher, in his black suit, stood everybody up when we came in. He looked worn out, too.

The service turned out to be on the mild side, with no loud crying or the preacher yelling about going to hell. A lot of the local folks filled the seats. I didn't really listen to much of the Bible reading and what the preacher had to say. I stared at that closed casket and wondered what my father would have thought of it. The flowers and all this fuss. He'd always been a down-to-earth sort of guy.

At the end of the service, the piano player started up again with the hymn "In the Sweet Bye and Bye," and we all marched out to the graveyard. The preacher read some more Scripture, said a few words, and ended with a prayer. People came by to shake my mother's hand, and most started leaving. I stood there by myself looking at my father's casket as they slowly lowered it into the red-dirt ground.

Nothing would ever be the same again. The happy days of childhood were gone. No swimming up there at the Rattlesnake Mountains watering hole. Trying to outrun the train crossing the trestle was over. I had to step into Dad's shoes.

I had to go to work.

3

★ ★ ★

HARD DECISIONS

I could see no alternative but to go up to the high school and officially drop out. Everybody already knew what had happened to my father, so there was no explaining to do. The principal didn't say much, but he expressed his regret and hoped I would come back.

"I understand your situation," Principal Irwin said. "We're all sorry about what happened to your father."

"Thank you," I replied.

"We've had a number of students drop out," he remarked. "Some of the older boys signed up for the military and that war in Europe. These are certainly tough times."

I nodded. "I'm afraid so. Everybody is feeling the pinch."

"What do you think you'll do?"

I scratched my head. "Well, I don't rightly know. There's not much around here locally that pays anything. I've got to make enough money to sustain my family."

"Sure," the principal said. "The WPA doesn't pay much, but I've got a suggestion that might help you. There's a special opportunity out in Oakland, California. A quick course at the Okmulgee Tech School will teach you to weld. You get good at welding, you could probably make a hundred dollars a week. That would sure put some bread on your mother's table back here."

This was quite a lead. I closed the door to his office and walked out of the building. Principal Irwin's idea was the first bright light I'd seen so far. Alice Anderson was standing at the corner of the building, waiting for me.

Alice had been part of my life since the second grade. She had long blond curls that hung down to her shoulders and blue eyes that sparkled even in the dark. Her face seemed faultlessly shaped right down to a perfectly rounded chin. I always knew she liked me, even in grade school, when I'd see her eyeing me at recess. In junior high, her girlfriends left hints that I was the apple of her eye. Of course, I didn't pay any attention to that chatter, but . . .

Alice started to grow on me. By the time we reached our freshman year in high school, I started taking her to the movies. One thing led to another, and we soon thought we were in love, whatever that meant. The truth was that we were serious, and the romance bug that bit us wasn't going away.

"What did the principal say?" she asked.

"He's always a nice guy," I said. "Irwin told me about a possibility in Oakland, California, where I could make a hundred dollars a week."

"A hundred dollars!" Alice's mouth dropped open.

"Yeah. That's what he said. I could learn welding. The brochure Irwin gave me said I could help build ships for the war effort. Now, wouldn't that be something?"

"Yeah," Alice said slowly. "But you'd have to move to California."

"Afraid so. The trouble is that there's nothing around here. A WPA job wouldn't pay a third of that salary, and who knows how long WPA might last? Welding would have permanent possibilities."

Alice nodded. "Frank, I don't think I could live without you. If you go off to California, I'd die."

"Look, Alice. We both got to grow up some, but then we could get married, and I'd bring you out to California."

"Oh, Frank!" She stood up on her tiptoes and kissed me. "Wonderful!"

"We got to keep this under wraps, Alice. No one can know that we're going to get married until I've got everything worked out in Oakland. Right now, I've never been out of the state of Oklahoma, and California is a long way off. I must go out there and take a look at the lay of the land."

"Sure. Frank, you are wonderful. Just wonderful." Alice kissed me again. "I'll write you every day."

"And I'll do the same. We can make it work, but the putting it all together is going to take time."

When I walked in the house, Mother was still sitting by the window, wearing her black dress from the funeral. I sat down across from her like I always did, but didn't say anything. I waited for her to speak. Finally, she turned around and looked at me.

"What did you find out, Frank?"

"I got a good lead while I was up there in the principal's office. If I went to California after taking a course in welding, I could make a hundred dollars a week."

Mother stared. "You're kidding!"

"No, I got a brochure and everything. All we'd have to come up with would be the bus fare."

Mother shook her head. "Oh my, I don't know how we'd do that."

I thought maybe we could ask the four adult children to chip in. If they'd help with buying the bus ticket, I could scrape up enough to get me started out there. As the principal described it, the government was frantic to find workers.

Mother sat there wringing her hands. Eventually, she said, "Frank,

I don't know what I'd do with you being gone. You're such an important part of life around here. On the other hand, we desperately need that money. It's a hard trade-off."

I'd miss everybody terribly, but I didn't know what else to do. Mother said she would call the girls.

She got up out of her chair more slowly than I'd ever seen her move and shuffled over to the phone. My father's death had another effect that I didn't expect: Myrtle Sisson was turning into an old woman.

4

★ ★ ★

THE BIG TURNAROUND

I'd never been out of the state of Oklahoma, but as the Greyhound bus sailed through Texas and New Mexico, I certainly kept my eyes open. Highway 66 wound through all kinds of towns on the way to California. Most were small and didn't look that different from Weleetka. Each one had a main street lined with old cars and store windows filled with items they tried to sell to struggling people. Many towns didn't look too prosperous; I saw a lot of windows boarded up. The flat plains of Oklahoma and Texas blended into the mountains of New Mexico and Arizona. We crossed what looked like the most barren desert in the world and eventually wound up in Oakland. One thought kept returning to my mind. When I turned eighteen, I knew it was possible that I'd be heading to war.

Everybody on the bus talked about the fierce struggle with the Germans. Sounded like the Nazis were swallowing the entire continent of Europe. Poland, Belgium, Norway, the Netherlands, and France had fallen like dominos. Everyone everywhere worried.

I got settled in the Oakland area, and in no time at all, I was in the Kaiser Shipbuilding Company Shipyards with a protective helmet on my head and an acetylene torch in my hand. Day and night, I welded together sheets of steel to fit on the battleships we were preparing for combat. The sparks flew as my torch blazed. Working night and day, I quickly got to like it—and certainly I liked the money it allowed me to send home. If General Patton could have seen me sweating and laboring like a faithful trouper, he would have been proud.

Of course, the letters from Alice Anderson came thick and fast. She kept me up on the goings-on around Weleetka. Not much really happened, but she made it sound exciting. I read them and reread them. Of course, I kept sending replies describing the happenings in the shipyard.

It seemed like my mother was making it okay now. Myrtle Sisson had always been an enduring, hardworking person. Mother was practical and could stretch what was cooked for supper into two more evening meals. We had always depended on my father and never thought Estes Sisson would falter. Even two years later, I still teared up when I thought about him and what had occurred. The pain lingered.

In 1943, as my eighteenth birthday approached, I knew I had business with the draft board. Even though I was in California, my obligations remained in Oklahoma, but I thought I ought to let the locals in Oakland know I would be registering for the draft back home. The draft board people proved to be all business.

"Sir," I said, trying to sound as adult as possible, "I'm about to turn eighteen."

"Well, that's fine," the rotund registrar said. "We love having boys like you come drifting by." He chuckled.

The man kept chewing on an unlit cigar. His suspenders held up a pair of pants about to avalanche. The man's fat, stubby fingers clutched an ink pen poised to fill out a form. The guy wasn't exactly a poster boy for the military, but he was certainly ready to sign up anyone who walked through the door. He said coldly, "Give me your name and address, son. I'll start filling out the papers."

"I'm only working out here because of the Depression. Actually, I'm from Oklahoma."

"Oklahoma!" the man snorted. "Why, you're one of those prune pickers come out here to sweeten the pie. You gonna register here or in Indian country?"

"Oh, I'm planning on registering in my home state."

He switched the cigar to the other side of his mouth. "Don't you be playing any games with us. If you don't get your name on the dotted line, we'll come looking for you. You can't hide from Uncle Sam."

"Oh, nothing like that. No, no. I'm not afraid of the military."

"Well, I'm sure you know you'll be drafted immediately. That war with Uncle Hitler needs fine young men, and even some who don't look so fine. Since you been out here in the shipyards, you going with the navy?"

"Sir, I can walk a lot farther than I can swim. No boats for me."

The fat man laughed again. "If that's the way you want it, start learning to march. Okay, you get on your way to Okie land, where the wind blows free and the red dust covers farms." He switched the cigar back to the other side of his mouth. "Good-bye."

There was no point in waiting around. As soon as I registered, they'd send me off. Getting on the next bus back to Oklahoma seemed to be the only thing to do. I figured I could tell them that I wanted to go to Fort Sill, Oklahoma, for training, and maybe they'd buy that suggestion. If nothing else, I'd be back with Alice after almost three years, and I couldn't beat that opportunity.

My welding days were over.

5

★ ★ ★

COMING BACK—
IN TIME TO LEAVE

The big Greyhound bus pulled in to the Weleetka station, and people began debarking. I was halfway out of the bus when I saw Alice running to meet me. She jumped up and hugged me for what felt like forever. I could hear several people laughing, and one man clapped. People were watching.

"Must have just gotten back from the war," someone said.

"Good for you, son."

I couldn't talk because Alice was kissing me. Her blond hair swirled around my face.

"You're home!" Alice gushed. "Thank God, you're finally here."

I took her hand, and we walked away from the bus station. "Seems like it's been forever," I said.

"Oh, an eternity!" Alice hugged me. "Does your mother know you're here?"

"No, I wasn't sure when I'd arrive. You're the only one that I told."

"I been waiting for you forever. I sat there on that old wooden bench for at least two hours. I couldn't do anything else."

I stopped and kissed her again.

"Thank you for all those letters," I said. "They helped me deal with feeling homesick. Every now and then, the ache would come back. That's when I'd sit down and reread everything you had written."

"Oh, thank you for yours," Alice said. "I got the picture of what that Alameda wharf looked like. What you were doing. Welding on those huge ships and all. What an adventure!"

"I've got to put that behind me now. I've just turned eighteen, and the draft will ship me out immediately after I sign up. I guess I won't be here long."

"Please don't leave me again," Alice begged.

"Sure don't want to."

We stopped right there on the main street of Weleetka and kissed again.

On the surface, the town looked exactly the same. People still drove the same old 1930s cars because the automobile manufacturers were now making primarily military vehicles. The stores on Main Street were just like I'd left them. But something was different. At first, I couldn't put my finger on what it was.

It took a while, but I slowly realized that what was different was *me*. I'd left a boy trying to help his family survive; I'd come back a man who'd learned how to make his own way in the world. The calendar said I hadn't lived that much longer, but in my head, I knew that I had matured. The army would soon slap a rifle in my hand and send me out there to die for my country. If that wasn't becoming a grown-up, I don't know what is.

The local draft board proved to be far more personal than that one in Oakland had been. Though some memories were fading, people remembered my father, Estes Sisson, and still had a good word for him. I told them that, if possible, I wanted to do my basic training in Fort Sill, three hours west of Weleetka by bus, and it was arranged.

The family all came in to see me before I left for the front. Fern had become a grown woman. Ruby showed up, as did Mildred. Buck and Bob were no longer little boys. They all gathered around and slapped me on the back. Mother had tears in her eyes when she told me what the funds I'd sent had done for the family. Alice couldn't be there; she had left with her family on a long trip. Her absence was a painful omission. On Sunday, we had a big outdoor picnic, talking and laughing all afternoon. Nobody asked about what I'd do next, because they all knew.

Ruby was not only the oldest but also probably the most thoughtful. Finally, near the end of the afternoon, she brought it up. "All we hear on the radio is about the war," my sister said. "Sounds frightening."

Nobody said anything.

"Somebody's got to go over there and kick Hitler in the seat of the pants," I piped up.

They all laughed, and that broke the tension.

"What do you suppose you'll be doing?" Ruby asked.

"I'm going to Fort Sill, where they do artillery training. I suppose I'll be shooting them big guns. Can't say for sure, but they tell me that when I finish there, they'll probably send me down to Camp Bowie in Brownsville, Texas."

"What's the difference between a fort and a camp?" Buck wanted to know.

"A fort is permanent," I said. "A camp isn't."

We finished up on some apple pie Mom had made. Laughed a little more, and then soberness set in. Ruby hugged me and left with tears in her eyes.

"Thank you for all you done for us," Fern said, holding me tight. "God bless you, Frank. God keep you." She turned and hurried away.

One by one, they came by and shook my hand or thanked me. And then it was over. My homecoming had turned into an emotional exit. Seemed like I'd just said hello to Alice and then good-bye. Once again, Greyhound did the trick, and when I next got off the bus, I was in Fort Sill and a private in the army. The lowest of the low.

Just as the officials at the draft office had promised, after four months at Fort Sill, I went to Camp Bowie for instruction in shooting the big guns. We learned how to fire the cannons and also what we would be facing in return. At first glance, there seemed to be little difference between the artillery branches of the U.S. Army and the German Wehrmacht. The American guns were a bit heavier than their German counterparts and generally had a longer range. The German 105-millimeter guns were almost like the American 105-millimeter howitzers, with little difference in range of firing. They told us there were enough similarities overall between each army's guns to allow the U.S. Army to equip two of its field artillery battalions with captured German equipment and take advantage of the enemy ammunition stock captured in France.

Though the weapons were alike, we learned that our army had the superior system. American artillerymen did not try to combat the Nazis' artillery by building bigger guns. The approach from the beginning was to build a better system of weapons, and it was working.

We were so busy learning the details of how to fire artillery that I had little time to write home or send letters to Alice. They ran my tail off and had me doing more exercises than I knew existed. I learned all there was to know about rifles and communications. By the time I finished training, I knew I was ready to go to war.

The thought of joining up with General Patton's Third Army left me with eager anticipation. From everything I heard, this was the general to serve under. Only later did we get a clear picture of what had been happening with Old Blood and Guts, as he was nicknamed, during this time. To say the general's butt was in the sling was an understatement.

In November 1943 Drew Pearson, the famous NBC radio news commentator, reported that three months before, during the Allied invasion of Sicily, the stepping-stone to Italy, Lieutenant General George Patton had slapped two soldiers in two separate incidents. Everybody listened to Pearson on the radio. According to him, the men were recovering in a field hospital when Patton walked in. The general's hard-driving personality and lack of belief in the medical condition called combat stress reaction, also known as battle fatigue and shell shock, led him to berate and strike the men because they were away from the front lines without apparent physical injuries. Prior to World War I, the U.S. Army considered the symptoms of battle fatigue to be nothing more than cowardice—faking illness to avoid combat duty. Soldiers who reported these symptoms received harsh treatment. In Patton's mind, nothing had changed.

Apparently, the general was speaking to patients in the hospital on August 3, 1943, and gave the wounded his best. Then he approached a soldier who did not appear to be physically injured. The man was sitting slouched on a stool in a tent ward filled with wounded soldiers. When Patton asked him where he was hurt, the soldier reportedly shrugged and replied that he was "nervous" rather than wounded, adding, "I guess I can't take it."

Patton exploded and slapped the soldier across the chin with his gloves. Then he grabbed him by the collar and dragged him to the tent entrance. He shoved the soldier out of the tent with a kick to his backside. Turning to the staff, the general yelled, "Don't admit this son of a bitch!" Patton demanded that the soldier be sent back to the front and added, "You hear me, you gutless bastard? You're going back to the front!"

Corpsmen picked up the patient and brought him to a ward tent, where it was discovered he had a temperature of 102.2 degrees. He was later diagnosed with malarial parasites. Patton was heard by a war correspondent angrily denying the reality of shell shock, claiming that the condition was "an invention of the Jews." Word of that incident, and a second one the following week, spread, soon reaching Commander General Dwight D. Eisenhower, who ordered him to apologize to the men.

The public was appalled, but many defended Patton's actions. Some wanted him gone, while others stated dogmatically that "war was war—forget the niceties." The whole incident became a hot topic of conversation, with speculation that Patton would be fired. While the general eventually returned to combat command in mid-1944, the slapping incidents were seen by Eisenhower, George Marshall (President Franklin D. Roosevelt's chief of staff), and other leaders to be examples of Patton's brashness and impulsiveness. Patton's career stalled, as former subordinates such as Omar Bradley became his superiors.

I didn't know what to think about the report. All I knew about General Patton had been hearsay, but I had nothing but the best thoughts about him. He was certainly high on my list of people I admired. It sounded like Patton had gone way too far, but I couldn't worry about it because I had to get on the job.

Following the slapping incidents, Patton had been put on the shelf by Eisenhower. Even the Germans were surprised that Patton had nearly disappeared. The general's dream had been to lead the D-Day invasion, but he was buried down south in Sicily, in obscurity. However, General Eisenhower came up with a shrewd move.

Rather than can Patton as punishment, he used him as a ploy to deceive the Germans. The story was released publically that General Patton was to head a mythical "First Army." Fake facilities and equipment, such as inflatable rubber "tanks" and "planes," were assembled in England to make it look like Patton was preparing for the invasion of Europe. The Germans were convinced that when the big invasion inevitably came, Patton would be right there in the thick of it. In truth, it was just a diversion that contributed to German military leaders' misreading where the Allies would land in Normandy, France, on June 6, 1944. D-Day.

We learned later that General Eisenhower had been holding back Patton to fool the Nazis. In fact, they completely misunderstood where he was. The Nazis were convinced the Allies would cross in the Pas de Calais area because it was the shortest distance across the English Channel. Seven weeks after the Normandy landing, Patton finally received the opportunity to lead the Third Army into battle in Europe. Like a charging bull, he sent his men into a powerful confrontation with the Wehrmacht.

Of course, I had no inside information on what was unfolding while I was making the rounds at Camp Bowie. Late in the training, I was told I would soon be on my way to Boston to board a ship and sail for England. I was going to war.

6

★ ★ ★

JUMPING OFF

We had been in Boston about two seconds when they lined us up to board the ocean liner that would take us across the Atlantic Ocean. I'd hoped to see some of the historic sites, such as the Old South Meeting House and Bunker Hill, but, alas, there was no time for sightseeing.

At the dock, soldiers laughed and joked. Almost everybody smoked. We milled around in a holding pattern until the orders were sounded. Then 650 men started shuffling forward and marching up the gangplanks to the SS *Nieuw Amsterdam*. We kidded one another, but once we were on the ship, reality set in. No one mentioned it, but we all knew: a high percentage of us would never come back. The *Nieuw Amsterdam*, christened by Queen Wilhelmina of the Netherlands in April 1937, was the jewel of the Holland America Line. At nearly thirty-seven thousand metric tons, she was the largest liner ever constructed in Holland up to that time.

Four years earlier, on May 10, 1940, Germany invaded and bombed the Netherlands. Within days, the country surrendered, and Queen Wilhelmina and the Dutch government fled into exile in England. The *Nieuw Amsterdam*'s usual Rotterdam–New York trips had already been curtailed due to the war in Europe; the ship was traveling between cities in Venezuela when word arrived that the Netherlands had been attacked. It was eventually converted into a military troopship, painted gray, and its luxurious interior replaced.

The ship's first-class restaurant had a Moroccan leather ceiling with brilliant glass light fixtures and gold-plated columns. There were both indoor and outdoor swimming pools. The features on this ship were so magnificent that they could make you forget you were about to come face-to-face with death.

Crossing the Atlantic took eleven days because the liner zig-zagged through the ocean to avoid German U-boat submarine attacks. We knew the possibilities were high that the Nazis would have their eyes on any ships headed for Europe. I tried not to think about it, but when I closed my eyes at night, I drifted away while saying a prayer: "O Lord, if I don't make it through this night, please take my soul."

We finally docked fifty miles south of London several weeks before Thanksgiving 1944. All 650 of us marched into a large building that would be our mess hall. I don't know what the Brits were thinking, but the facility had limited toilets. Poor planning indeed. Certainly that created a little tension for so large a group. We were told to overlook such inconveniences because the military was planning a big Thanksgiving celebration for us.

However, one problem existed that no one had paid any attention to or recognized. The turkeys had been frozen, and then thawed out, and then refrozen—several times. Apparently, no one knew what happens when a bird is refrozen once, much less a number of times. They were about to find out.

The men filed past the serving line, having their metal trays filled with dressing, mashed potatoes, green beans, a touch of cranberry sauce, and, of course, turkey. We laughed, ate, kidded one another, and talked about home. Some of the men speculated about what we might find in France. We knew that the Normandy invasion, less than six months prior, had proved highly successful. We had not just held on but pushed the Germans back substantially. Turned out the Americans had made a penetration three miles wide and a mile deep on the first day. A few of the guys heard that Patton was roaring along and making the Germans pay for what they had done in France during their four-year occupation.

The Third Army had been reactivated to combat status on December 31, 1943, and shortly after became General Patton's command. Patton nicknamed the outfit "Lucky," and the name stuck. By March 21, 1944, the officers and remaining headquarters staff had been assembled. The army grew quickly as convoys from the United States came ashore. By May, the Third Army consisted of four corps divided into seven infantry divisions and six armored divisions. The total strength of Patton's command grew to 250,000 men. I was one of them, part of a developing force that would charge across Europe.

About forty-five minutes after we finished our Thanksgiving dinner, we began to feel strange. Some men complained that their stomachs hurt. Not a few doubled over, groaning and moaning. I, too, could feel a train roaring south of my stomach, and I knew where it was going. Men started running for the bathrooms. A mad scramble began.

Unfortunately, the line had already formed far too long for me to think I could make it. How I ever stood there and held on, I'll never know, but I could see the handwriting on the wall. Something had to be done fast. We were in the midst of a diarrhea epidemic.

I walked up to the sergeant. "Sir, you got to do something, or you're going to have a revolt on your hands. Every one of the six hundred fifty soldiers in this place is running to three or four bathrooms. The lines are stretching over the hill, and the men can't wait."

"Yeah," the sergeant growled. "I've been watching the problem. I'm going to see if I can get something done." He walked away quickly.

I sat down and laid my head on one of the tables, feeling miserable.

About five minutes later, an announcement came over the mess hall speakers. "We have requisitioned a tractor that is digging a trench out here in the field at this moment. It will be long enough in length to accommodate every soldier immediately. If you're not too proud, you men can line up along the side of that ditch and take care of your business. We're sorry about this imposition, but we can't do anything about it."

I thought God had smiled on us. We might survive.

The next morning, we were still limping around, but by afternoon, most of the men were recovering. I struck up a conversation with one of the sergeants.

"You saved the day by bringing in that tractor and cutting a swath through the field," I said appreciatively.

He shrugged. "What a mess."

"You got a picture of what's going on over there near the front?" I gestured toward the English Channel.

"Oh, you can bet that they're waiting for us," he said. "You see, the Nazis fell for that ploy that Eisenhower came up with to make them think Patton was running the fake First Army. They figured Patton had thirty divisions lined up near Dover. The Allies called it Operation Fortitude. When the big landing came at Normandy, we kicked 'em in the butt."

"Where do you think we'll go?" I asked.

Only later did we learn that we would end up in the Saint-Lô area. When Hitler invaded France in 1940, the Seventh Panzer Division, commanded by the celebrated General Rommel, entered Normandy with the objective of capturing the Port of Cherbourg.

The German army quickly occupied Saint-Lô because the town was a strategic crossroads. We had to hit the ground in France before we really understood what this meant.

"Interesting," I said. "The town must have gotten bombed."

"Oh, yeah!" the sergeant said. "With the start of the liberation, Saint-Lô suffered two attacks during the fight for Normandy. The first was the bombardment of the city by the Americans during the nights of June 6 and 7. The second was the fight for the liberation of Saint-Lô on July 17, during the battle for the area. This time the city was bombed by the Germans, trying to maintain their position to the south. Saint-Lô was almost totally destroyed by American bombing during a phase of the battle for Normandy. Of course, today we call that Operation Cobra."

"We're sure going to be in the thick of it," I said.

The sergeant looked at me intently. "That's the biggest under-statement of the day next to whoever thought this place had enough bathrooms for six hundred fifty men."

7

★ ★ ★

UNCOVERING THE FACTS

Throughout early December, we received information on what to expect when we hit the European shore. Some of it came directly from officers, while some was just gossip, but the picture was beginning to take shape. The bottom line was that our soldiers were marching right along, and our battle plans were working.

The army realized that a major advance south from Saint-Lô marching toward the Loire River could set up a charge into the Cotentin Peninsula, and this offered a number of advantages. The Allied armies would have a secure right flank. We were told that French hedgerows might give us as much trouble as any other factors. Apparently, these tall, bushy outcroppings were everywhere, and we had to maneuver through the thick entanglements that were used as fences. Front-line casualties mounted because of the problems in overcoming the Normandy hedgerows. First Army would end up requesting twenty-five thousand more infantry replacements as a result.

Still, we heard the Germans were getting it in the teeth. The rumor was that the German losses in France totaled almost two thousand officers and eighty-five thousand enlisted men. Apparently, the Germans could replace no more than 12 percent of their losses. On the other hand, we heard that the German Panzer Lehr Division was on the move, and these tank attacks were hard to stop. We weren't sure what to expect because it seemed like a good news, bad news situation.

But we took it all in stride. The 667th Field Artillery, Tenth Armored Division was ready to enter the fighting. We were instructed that the Saint-Lô area was a central point where the roads ran in all directions. Controlling the city and those roads was a key factor in maintaining the entire area. The Germans understood the significance of this city and those crossroads as well as we did. They weren't about to give up without a big fight. Four thousand of our men had already fallen. Ninety percent of those casualties were infantry. Looked like we were going be part of that struggle. We were standing around talking about the situation when mail call sounded. Of course, we dropped whatever we were doing to line up to see if we got any letters.

"Soldier, you got a letter from home!" the sergeant yelled out.

I jumped forward and snatched it out of his hand. Sure enough. Alice was updating me on life in Weleetka. I read it quickly, reread it, and then reread it again. The basketball team was winning and the oil field still booming. She'd seen my family a number of times, and all was well there. She ended by telling me how much she loved me and missed me. I read it again.

Some of the men had wandered into a small village nearby. The villagers seemed overjoyed to see Americans and treated us like the saviors of the nation. A couple of years earlier, the Nazis had bombed British cities and towns, leaving Londoners sleeping in the subways. They knew then that the Germans were knocking on their door and were scared to death about an invasion running over them. We were seen as a vital part of a crusade to stop their advance. Because so many of our soldiers were under twenty, the welcome felt like a return home.

An announcement rang through the entire hall. We were to prepare our gear immediately for deployment. The actual time and date
would come later, but we were on a standby basis. No one could leave
the area. I started arranging my canvas bag and prepared for the big
signal that we were leaving, but it didn't come. Time began to hang
heavy.

I sat there next to a guy who said he was from Philadelphia, and
the two of us started talking.

"What's back there in that big city?" I asked.

"Philly?" the soldier said. "Lots. Was born there. Of course, my
parents immigrated there in the midtwenties. We came from Russia."

"Russia?" I blinked. "Never met no one from Russia before."

"Oh, we had to learn the language and all. I was so small, I didn't
know much about my parents' struggles, but people at the synagogue
helped us."

"Synagogue?" I said. "You're a Jew?"

"Well, sure."

"What's your name?"

"Cohen," he said. "Eli Cohen. And yours?"

"Frank. Frank Sisson." I shook my head. "I never met a Jew before."

"You got to be kidding."

"No, really. I just haven't."

"Where you from?"

"I come from Weleetka, Oklahoma."

"Well, what kind of people do you have in Weleetka?"

I shrugged. "White folks. Of course, we have Indians. Lots of
Cherokees around our town."

"Don't they read history books down there?" Cohen asked.

"Unfortunately, I had to leave high school when I was fifteen and
a half because of the Depression. Had to feed my family. I guess I
never read any of that history."

"I see," Eli said slowly. "You have *heard* of the Jews?"

"Oh, sure. We studied about the Jews in Sunday school."

Cohen laughed. "We've come a long way since then. You should know that the Russian government and the Russian Orthodox Church went after us. Stole our land, took our money, and killed some of our people just because we weren't Christians."

I shook my head. "Boy, never heard any of that story. That's terrible."

The guy laughed. "I'm sure not an Indian, but we have lots of Jews in Philadelphia. People like us who left Russia because of the pogroms."

"Pogroms? Do you mean programs?"

"*Pogroms*, friend. A massacre of the Jews."

"Are you kidding me?"

The soldier looked at me harshly. "Check it out. You'll find that through the centuries, the Christians persecuted the Jews many times. They don't talk about that history much, but it's certainly out there. Reading that story will be worth your time."

"Wow! You're telling me things I've never heard of before. And they were doing that in Russia?"

"Hitler's doing that right now in Poland, Germany, and all over Europe. The Nazis are trying to kill our people."

I stared at this man from Pennsylvania. No one had told me about such a horrible thing as killing people just because they were of another religion. I kept rubbing my chin and looking at Eli Cohen.

"I guess we just never heard that story out there in Weleetka. I'll sure read up on it. That's an important piece to remember."

"Private, I got drafted into the army like everyone else in America, but I'm here because we know what they're doing to the Jews. You haven't heard much about it in the newspapers and maybe never in Oklahoma. The Jewish people have relatives trying to get into

America right now to escape the killing, and the Roosevelt administration won't let them in. Did you ever hear about that?"

I kept shaking my head.

"Well, that's a fact. I'm on my way to Europe to do what little I
can to save our people. The Nazis have been rounding them up and
putting them in camps. That's one of the reasons why I'm here."

I nodded my head and walked away. Why hadn't I heard of such
a thing? I felt completely dumbfounded. One thing was for sure: no
longer was I fighting just because I got drafted or the Germans were
running loose across Europe. I was also in this war to stop those mur-
dering Nazis from killing Eli Cohen's relatives.

8

★ ★ ★

CROSSING

On Christmas Day 1944 I started across the English Channel.

Christmas had always been a big deal at home. On Christmas Eve we'd go to a church and sing Christmas carols, and the preacher would talk about what happened on this very night so long ago. The little choir always sang "Silent Night" while someone lit candles all over the church. Mom would fix some hot potato soup, and we'd sit around speculating whether Santa Claus would come down the chimney, because we hadn't particularly been such good boys and girls that year. I knew for sure that Santa wouldn't be coming down my chimney this year.

"Okay, men." The voice over the mess hall's speaker system crackled with authority. "This is the big one. Won't be nothing like the trip over, where you lollygagged and acted like rich playboys. Won't take us long to get over the Channel. Once we get started, it'll probably be around forty-five to sixty minutes. You'll be on one of the ferries we've requisitioned for the crossing today. When we hit the beach, you must be ready for whatever is there. We don't expect the enemy to be around, but they can still fire artillery, and the Luftwaffe of the Third Reich can come swooping down out of the sky right at you.

Those Messerschmitts are a dangerous machine. You've been taught to pay attention. Do so!"

I could tell that some of the men had begun to get restless. A few looked almost terrified. The army had seen the fidgets before and wasn't taking any chances. Soldiers with their rifles loaded stood at all the doors. Nobody was going to have a chance to make a break for it.

I looked over at the Jewish guy I'd talked with earlier. Eli Cohen sat there as cool as a cucumber, as my mother always said. Cohen seemed to have more resolve than many of the soldiers around him. I guess his reasons for fighting were more personal than for most of us.

"Okay, men. Line up. The trucks will take you down to the dock."

We stumbled out the door, trying not to show our hesitation. Soldiers piled quickly into the back of the trucks. Talking stopped.

When we reached the loading area, I saw a military chaplain in an alb with a stole draped around his neck standing with a group of Roman Catholics, who were all kneeling. He had his hand in the air and appeared to be blessing the men. As best I could tell, a chaplain's assistant was moving among the soldiers passing out some sort of flat bread and holding a chalice. I wasn't a Roman Catholic, but this wasn't the time to quibble over church membership. I wanted in on all blessings that were going around. I'd need them today.

Near the back of the gathering of soldiers, I dropped to my knees and waited for the server to come by. The chaplain's assistant served me like the rest of the men. I started praying for my safety and well-being as fervently as I had ever prayed in my life. Men around me were doing the same, and I could hear them mumbling their petitions. I looked up, and the priest in the white alb placed his hand on my head.

"God bless you, my son," he said and moved on.

I took a deep breath and got up. I returned quickly to my group of soldiers already about to board. The 650 men started filing toward the large ferry. In no time flat, I was marching up the gangplank and into the ship.

By the time I got on deck, the inside cabin looked full. The whistle blew a long, mournful blast, and the convoy started to move. No girlfriends or wives were down there waving; the scene was all military. The port disappeared slowly into the early morning fog as we pulled away.

I leaned against the side of a cabin and wondered if one of those Messerschmitts might come dropping in on us. Not a pleasant thought. The wind had become much colder, and I wanted to get inside, but I could see through the windows that men had filled every seat, packed the aisles, and taken every conceivable space. I hung on and stood there shivering.

When the outline of the European shore appeared, I didn't know whether to be glad or worried. The biting cold had been getting to me, but on the other hand, I knew the far horizon would have smoke hanging across the hills. The ferry docked, and they hustled us off. Trucks were running and waiting for the 667th Field Artillery, Tenth Armored Division.

Instantly, I was in a different world. Everywhere I looked, everything around me had changed from the place I grew up in. Oklahoma had been a state for not quite forty years, whereas I could tell these quaint French homes—the few that were still standing—had been built hundreds of years ago. We quickly started down a winding dirt road. Many of the villas were stacked together in odd arrangements, like no one had planned anything. They must have just added on as the need popped up. Some of this jumbled assortment had gaping holes in their roofs, the handiwork of bombshells. I was sure that the local people were hiding from the invasion flying past their doorstep. No one was in sight.

We hadn't gone far when I heard the roar of explosions. I couldn't tell whether it was howitzers or German bombs, but the blasts sounded ferocious.

"Where we headed?" I asked a sergeant sitting across from me.

"Don't know for sure, but I think we'll stop in the Saint-Lô area," he said.

"I thought the town got leveled," I said.

"That's what they're saying," the sergeant said.

"What about the big guns?" I asked. "The howitzers?"

"Probably take a day or so to get them up to the front. Don't worry. The big boys will have something for us to do."

The men around him laughed. "You bet!" someone chimed in.

We had traveled about five miles when the explosions opened up full force. Sounded like demons from hell were after us, with the road shaking a number of times. The entire situation was quickly becoming scary as hell. However, in the back of my mind, I believed General Patton knew what he was doing.

We knew Patton expected his officers to pay attention to the health and contentment of their soldiers. Rations were to be a major issue for an officer. In actual combat, the officer should be the last to seek shelter and the first to move out. The general insisted that his officers watch for any signs of sickness or nervous strain. In other words, no matter how the ground shook, our well-being was an officer's top-drawer concern. Somehow that didn't seem quite as impressive when the ground was shaking.

As we bounced along, I thought about how Operation Fortitude had fooled the Germans. The idea had been to make them think our big landing would be in the Pas de Calais area rather than Normandy. Of course, I learned much of this later; often, we didn't get clarification until a significant amount of time had passed after the event. All kinds of elements had been employed to convince the Nazis that was where we were going. Because Calais was only twenty miles from the English coast, that beach was the most logical place to hit. Eisenhower's big gamble was sensing that the Germans never doubted for a moment that Patton would be in the thick of things on D-Day. But when the actual invasion began, five thousand ships and 130,000 soldiers came flying across. British field marshal Bernard Montgomery oversaw the seaborne assault as well as commanded the Twenty-First Army Group, made up of all Allied ground forces taking part in the invasion codenamed Operation Overlord. Monty had performed well. I knew we owed a debt to the men who made that initial, successful landing. As we bumped and jostled down that dirt road, I could only hope our assignment would prove as fruitful.

9

★ ★ ★

THE WAR

The trucks stopped, and the crew bailed out. Somewhere off in the distance, artillery was firing, and smoke curled up into a dark sky. We immediately began scouting the area to find a high point where we could hook up the wire lines that gave observers the best view for directing where our cannons should fire. No one seemed to know for sure where the front battle lines were, but it couldn't be far away. Out there somewhere was a dead man's land separating the combatants.

My job was to string communication wiring from high observation points back to the howitzers, so that their firing would be as accurate as possible. Once we got an area set up, our big guns could exact real damage on the enemy. However, the job wasn't done once the wire was in place. I had to maintain the line while the Germans tried to cut the wire every chance they got. The job could get tricky if a German sniper was hiding in the trees waiting for us to show up to repair a cut line. One shot would be enough.

If a line transmission went dead, I had six men working with me whose job it was to fix the problem. We'd start running down the raw wire. When we discovered a break, we'd examine how the wire was severed. A jagged break told us a number of things could have happened. If a tank ran over the line, it was torn for sure. A truck could have happened by and torn the connection loose. However, when we found a clean cut, we knew for certain that Germans had clipped the wire. In that case, we'd look for cover because a sniper was probably hiding in the brushes waiting for us to show up. That was one sure way to get killed.

We knew that the successful acquisition of Normandy and Brittany gave the Allies access to more than five hundred miles of French coastline with many port facilities. Immediately, men and troops had been rolling in. A month after D-Day, 500,000 tons of supplies and 150,000 vehicles had come ashore. Headquarters were set up for General Bradley's First Army that would be transferred quickly to General Patton when he arrived. By summer, the Germans still had not figured out that Patton wasn't in the Normandy landing or part of establishing control in this area. They were looking for him to show at Pas de Calais.

However, the security situation then was far from an established fact, with a number of Allied leaders still fearing the Germans might push us back into the sea. We had not taken as much land as had been planned. The Nazis had destroyed many of the ports while retreating. Not one working port had been captured yet, which meant that supplies had to come in through beaches and that limited the types of ships we could use. Moreover, the tides of the English Channel proved to be a problem. We had 650,000 German troops staring us in the face, and that was no small force.

What kept us in the battle was both the air and naval support that pounded the Germans and kept them at bay. Allied airpower broke up German ground movement during the day and even at night. It later turned out that the Nazis were surprised by the long range and accurate fire from our warships that remained off the coast.

I saw a sergeant walking toward us. I knew more leadership was needed and hoped he might have something in mind. I came to attention and saluted.

The sergeant shook my hand. "Congratulations, Private First Class Sisson. You have just been promoted to the rank of specialist."

"What?"

"You are now of sufficient rank to manage enlisted men under you," the sergeant said.

"But I haven't been here any time at all," I protested.

"In a war, the big boys are more concerned with getting the job done than they are about protocols. You'll need to be in charge of the six men working with you. They figure you can do the job, so you got picked by command."

I shook my head. Maybe there had been a mistake?

"Put this specialist SPC insignia on your uniform, and while you're at it, take a hike up that hill." He pointed to a rise not that far away. "If we stay here, we'll need to use that observation point for our cannons. Take some men with you."

"Yes, sir." I saluted slowly and immediately began fixing this change of rank. I hadn't expected any sort of recognition and didn't really know what to think. Here I was, a boy from Oklahoma, being put in charge of other men. Left me a little unsettled.

The men were standing around talking, smoking, waiting for something to happen. I didn't know a one of them. I walked up and said sternly, "I need six men to go with me up yonder hill. You can volunteer, or I'll select you."

"Well, look at that," a private said. "They've already promoted one of us to being the new boss."

"Anyone want to go with me?" I looked harshly at the private who made the crack. "That's how you get promoted."

He didn't say anything.

Several men picked up their rifles. "We'll go," one fellow said and pointed to his buddy.

A couple more joined in.

"Okay," I said. "Let's move out."

We walked to the turn in the road to get around the hedgerow. Getting through one seemed almost impossible. Now, on one hand, a hedgerow provided formidable cover. But once you broke through, you were exposed if someone on the other side was waiting for you. Obviously, they made a perfect cover for German machine gunners.

General Omar Bradley said these hedgerow landscapes were "the damndest country I've seen." Was he ever right!

Once inside the first field, we started advancing carefully by staying next to the shelter of the bushes along the side of the land. We got through two fields with some effort and could see that the top of the hill wasn't that far away.

"If we settle in this area with the big guns, we'll probably have to come back here and string wire along the edge of the field," I said. "We need to make note of where we are because we may well have to return this way."

The men nodded, and we started out again. After we got across the next field, we came to the base of the rise. The hill wasn't all that high, but it certainly provided a visual perspective on the area. The problem would be the bushes covering the area.

"I'm not sure I want to stick my neck out for a climb," one of the men said defiantly. "We could be sitting ducks up there on top."

I remembered what Patton had said. The man in charge had to be the first to go forward and the last to retreat.

"We're going up that hill," I said firmly. "When you boarded that ferry, you already had your neck sticking out. Let's go."

The guy smirked. But he picked up his rifle.

I started up the hill without looking back. I could only hope the men were behind me. This leadership business was new to me, and I wasn't real happy about being in charge of other soldiers. The truth was, I was barely over being a kid myself, all of nineteen, and now I was responsible for six other guys, but then again, I had no other choice. We got halfway up, and I counted heads. They were all there. We kept on moving. At the top, an outcropping of rocks provided a good observation point. The men sat down and looked around.

"What do you think, Mr. Specialist?" the soldier asked in a smart-alecky voice.

"I think this would be a good place to get your ass blown off," I said.

The guy looked surprised that I had called his cards. After that, he shut up.

We were surveying the scene and estimating how much distance this vantage point would give us when I noticed an airplane circling. I looked again.

"Doesn't look like one of ours," one of the men observed.

"I think that's a Focke—a German reconnaissance airplane," another man said.

"Yeah, and he's coming our way!" someone shouted.

The men hit the ground. Some rolled under a couple of boulders. They scattered.

The Focke-Wulf was coming straight at us. I guessed the pilot must have seen our movement. I slid under an old fallen tree trunk. The plane started firing. Dirt flew in every direction. The airplane mowed down bushes on top of the hill and then abruptly shot straight up into the clouds. The roar of his engines was deafening. We lay there waiting to see if he would buzz us again. He didn't come back.

The six men didn't move for quite a while. They finally got to their feet, looking a little shaken.

"Wow, that was close!" one guy said, brushing dirt off his pants.

"Far too close!" another guy said.

I noticed the smart aleck's face was white.

"Okay, let's get down that hill," I said. "The Nazis know we're here. No point in giving them any more shots. Let's move it."

We started back, with everybody looking tense. The men clambered down the hill in record time. When we got to the bottom, I turned to them and said, "Welcome to World War II."

The smart aleck stared at the ground.

10

★ ★ ★

MEET GENERAL PATTON

After the war, people often asked me about my opinion of General George Patton. I can tell you unequivocally that I admired the man. I don't know of any other soldier in our unit that didn't feel the same way. Sure, he was rough and tough, but we knew that he had our best interest at heart.

Did Patton have trouble keeping his mouth shut? Oh, yeah. Probably his biggest problem was popping off when he should have been speaking diplomatically. His quips not only got him in trouble but also nearly got him kicked out of the army. He just said whatever ran through his mind when he should have kept his jaw locked.

Everyone knew that Patton didn't like or trust the Russians. In his opinion, as soon as we finished off the Germans, the American military ought to turn its guns on Moscow. I'm sure that Supreme Commander Eisenhower worried Patton would start World War III before World War II was even over.

Patton's forcefulness was a sign of his tenacity and resolution, but sometimes it got him in trouble. One time was a speech he made to a women's group in England. Eisenhower had warned Patton about making public statements, but for some reason, Patton decided to

ignore the order. On April 25, 1944, he was invited to speak to a la-
dies' club in the town of Knutsford. Assured that his remarks were off
the record and wouldn't be reported, Patton praised the war efforts
of the British and Americans, predicting victory in the immediate
future. He *did not* mention the Russians, who sustained far more casualties than either Britain or the United States and essentially maintained the war against Nazi Germany single-handedly while America
was building its military during 1942 and 1943. It took two and a half
years for us to be ready to attack Germany from the west while the
Russian army was doggedly and courageously fending off the Wehrmacht on the eastern front.

The omission of this important component in the Allied Front
was seen as a rebuff to the Russian army and country. Around the
world, the response to Patton was harsh. Eisenhower sent him a letter registering his growing frustration with Patton's inability to exer-
cise self-control. Although Ike decided not to relieve the general, the
concluding sentence of his letter warned, "I want to tell you officially
and definitely that if you are again guilty of any indiscretion in speech
or action that leads to embarrassment for the War Department, any
other part of government, or for this headquarters, I will relieve you
instantly from command."

I think the soldiers in the Third Army understood the situation.
Patton had disobeyed orders, shot off his mouth, and jeopardized
cooperation. Eisenhower couldn't have it. We liked Patton the general, but not his from-the-hip comments.

On the other hand, General Patton believed that his speeches
and appearances before his men helped morale. He made as many
of these pep talks as possible, which everyone knew would be laced
with profanity. He held the viewpoint that you couldn't run an army
without profanity. Once he got rolling, the air turned blue. I wasn't
there when he delivered the following speech, but the words were

etched forever in the minds of the men who attended: "I want you men to remember that no bastard ever won a war by dying for his country. He won it by making sure the *other* dumb bastard dies for his country. All this stuff you heard about Americans not wanting to fight, wanting to stay out of the war, is a lot of horseshit."

That was just for starters! I picked up some of his remarks from the newspaper. The Brits particularly enjoyed quoting him. Patton would often end his pep talks with something like: "I'm not even supposed to be in England. Let the first bastards to find out be the goddamn Germans. I want them to look up and howl, 'Ach! It's the goddamn Third Army and that son of a bitch Patton again!' All right, you sons of bitches, you know how I feel. I'll be proud to lead you wonderful guys into battle anywhere anytime. That is all!"

Does that give you a little feel for General Patton's pep talks?

The men all got a bang out of hearing a general sound off like a bartender. They knew the press would pick up these verbal assaults and loved the impact his comments would have back home. Eisenhower wasn't so enthusiastic and told Patton to keep his opinions to himself without express permission from the top. Of course, Old Blood and Guts didn't pay attention to Ike's directive, and that finally got him kicked to the bottom of the stairs.

Colonel Leslie Cross of the Forty-Third Reconnaissance Squadron had been given a mission of occupying a five-mile front along the Moselle River, in Luxembourg, when he received word that Patton was driving to his headquarters. I learned from one of the attachés who was there that Cross wanted to meet the famous general but was also apprehensive about seeing such a lofty figure. The lead jeep arrived first, with two majors carrying tommy guns ready to fire. Next came Patton's jeep, flags flying. Snapping to attention, Colonel Cross saluted with precision. The general returned the salute and extended his hand. They broke into small talk. Cross was surprised that Patton was head and shoulders taller than he was. He found the general to have a most commanding appearance.

They went into the situation room, where Patton began studying their maps of the area and asking questions. Colonel Cross felt exceptionally nervous answering the renowned general's inquiries, but he did the best he could. To his relief, Patton agreed with his answers. They shook hands, took pictures, and then General Patton's jeep stood ready to leave. With a salute and a wave of the hand, Colonel Leslie Cross watched his commanding general's jeep disappear down the road. The entire staff, having experienced an overpowering moment, felt a sense of relief.

After all of these years, the image of General George S. Patton stays in my mind as a supreme example of fortitude, discipline, and determination. He inspired devotion. During the passing decades, history embraced Patton even with his defects. He was a man of contradictions. Patton was a swaggering, pistol-packing, profane man who was also deeply religious. While he could scream and shout, underneath he had a kind heart. In battle he could become hotheaded, even ruthless—but behind his impulsive actions was a studious and exacting military student.

At the end of the war in Europe, Patton wanted to go to the Pacific and fight the Japanese, but his requests were ignored, and he wound up the governor of Bavaria. Unfortunately, that assignment didn't fit his temperament well. During a press conference, he made an off-the-cuff comment comparing the Nazi Party with the American Democrats and Republicans. General Eisenhower immediately removed him not only from the governorship but also as head of the Third Army. He was assigned the task of writing a history of World War II. He had gone from the top to the bottom. In one of his last comments, he said, "I love war."

He truly did.

11

★ ★ ★

WINTER SETS IN

That night, after our reconnaissance up the hill, a blizzard blew in straight out of Siberia. Sometimes the Oklahoma winter sky would turn purple, and the snow drifted everywhere. But those winters didn't even hold icicles to what hit us that night. The temperature dropped to 70 degrees below zero. Yeah, you heard that right: we were going to war in minus-70-degree weather. The wind kept whipping up drifting snow, and I thought my lips would freeze off. We had on everything we could lay our hands on. I was under so many layers that I could hardly move, and even then, I thought I would end up a block of ice.

Strangely enough, the sky looked like it was ablaze. The winds of war were shooting up fire into that frozen sky like it was the Fourth of July. The fire in the clouds made a strange contrast to the blizzard on the ground. I worried that my fingers would refrigerate and turn black. I knew the cold could be as deadly as a German Mauser K98 rifle. Far off in the distance, we could hear cannons blasting away and the constant cracking of gunfire. We had to be close to the front line. No comfort in that thought. Terrible weather didn't slow down the war a notch.

I had no idea who the guy standing next to me was. I imagine he'd showed up from some other unit and been assigned to us. His lips were blue, and he kept rubbing his cheeks. The man's eyes appeared hollow and red.

Suddenly the guy whimpered, "I-I-I don't want t-to die."

"What?" I said.

"I-I'm afraid." The private could barely speak. "I don't think I'm going to make it."

"What'd you say?" The sergeant whirled around.

"I don't know. I'm afraid . . ."

"Shut up!" The sergeant snarled and slapped him in the face. "Listen, you son of a bitch! You're not going to die any sooner or faster than anybody else, and you'll not freeze to death if you keep your mouth shut. Now shape up and get tough."

The private kept blinking and started rubbing his cheeks.

"You hear me?" the sergeant shouted. "Stop it!"

The soldier abruptly had a shocked look on his face. "Y-y-yes, sir," he mumbled.

"Now, listen to me!" the sergeant yelled at the squad. "We're going to load up in a minute. Sit close to each other in the truck. You'll stay warmer that way. The convoy's going to get closer to the front, and then we're going to blow the hell out of the Nazis. Got it?"

The men mumbled their yeses.

An older guy I always called Mr. Dobson nudged me. "Here's an old worn blanket. Wrap your feet in it. Don't want your toes to get frostbite."

Randy Dobson was thirty-five, much older than most of the other soldiers. The average guy looked like me. Farm boys. Kids just out of high school. Nobodies. Most of us had never been out of the state we were born in, and here we were in France or Belgium or wherever the hell we were right then in this frozen countryside. But Dobson was older and had been around the barn a few times. He had a much better grasp of what was going on, and I wanted him to be my partner in whatever assault was coming down the road, so I treated him with a great deal of respect. I always called him Mister because that's what we called the principal at the high school.

The truck fired up, and we piled in. The gears ground with a roar, and we started bumping down the dirt road. I leaned over to Mr. Dobson. "Know where we are going?"

Dobson knew that we'd completely outfoxed the Nazis, and they were scrambling to readjust to the fact that we not only had landed on Normandy but had pushed through their lines and established ourselves. Today they were having to recognize that the First Army was pressing on toward Paris. Dobson imagined they were in a panic. Dobson knew we had to give General Eisenhower and old Monty credit for outsmarting the Germans.

"Sounds like the cannons are getting louder," I said.

"Oh yeah," Dobson growled under his breath. "We're getting there."

After a few minutes, the truck stopped, and the orders were sounded to pile out. The sergeant stood in front of the men.

"Okay, boys," he began. "The howitzers are already in place. Your job is to keep them firing!" he shouted. "Constantly! We're going to scare the living hell out of those German bastards and splatter them over the countryside. They thought they owned the European continent. Well, we're going to show them that they don't own shit. Keep your eyes open 'cause they got snipers that can shoot, and we don't want no dead men manning these big guns. Now, each of you select a partner. You'll cover each other's backs and make sure you keep functioning without a hitch. Pick your man."

Instantly, I grabbed Randy Dobson's arm. I knew I needed an

older man looking over my shoulder to make sure I didn't do something stupid and get shot. Mr. Dobson nodded at me and smiled. I knew I was hooked up with the right guy.

My father had always been my buddy. Those years that I worked in Oakland as a welder, I had missed him so often because he always knew what I should do. I could only hope that Mr. Dobson had those same smarts and cared like my old man.

"Dobson!" the sergeant called out. "You're in charge of this unit of men for the time being. You'll need eventually to find a place to bed down tonight. Some of these men will be involved in firing the howitzer 105s. Others will need to stand guard watching for snipers. We don't want no Germans surprising us none." The sarge looked around. "Everybody got it?"

The men mumbled a cold "Yes," and we began to settle in.

The sky had turned even redder, but at least the wind subsided some. The men started finding their places.

"Specialist Sisson!" The first lieutenant standing at the edge of the lineup of the big guns gestured for me to come forward.

I saluted.

"You boys need to know that we're not gonna need to string them wires at this location," he said in a Texas drawl. "I can see you all is a load of rookies. We're going to be shootin' so loud it might blow your pants off. Don't let the noise bother ya. That's just the outgoing mail. We're a-kickin' them Nazi asses. So, you kids be careful now, ya hear? That's just the message flying down the line."

I nodded. The Texan hitched up his pants. "You can help load shells into them howitzers. Once we start firing, we're not going to stop for the rest of the day."

"Yes, sir. Where's the ammo?"

He pointed to a stack of wooden boxes piled up at the edge of some trees. "Several thousand rounds over there. We're gonna start pretty quick."

"Got you." I saluted.

The shells for the 105-millimeter cannons weighed around 110 pounds each. Carrying them back and forth was not an easy task for one person. It was easier with two men. Our 155-millimeter howitzers were self-propelled weapons, which meant they could be moved relatively easily as the battlefield changed. From what we were hearing, the Allies were steadily pushing back the Germans. We knew our position was important and could make a difference.

Mr. Dobson looked at me and grinned. "Okay, tiger. You ready to haul those heavy shells alone? Or would you like a hand?"

"Are you kidding? Maybe the hard work will warm us up just a tad."

12

★ ★ ★

THE KILLING MACHINE

Once the cannons started firing, the rumble was nonstop. We tried to plug our ears, but you couldn't escape the detonation and the thunder. Constant bombardment drowned out even my innermost thoughts. Mr. Dobson and I supplied a stream of shells to the cannons as quick as we could carry them. All I could do was sling those heavy mortar shells toward the howitzers and the soldiers firing the big guns. The ground shook, and our teeth rattled, and after a while, even my legs started to get the shakes. But we kept at it.

In the fiercely cold weather, the barrels on the big guns got hotter than a firecracker. The heat felt like someone had turned on a furnace downstairs and left the basement door open. Maybe, just maybe, we wouldn't eventually freeze to death. By the late afternoon of the action, we had fired close to two thousand rounds. The sound became almost impossible to endure, but we didn't stop. I wondered how the Germans didn't go completely nuts.

When we took a break, Mr. Dobson and I walked far enough away that at least we could talk some, but the constant blasts made it hard to understand each other. The dirt road was snow packed but had withstood devastation from the ice. Seemed like a durable path.

We had to be careful that we didn't end up getting exposed to some enemy sniper waiting for soldiers like us to come walking out of the bushes. Finally, we sat down on the trunk of a fallen tree knocked down by the bombing. Mr. Dobson told me that General Patton had surveyed the road situation clear back to ancient times. Apparently, Patton discovered that far back in the eleventh century, William the Conqueror, then the duke of Normandy, studied the local roads to discover which trails were always usable so that he could travel in his war operations in Normandy and Brittany. To this very day, those same roads provided transportation no matter the weather or the circumstances. Strange as it might seem, nearly a thousand years later, we were on the identical paths and trails William the Conqueror rode down in his preparation to invade and defeat England and seize its throne. Patton obviously knew what to expect.

"Got any cigarettes?" Mr. Dobson asked.

"Sure." I pulled a pack out of my pocket and flipped one out.

We both lit up and leaned back.

"You know every time one of those hundred-ten-pound shells go flying off, we might have killed who knows how many men?" I said.

"War is a killing machine," Mr. Dobson said. "That's just the way it is. I'm sure the general knows that fact. Makes you either an atheist or a believer. I think most end up calling on God to pull them out of the ditch."

"You think Patton's a religious man?" I asked.

"Sure," Mr. Dobson said. "I understand that the first Sunday he was in Normandy, he went to a Roman Catholic field Mass. A slight drizzle had settled in, and they had to kneel in the mud, but the general was down there on his knees just like the rest of the men. In the background, the guns were blasting, and the sky was filled with airplanes and bombers zooming overhead, but the worship service continued on without a hitch. Patton stayed right there to the end."

"Interesting," I mumbled to myself.

But my mind was actually somewhere else. War pushes one to think about the ultimate issues—such as death.

People were getting killed everywhere, and I knew I could always be next, but I had found a passage in the Bible that spoke to me at such moments. I wondered if these words could make me bullet-proof. I know that sounds a little silly, but when you're looking death in the eye, you want something you can hang on to that might make a difference, and this particular Psalm seemed to have my name on it. I knew that when the going got tough, I could pull it out and read the verses. Comfort and solace resided in that thought.

Mr. Dobson got up and started walking back to the howitzers. I waited until he was down the road and then pulled out this page that I had cut out of a Bible. I read it again:

PSALM 91
Though a thousand fall at my side,
Though ten thousand are dying around me,
The evil will not touch me.
I will see how the wicked are punished
But I will not share it.
For Jehovah is my refuge!
I choose the God above all gods to shelter me.

I read those lines several times, and then I slipped the passage back into my shirt pocket. I knew no greater comfort and assurance than that promise. Patton had knelt in the mud. I was praying in the snow. "God, please be our shelter."

There wasn't much sun breaking through the winter clouds, which were edged in red from the fires erupting across the front lines. It certainly wasn't any warmer, and the sun was moving toward the horizon. Our unit needed shelter for the night.

Mr. Dobson walked up to me and shouted, "The sergeant says they'll be firing all night! Won't give them much time to sleep. We got to find housing for our men. He tells me it is safe to go back to that little village of Ciney, and we can use his jeep to get there."

"Let's go," I said.

We piled in and took off. In the distance, I could see the steeple of a village church. A few houses appeared as we got closer. The roofs were steep, with slate shingles and tall chimneys. Smoke curled up out of every one of them. Most looked like they were built out of rocks and stones gathered from the fields. The windows, most of them shuttered, were tall and narrow. Many of them had smaller rooms attached that looked like they had been added on decades later as an afterthought. The high-steepled church had bells, but the whole outfit was at the back of the building. The front of the church looked like it had just been chopped off. It certainly didn't look like anything I was used to seeing.

We pulled into Ciney central and could see townspeople pushing back their curtains and staring out the windows at us. The streets were empty, and I guessed that the locals weren't sure what we were up to. One older gentleman with bushy white hair came running out of one of the houses. He waved at us like he was trying to stop a train.

Mr. Dobson went over and began talking to him because he had some grasp of German. I could tell he must be the mayor or some official of the Belgian town. The man kept nodding and bowing as if Dobson were some exalted foreign leader dropping in for a visit. The man swept his arms around like he was inviting us to use the entire village. Dobson smiled and nodded as though he'd struck a good deal.

Finally, Mr. Dobson came back to the jeep. "Good God, I'm about to freeze my butt off. That character was the lord mayor, the *maire*. Name is Aleron. Arno Aleron. Says the village is ours. I told him we'd be bringing the soldiers in momentarily. They're expecting us."

"Where we staying?" I asked.

"It's a small cobblestone cottage," Mr. Dobson said. "Just up the street."

"Well, let's not dillydally. Too damn cold for any waiting around. Let's go get the men."

13

★ ★ ★

PARIS SURVIVES

When we awoke, the big guns were still booming. The night sky had almost turned into day, and silence had turned to pandemonium. Pellets of snow and ice bounced off the windows in dull thumps. I realized immediately that this quaint little room had a different smell. Not that it was unpleasant; the scent was more like the remnant of a thousand cooked meals blended together with smoke from the wood stove. The small cottage hadn't seen warmth in days, and last night made no difference. When I peeked out beyond the covers, a cloud rolled out. My breath had turned into a fog machine.

Mr. Dobson got up first and built a fire in the old stone fireplace. A little warmth could sure go a long way in making you feel human again. I pushed aside the feather-stuffed covers and slipped my woolen socks into my boots. Someone had set a loaf of bread and a hunk of cheese on the table while I was sleeping. A small pitcher of milk stood beside the plate. Probably the people who owned the house appreciated our presence more than I realized.

"Well, look at who finally woke up," Mr. Dobson said. "A true man of leisure."

I mumbled and groaned but didn't really say anything. Getting out of that warm bed, I hobbled over to the window and looked out. Several of our men stood outside talking. Something must be going on. With the brutal cold being what it was, I knew they wouldn't be out there long. Mr. Dobson had already sat down at the table and cut off a piece of the cheese. I walked over and sat down at the other end of the table.

The endless explosions throughout the night had made it difficult for both of us to sleep. We weren't sure of what was coming next or where they'd be sending us, but we expected to have our orders soon. All we could do was wait.

The wind had picked up, and the windows kept rattling. I didn't relish the thought of going back out there in the bitter cold. In boot camp, they'd told me that it was going to be a "hot war." It sure hadn't been that way yet. I'd never been so cold in my life. Dobson agreed that we picked the wrong winter to start a fight.

The door flew open, and the first lieutenant from Texas stomped in. He immediately rushed to the fire to warm his hands. "My God," he choked. "I'm turning into an iceberg."

"Yeah, doesn't seem to be warming up at all," Dobson said.

"You been around this war quite a while?" I asked. "How long you been in the fight?"

"I landed on Normandy," the lieutenant said in a straightforward way that still sounded bleak. "I was one of the survivors, and there weren't that many of us in my outfit that made it."

"So, you been with Patton all this time?"

"Well, sir," the Texan drawled, "we all heard that Patton didn't join the party until July 28. The story is that headquarters held him back to make the Nazis think we were going to land at Calais or some such place. The general got in trouble for slapping a couple of soldiers, but they used him to deceive the Nazis. Patton took control of the Third Army well after the Normandy invasion."

"I see," I said slowly. "Many of us been in boot camp and then went through training in artillery, and we don't know that much about what's been going on. We got bits and pieces but don't have a clear picture of how the war's unfolded. I heard Patton had driven clear to Paris."

The tall Texan took off his helmet and scratched his head. "Sure. I imagine the newspapers back home been having a time keeping up with the fast-moving story. Let me fill you in on some details. When Patton took the command, he started the Third Army kicking them Germans' asses like slapping fleas on a dog. Them Nazis didn't know what hit 'em. Why, in two weeks he had them goin' backward clear to the Loire River and moved beyond Le Mans. Beatinest thing I ever saw."

"Patton made that much difference?" I asked.

"Don't have to be a damn genius to conclude that," the Texan said. "By the time that campaign ended on September 25, the Third Army had cleared out the enemy from the Moselle River north of Metz and established beachheads on the north and south of Metz. We was knockin' 'em to death."

"I was getting ready for the war when all of that happened," I said. "So, you kept plowing ahead across France with nothing stopping you?"

"It was mighty tough fighting," the lieutenant said. "But we went after them to beat the band. The First American Army and the Second British Army made parallel drives across northern Europe and got onto the Belgian border. The Russians got across Bulgaria and started a new offensive south of East Prussia. If Uncle Hitler had any sense, he'd have seen the writing on the wall and sued for peace. We was a-coming after him."

Mr. Dobson nodded. "Must have been exhilarating."

The Texan rubbed his chin. "Well, I wouldn't exactly use that word, but we were making significant progress up until about September 25. Then we hit a big slowdown. That period up through November 7 was difficult for the Third Army. We found ourselves fighting with inadequate means and had to assume a defensive position. Seemed totally unproductive. The Germans weren't fooling around and sure weren't going backward anymore."

"What did you make of it?" I asked.

"The Germans bore down on Montgomery's Twenty-First Army Group," the lieutenant continued. "Old Monty spent his time working on the port of Antwerp. At the same time, the Russians entered Czechoslovakia and took over Budapest, Hungary. Seemed to me we were sitting out here twiddling our thumbs."

"You are telling me details I've never heard before," I said.

"Yeah." The Texan shrugged. "You learn more about what was going on after the battle is over than you knew at the time. Guess that's just the way it is."

"When did things change?" Mr. Dobson asked.

"About November 8, we got back in gear. The Third Army had never been a lethargy-minded bunch. The weather wasn't on our side, but we shifted into gear and were ready to move out. One thousand thundering big guns started the offensive, and we headed out through the fog, rain, and even flooding. By mid-December, we were aiming at the Rhine River. Can you believe that? The Rhine River!"

"Wow!" I exclaimed. "That's exciting."

"The Eighth Air Force sure gave 'em hell. One thousand bombers pounded the Nazis for three days. We were moving right along. Back on August 18 the Third Army had been only around thirty miles from Paris. Reconnaissance reported that the Seine River was filled with barges. We figured they were probably there to remove the Nazi troops from Paris. Our Supreme Headquarters in London sent out a radio message telling the citizens of Paris to be ready to rise up against the Nazis and that we'd be sending them a signal tellin' 'em when to charge. Now, wouldn't you think that might send Hitler runnin' for the nearest bathroom?"

Mr. Dobson and I laughed. The Supreme Headquarters, by the way, was where General Dwight Eisenhower, as the commander of the Allied Expeditionary Force, was orchestrating the war in the European theater. Later it would move to France, and then, in the closing weeks of the war, to Frankfurt, Germany.

"By August 21, the population of Paris went after the Nazis," the Texan continued. "Man alive! The Germans knew they better get the hell out of town. Turned out all those barges in the Seine River had been intended for the invasion of England, but the Germans couldn't pull off the incursion. The citizens of Paris were shooting from every corner in the city."

"And you were right there in the midst of it?" I asked.

"Isn't that somethin'!" the lieutenant exclaimed. "Third Army patrols rolled into Versailles. The only problem, we had come with the Fifth Armored Division when they advanced along the Seine toward Louviers. They were attacked on both flanks and caught some heavy artillery coming from across the river. That particular group of Nazis still had some fight left in them, but they didn't last long. Of course, the big story is what General Dietrich von Choltitz didn't do that saved Paris."

"Choltitz?" asked Dobson. "Never heard of him."

"General von Choltitz was the last commander of Nazi-occupied Paris. Hitler commanded him to blow the city to pieces. Interestingly enough, Choltitz refused. Explosives had been set all over the city and only awaited his pushing the button. The general didn't."

"Really?" I asked. "Why?"

"Several stories floated around. Apparently, Choltitz had affection for the history of Paris and thought Hitler was crazy. He turned the city over to the Free French forces."

Mr. Dobson said, "Helps to have the big picture."

"I'll tell you another interesting little story," the lieutenant said. "Elements of the Eighty-Third Infantry Division were working the area around Rennes and Orléanais. The citadel at Saint-Malo on the Brittany Peninsula fell, and the Germans surrendered. The rumor was that they ran out of ammunition, but that wasn't the real story. They ran out of water!"

"You're kidding!" I said.

"Naw. An enlisted man in the Third Army was taken prisoner and put on KP duty. He discovered that one of the Germans working in the kitchen had lived in the United States and spoke English. Turns out this German didn't like the Nazis and wanted to turn on them. He and the American opened up their water supply tanks and brought a shortage down on the Nazis. That's the real story."

"Fascinating," Dobson said. "So, when did Paris actually fall?"

"August 25," the Texan said. "See all the fun you boys missed out on by not showing up until Christmas? We was just tearin' the countryside apart."

The door burst open, and a major stepped in. "Lieutenant!" he barked. "Just got a radio report. We're moving out right now. Something big is going on. Don't know what it is, but you need to get everybody on the road. We're moving to the town of Erezee." The major turned back to the door and stopped. "And I mean *right now*!"

14

★ ★ ★

DISASTER LOOMS

By the time we got outside the house where we'd spent the night in Ciney, our men were coming out of their quarters and filling the streets. Trucks were pulling up, and the thoroughfares were filled with activity. Obviously, something big was going on. I walked to one of the sergeants standing by an M4A4 Sherman tank that had pulled in during the night.

"What's happening?" I asked.

The sergeant fixed me with one of those "None of your business!" looks, but replied, "Something important is unfolding up north. We're pulling out and going in that direction."

"Know what it is?"

The sergeant shrugged. "Nope."

I walked on. Generally, we didn't know what had happened until after the battle was over. That was just part of the deal.

Mr. Dobson gestured for me to come over. He knew we were going in one of those '43 Dodge WC63 6x6 troop carriers. They would leave as soon as the truck was full.

I nodded and climbed on, moving to the front, where space was vacant. The truck kept filling with men of the 667th Field Artillery.

"Okay!" the sergeant yelled from the street. "This one's full. Let her roll."

The truck started up and rumbled down the street. The locals were standing in their doorways watching. Some waved. Some just looked.

The men broke out their cigarettes and talked among themselves. I just listened. I was thinking about how we always followed along without knowing where we were going. I wondered if the German soldiers thought the same way. We'd heard they were highly regimented and disciplined. But I thought they must be struggling with the many defeats they'd been handed along the way. From 1939 to 1941, their army had knocked over every country in Europe. Now the average soldier had to know they were losing it all in a hurry. Must have been hard for them to keep fighting when we were crawling down their throats.

Mr. Dobson nudged me. "They are saying that the town of Erezee is some distance away. It'll take us a while to get there."

"Got it," I said. "Let's just enjoy the ride."

Mr. Dobson laughed. "You boys from Oklahoma sure are easy to please."

Our trucks rumbled into Erezee, which looked much like Ciney. Same houses, same streets, same quaint window boxes now filled with snow. The town seemed inviting except for the distinct barnyard smell floating down the street. Somebody was raising milk cows on the backside of those houses. The men piled out of the truck and dusted themselves off. The village looked secure. We lined up for instruction.

"Okay, men!" the lieutenant called out. "At ease."

The men relaxed.

"We're not sure how long we will be here, but find your quarters in any of these houses. The area is safe, but don't get complacent.

Keep your guard up. The enemy isn't slowing down. We may not be here long, so stay ready to move out."

Off in the distance, I could hear the rumbling of the big guns being driven down the back road. As best as I could see, we had moved the entire outfit to the north. I walked over to a lieutenant standing there.

"Sir, I'm Corporal Sisson. Been given charge of a three-quarter-ton truck, a driver, and six linemen. Our job is to hook up the telephones from a high point for observation and send reports down to the howitzers. Will that be needed here?"

"Don't think so," the lieutenant said in a Boston accent. "We may not be here long."

"Can you tell me what's actually going on?"

The lieutenant said that it all started back on December 19. General Eisenhower called a conference in Verdun, France, to deal with a breakthrough that Field Marshal General Gerd von Rundstedt and the Nazis had made, called Operation Wacht am Rhine, or Watch on the Rhine. General Patton had already speculated the Germans might well strike forcefully in the North, and they did. We were part of a campaign to stop this German offensive.

"Is it serious?" I asked.

"Damn serious!" the lieutenant said. "All of this problem was preceded by an assault on the VIII Corps on December 26. The Germans counterattacked in the Ardennes that day, forcing us to give ground. A little farther to the north, there was a heavy assault on the V Corps. Part of the problem was that the Ninth Bomber Command couldn't fly because of the lousy weather. The next day, there was increased activity, and some enemy penetrations had been made. That night, the Luftwaffe hit the whole front with strafing and bombing. Soon the reports came in about parachutists being dropped behind our lines. You can see that something was up."

"So, we're now caught up in this situation?" I asked.

"You bet!"

He continued, "The weather hasn't helped, and limited our ability to observe their buildup. Of course, it's been colder than almost any time in history. In the midst of these circumstances, Field Marshal Rundstedt came barreling in with a furious charge. We discovered that there were heavy rail and road movements around Trier and the town of Homburg. The Germans were bearing down. All of this was executed masterfully by Rundstedt. Got to give him credit. They say he's one of the top brains in the German military.

"From the information we had, it appears that we are moving our headquarters to Luxembourg to deal with the situation."

"You've been there?" I asked.

"Yes. I once met an American woman who had married a Luxembourg doctor. Her father was a professor at Harvard, and she was a graduate of Vassar. I understand the Nazis took him to Germany as a hostage. I fear for what's happened to her and their two children during the battle for that area. They may be living in rubble. The Fourth Infantry Division has been holding that ground where she lived. Bad fighting there. You must realize that the Nazis have been beasts, with no end to the atrocities they are capable of committing. The people in Luxembourg have lived in dread and fear of what their German conquerors might do to them."

"Yes, sir," I said and walked away.

Mr. Dobson was standing across the street talking to an old man and his wife. I could see they seemed to be particularly gracious and kept gesturing for him to come inside. Dobson was nodding, smiling. Finally, he turned and waved me over.

The couple were small and dressed like most of the locals. The man wore a blue smock that hung down over his blousy trousers. Simple but adequate. The woman's plain, worn dress hung down to her ankles. She had on a simple bonnet with thin strips of cloth tied under her chin to keep the covering from blowing off. Both had on wooden shoes with heavy wraps around their ankles. Even with shawls draped around their shoulders and upper bodies, they certainly weren't dressed for this subzero weather.

"Corporal Sisson, I want you to meet Monsieur Aubin Ganelon and his wife, Orva. We are going to stay with them."

I made a formal bow, and Monsieur Ganelon rushed out to hug me. I was taken aback.

"They are delighted to see us," Mr. Dobson said. "They speak English and want us to call them Grandpa and Grandma."

I laughed. "Okay. I can do that."

The old man and his wife clapped their hands and laughed.

"Come in." Madame Ganelon swung the door open wide. "Come in. We have a little glass of wine waiting for you."

We followed them inside. The small house looked much like where we'd stayed in Ciney. A large fireplace in the center of the front room already had a nice fire burning. The smoke stains on the kitchen walls rose to the ceiling, where burning candles and wood fires had etched black streaks across the timbers. Two little bedrooms were attached to the back wall. Even though the house was small, the space was plenty for us.

"You will like this wine," Monsieur Ganelon said. "The grapes are from a vineyard behind our house. We grew them ourselves. Here, sit down. Sit down."

Mr. Dobson and I pulled up to the table. Madame Ganelon set down in front of us two glasses etched with the designs of the forest. They were obviously the finest in the house.

I took a sip. The red, sweet wine had a nice taste. "Excellent. Please tell us about your family."

Aubin Ganelon stiffened. The smile disappeared. Grandma Orva's lower lip started to tremble. It was as if a suffocating blanket had been dropped over them. Quiet hung heavy.

"W-we had a s-son." Aubin could barely speak. "They lived across the street."

Grandma Orva sank into a chair. She bent over, covering her face with her hands.

"Th-three days before you arrived," Aubin said and then stopped. Finally, he began again. "My son and his wife had two children . . . an eight-year-old boy and a girl, five." He caught his breath. "Three days ago," he began again, "the Nazis forced their way into my son's house. They killed him, his wife, and the two children." Aubin broke down sobbing.

Dobson and I immediately got up and hugged them like they were our own family. We held them tight as they moaned and wept. We couldn't help it; both of us began crying with them. For a long time, we held them. Eventually we all sat down at the table together. No one could speak.

Mr. Dobson picked up his wineglass and held it aloft. His voice was steady, carrying a noble salute. "We drink to your son and his family. May God always bless their memory. *Respectueux. Tichin, tichin,* respectfully."

We each picked up a glass. *"Tichin, tichin."*

15

★ ★ ★

THE BATTLE BEGINS

When I awoke, no one had to tell me that the temperature had remained at the bottom of the thermometer. Funny how your body takes over first thing in the morning. I had to bolt out of bed in a hurry!

"Grandma Orva, do you have a restroom?"

She took me by the hand and led me to the back door. "Look," she said, pointing.

What looked like a million miles away stood a little house with a crescent carved on the door. Did I know the place? You bet. We had one of those out back in Weleetka, Oklahoma, with the same crescent on the door.

"Thank you, ma'am," I said and opened the back door. One whiff, and I thought my lungs would freeze. I took off running like a terrified deer. I am certain that I set a Guinness World Record for speed coming and going from the little outhouse out back.

Grandma Orva fixed us a breakfast, but as Mr. Dobson and I watched, we could see they were sharing from the bottom of the barrel. The turmoil of the war and the chaos created by the Nazis crashing through their town had left them with very little. I surmised that they must have hidden some of their supplies to have come up with anything. Still, they treated us like we were honored guests sent by the king. We had our own private food supplies, but we ate what they offered so as not to embarrass them.

Mr. Dobson and I had already discussed leaving all of our meal packets and supplies with the Ganelons when we left. We wanted to make their lives easier in any way we could. Hopefully, we could give them supplies to carry them through the tough days ahead.

We didn't bring up their son and his family again, and they didn't touch the subject. War spread death everywhere, but the losses in anyone's family remained private. They were too painful.

No further instructions had come in about what our next move would be, so we had no alternative but to wait. Around nine o'clock, the five wiremen that worked with my unit came over to check in and see what was going on. They were a friendly, joking bunch. Good guys to work with. Of course, Mr. Dobson was already there.

The first guy to arrive was Jack Postawaiet. Jack, from New Jersey, had trained as a barber before he joined the military, though that wasn't his occupation. The inflection in his accent told you he was from the East. I'm sure he thought I sounded like a boy from the South. Jack liked to talk and could jabber a mile a minute. He was excellent with a pair of scissors and kept all of us in good haircuts. I guess he figured that his nonstop storytelling made his customers relax while he clipped away.

Snuffy Smith came rolling in next. Snuffy grew up in Montana on a ranch. If there was anything he didn't know about horses and cows, I don't know what it could be. He must have grown up with a rifle in his hand. Snuffy was a crack shot and made a good sentry. He didn't talk much, like Jack did, but seemed like a soft-spoken cowboy. I had no idea how he picked up the name Snuffy, but I assume it must have popped right out of the funny papers.

Walt Brandon came in with Al Jackson. They had paired up earlier and stayed in the same house. Brandon's intent when the war was
over was to become a preacher. He was a really straight sort of guy;
the only cussword I ever heard him say was a "Damn!" when his finger got caught in a door. Hell, that wasn't bad, because everybody
cussed in the army. But Walt was honest to a fault. Didn't touch booze
and stayed away from the dirty jokes. He took a lot of ribbing, but I
respected him. After all, I always carried that passage from Psalm 91
in my pocket and a cross attached to my dog tags.

Now, Al Jackson really was a character. Al smoked day and night.
You'd have thought smoke was coming out of his ears. Jackson was
the Camel's king of the military, leaving those crushed cigarette packs
wherever we went. He wasn't much for work and never volunteered
unless cornered. If it was possible to avoid a job, Al knew how to do
it. His interest was actress Betty Grable, and he kept pinups of her
in every bag he carried as well as a folded-up one in his shirt pocket.
That one had been creased so many times, it was about to fall apart.
Al talked endlessly about how Betty was the highest-paid actress in
Hollywood and that he forgave her for marrying the trumpet-playing
bandleader Harry James instead of him. I had a feeling that by the
time the war was over, no one would want to hear anything more
about the box-office queen ever again.

The last guy to show was Mr. Parker. His full name was Faye
Pearl Parker, but no one had the nerve to call him Faye. Or Pearl.
That would be inviting trouble, since Parker was about six feet tall
and weighed around 225 pounds. Who wanted to get in a wrestling
match with him, much less a fistfight? Mr. Parker was losing some of
his hair, but that didn't dampen his attitude. He was as strong as a bull
and could lift almost anything. No one ever challenged Mr. Parker.

Each of the men already knew his assignment when we started

stringing wire to hook up the cannons to an observation post or to the company commanders' switchboard. Even though I was in charge, and a corporal when they were privates, I felt strange leading the group. But I knew I had to stay in charge.

"Anyone know where we're going?" Snuffy Smith asked.

No one did.

"I'd sure like to know," Snuffy said.

The men kicked the possibilities back and forth. Of course, none of us really knew anything about France or Belgium or anyplace else, really. Mr. Dobson was the only one who had traveled outside of his home state. I never had until I went to California.

Al brought up Betty Grable again and started wondering about her measurements. We'd already heard so much about her that no one wanted to go down that alley. Walt Brandon suggested that wasn't an appropriate subject to talk about and got booed.

We mainly sat around and laughed until the door opened and Sergeant Maddox walked in. Everyone jumped to his feet and stood at attention.

"At ease, men."

There had been another change of plans. Apparently, the Germans were pouring on the heat up there in the Ardennes Forest area encompassing Belgium and Luxembourg, as well as parts of France and Germany. Also, the scuttlebutt was that the British field marshal, Montgomery, had to be appeased. The fact was that old Monty seemed to be dragging his feet by not attacking. Anyway, it appeared that Luxembourg was going to become our headquarters, and General Eisenhower needed the Third Army's help in containing the Germans. They wanted us to hit the enemy with everything we had. Moving fast was now important. We were going to pull out, start up north immediately.

"The weather's about as nasty as it gets," I observed. "Can we move forward in minus-seventy-degree weather? I mean, think of the ice-impacted roads and—"

The sergeant cut me off. "We must. That's it! Any more questions?"

Mr. Dobson held up his hand. "Is there a name for the target area?"

"Yeah," the sergeant said. "Bastogne."

16

★ ★ ★

THE SKY TURNS BLACK

The men piled out of the quaint little houses they had stayed in and assembled on the streets. Time had lost meaning, and they weren't sure what the date was. Citizens of Erezee kept waving and applauding us. They were genuinely positive because they had experienced the terrors that the Nazis spread across the small village. Grandpa and Grandma Ganelon kept hugging us, thanking us for the food we'd left them, and wishing us the best.

I couldn't help but stop and look directly across the street where their son and his family had once lived. No light shone through the dark windows. A wilted, frozen funeral wreath still hung on the door. For a few moments, I couldn't look away.

Mr. Dobson and I hugged the Ganelons, blessed them, and walked away slowly. I took one last look and saw grief lingering on the old couple's faces. They waved affectionally as we left. I could never forget those two who had cared for us. They would remain symbols of what this awful war was about.

Trucks started pulling up, and we began to load. The six men in my unit rode in the same vehicle with me. We would have work to do when we arrived at our destination and needed to stay together.

The trucks filled quickly, and finally our caravan started down the snow-covered road. We kept waving from the back of the vehicles, and the citizens of Erezee kept saluting and wishing us well.

The trip turned out to be a slog: eight hours bouncing along roads full of potholes and scattered debris. It didn't take long to realize that we were getting closer to where the fighting had been intense. The freezing wind made us wrap mufflers of every sort around our faces. The weather seemed forever below what anyone had ever known.

"Look at that!" One of the soldiers near the rear pointed to a wrecked German vehicle that looked like it had been hit by a big shell. "God help us if one of those mortars comes our way!" A dead German soldier was hanging out through the shattered windshield and bent over the battered hood of a one-ton German half-track, a troop carrier with tracks rather than tires. He looked like he'd been frozen almost instantly. Blood ran partway down the hood and then seemed to have turned to red ice quickly in the cold.

The farther we went down the road, the worse it got. Body parts were hanging off trees like grotesque branches. Destroyed German tanks and vehicles lined the sides of the road. Some of the ugly scenes were covered with snow, but frozen hands or arms still stuck through the icy banks at odd angles.

The truck kept bouncing along without slowing for these disconcerting sights. Finally, we turned and drove past an ice-covered lake. In the middle of it, a dead German soldier was frozen in place, his upper torso standing up immobile. Our men stared at these scenes they couldn't avoid, almost uncomprehending of what they saw. No one, under any circumstances, should ever experience such sights. I thought some of the men might vomit.

I was tougher than most of the guys because I had grown up around death in Weleetka. Not only my father's death, but when I was ten years old, I had been around the local funeral home often enough that the funeral director had me help on occasion. Once, a drunk had stumbled onto the railroad tracks just as a train came flying by, mangling him beyond recognition. The funeral director handed me a sharp stick and a small basket and paid me to walk around and pick up what was left of the drunk. Wasn't a pretty job to get paid for, but I did touch the reality of death up close. While our truck jostled down the frozen road, I looked at those awful scenes in a more accepting way than some of the other men could.

One thought was running through the crew's minds. We hadn't lost a man yet, but they had to be thinking that losses were coming. Every soldier had to consider if he could be next. Would he be the first victim? Would a shell unexpectedly drop on us and take him out? Would a German Messerschmitt come diving into our location and blow one of them into a thousand pieces? Sure. That was simply the way of war. Good people got killed by bad actions. And none of us was exempt.

Eight hours later, we pulled into a clearing in the forest. The trucks stopped, and the men got out. Sergeant Maddox came around from the first truck, and the men knew to line up and stand at attention. The sergeant walked toward us with a no-nonsense stride that meant he had something important to say.

"At ease!" Sergeant Maddox began. "The Germans are pouring everything they've got into the area around the Ardennes and the town of Bastogne. We've come up behind them and are going to blow the living hell out of these bastards. Our cannons are being set up right now, as you can see. The Germans haven't figured out yet that we are here. So, you get to have a good night's sleep. Unfortunately, there's no houses around. It's gonna be tough. Dig in and make those sleeping bags work for you. In the early morning, we get down to business. That's all."

I watched the men look around. They were trying to find fallen trees, trenches, anything they could crawl under or into to keep the snow and wind off of them. Of course, the sleeping bags were waterproof and insulated, but the temperature was still down there at the bottom. Nobody wanted to think about what a difficult night was ahead of us. Men started building fires, and everyone huddled around the flames. There wasn't much talking.

An eerie stillness hung over the area. The sunrise nearly disappeared in a smoky sky that made the sun look like nothing more than a small glowing lightbulb peering through a gray haze. Snow had piled up again during the night, covering everything in sight. I wasn't sure what it meant, but I knew a major disruption was coming down. If nothing else, our howitzers would soon make the ground shake.

Someone had started a fire, and the men gathered around eating out of their mess kits. Keeping our hands bundled and trying to eat at the same time proved to be a challenge. We were finishing up when Sergeant Maddox walked up.

"I see you boys got a good night's sleep," he said sarcastically.

"Yeah, if you don't mind sleeping with a polar bear beside you," Snuffy Smith wisecracked. "I always enjoyed cuddling up to an icicle."

The sergeant laughed. "Don't worry. We're about to heat up the situation."

"What's going on?" Mr. Dobson asked in that more mature voice he always spoke with.

"The VIII Corps headquarters were situated in Bastogne with a ninety-mile-long front," the sergeant said. "Only three infantry divisions were holding things down, with the Fourth Infantry working the south side and the Twenty-Eighth in the center. Well, Rundstedt's troops came busting through like runaway bulldozers driven by madmen. The Fourth and the Twenty-Eighth were badly mauled.

The One Hundred Sixth Infantry was a new division with only ten days' combat experience when the Nazis came exploding through the front line. They got knocked on their asses. They had English-speaking soldiers in each unit that came charging at our lines yelling every filthy name they could call us over loudspeakers, trying to intimidate our men. They came in wave after wave of tanks and infantry, and firing with every possible weapon. They took no prisoners but shot our men who surrendered. An artillery observation post was overrun. Our soldiers were immediately lined up in a field and mowed down by machine guns. Those boys were a unit just like yours."

A grim silence settled over us. The men stared at one another.

Maddox continued, "Our men reported that many of the Germans were tanked up on dope or booze. They were half crazy and shooting everything in sight. Rundstedt dropped paratroopers behind our lines. They came floating down speaking English as good as we do. You think those Nazis weren't deadly when they walked up looking and talking like one of us? The entire conflict turned into a battle that could affect the future of the war. The situation is serious."

"What's the next step in all of this?" I asked.

"If the Germans can cut our front in half and drive to Liège and Antwerp, they'll be in a position to destroy our army," Sergeant Maddox said. "We can't let that happen. You men got to get out there today and help General Patton come up behind the Germans and stop this assault on Bastogne."

The men looked at one another. No one had to say anything more. We were staring down a German gun barrel. If the Nazis prevailed, we'd be looking at disaster. We couldn't let that occur. The sergeant saluted and walked off.

We knew the situation demanded all we had.

17

★ ★ ★

TENSIONS EXPLODE

Sergeant Maddox took me aside to discuss our current assignment. Snow continued to fall, and the temperature hadn't risen a smidgeon. We had to stand under a tree to keep from landing in snow up to our knees or higher. The wind had picked up, and the conditions were miserable.

"Corporal Sisson, we must get this wire strung as quickly as possible. Communications is vital at this moment. I want you and your men to climb that hill over there." The sergeant pointed to the highest outcropping of rocks and trees in the area. "We need to get this unit connected to headquarters as well as make sure we can identify who might come down that road. The Nazis are running loose, and we can't afford to let them catch us off guard. It'll be a while before we start the big guns, so you can get a head start. Get your men out there."

"Yes, sir," I said. "We'll start out immediately."

Sergeant Maddox saluted, then turned and walked away.

I walked back to my unit, waiting around the fire. "I've got the assignment. We are going to string wire from that big hill down to the howitzers." I pointed to the lookout area. "Headquarters wants the job done fast. Let's head out."

No one said anything. Snuffy Smith slung his rifle over his shoulder. Al Jackson tossed his first cigarette of the day into the fire and walked off. Walt Brandon, the aspiring preacher, seemed to be mumbling something under his breath. I figured he was praying, because he always did. Mr. Parker rubbed his chin thoughtfully but said nothing.

I could tell that each man was feeling the tension of walking into a possible trap. Sitting up there on top of an observation point made them a prime target, and they knew it. Before this moment, the war had been an idea. Now it was a cold, hard reality.

"Okay, follow me." I waved for the men to line up and start pulling wire.

We left the icy road and started through a field. Staying close to the border of the hedges and the fence line, we began dropping the wire into the snowbanks. Everywhere, the snow was at least several feet deep. Mr. Dobson was anchoring the back end. I was on the truck carrying the large spool of wire, and the rest of the men were guiding where it fell. The snow picked up again. Within a few minutes, the cold was getting to all of us. The only helpful thing the snow did was cover where the wire had been laid down.

The men started grumbling and cussing at one another. I knew their hands were cold, but much more serious, they were obviously worried about getting shot by a sniper hiding in the bushes or sitting in a tree. The crew was on edge, and each man's irritation had to be increasing.

Just as we came to the edge of the field where the incline started up the hill, Jack Postawaiet started yelling at Al Jackson.

"Watch what you're doing! You're going to get the wire twisted!"

Jackson stopped and stood up. "Mind your own business, big mouth."

"Listen, you son of a bitch! Don't tell me what to do!"

"Screw you. You don't know shit!"

Postawaiet threw his shovel on the ground and swung his fist wildly at Al. He missed, then slipped and fell in the snow. Jackson was immediately on top of him. The two men rolled over in the snowbank and got back on their feet. This time Jack popped Al in the mouth. They were slugging it out like two prizefighters.

I had to break it up before someone got hurt. I leaped off the truck and fell face-first into the snowbank. The blizzard had covered the ice. Snow heaped up over me, and I couldn't get my footing. I started crawling as fast as I could, trying to get back on my feet. The best I could do was crawl in between them.

"Stop it!" I screamed. "I mean it! Quit!"

I put my arm around one soldier and slid my other arm around the other's waist, pushing them apart. "What in the hell are you doing?" I shouted. "You aren't the enemy! The real enemy is out there watching you, you knot heads! Stop it!"

Each man took a step back. Their clenched fists opened. For a moment, they stared silently at each other. To my surprise, each abruptly dropped his head on my shoulder and started to weep.

"Look, guys," I said. "Take a breath. We're all under terrific tension. Don't take it out on each other. Now, shake hands, and let's get on with it."

They wiped their eyes and went back to pulling the wire. War can do strange things to strong men. It's not like in the movies. When you know that any second you can get killed, that singular fact wraps around your thinking and turns you inside out. Your emotions create fear. You get spooked, weird, reactionary. War simply does that to you.

Once we started up the hill, slipping became another real problem. The men had to grab bushes and small trees to keep their footing.

It took all of Mr. Parker's considerable strength to get the wire laid down and in place. We had to keep watching for possible snipers or German infantry trying to creep up on us, but we finally got to the top. The snow didn't let up.

An outcropping of jagged rocks made an excellent observation post. We hooked up the wires and got the setting ready for operation. With binoculars, I could peer far down the valley to see if the enemy was coming. The outpost was ready.

"Al, I'm going to ask you and Mr. Parker to man this position until they send someone else up here to take over," I said. "One of you can watch while the other stands. Keep changing the duty so you'll stay alert."

Both men nodded, and the rest of us started back down the hill. Halfway down, the big guns started firing. Fire and smoke immediately filled the air. Each time a blast went off, I could feel the tremor beneath my feet. We got back to the truck and returned to where we started.

A young lieutenant was standing there around the fire, apparently waiting for us to come back. We pulled up, and the men jumped out of the truck.

"We're hooked up," I reported. "Ready to roll."

The lieutenant nodded. "Good. See anything?"

"No, sir."

"Hmm." He rubbed his chin. "No tanks coming this way?"

"None."

"Okay," he said slowly. "That's good."

"Who you looking for?"

We knew the Panzer Lehr Division 130, led by that tough cookie General Fritz Bayerlein, was trying to ram its tanks down Allied throats. American generals knew they were on the move.

"Tell me more about this panzer attack," I said to the lieutenant.

"We understand their ultimate objective is to break through and attack Antwerp because this is the main entry point for Allied supplies, including oil. If the Germans can capture that area, they believe they will be in a position to force us to make peace with the Reich. Bayerlein is leading the assault. We suspect he is also heading for the Meuse River. This important river winds through France, Belgium, and the Netherlands."

"They're a strong unit?" I asked.

"We believe they've got five thousand combat troops with them and are supported by five thousand supply and support men. They are probably the best German armored unit in the Wehrmacht."

"Wow! We'll sure be keeping our eyes on anything that looks like that Panzer Corps."

"The weather's been so bad that it's kept our airplanes on the ground, which only complicated identifying where the panzers are going. If the clouds part, we'll be in a much better position to follow them."

Back on December 16 the Germans had come barreling down on the Allies and greatly outnumbered our men. The Germans were driving to open an avenue through Marnach, Luxembourg, and open a critical route through a small village called Hosingen. Fighting against superior numbers, our troops kept the Germans tied down in bitter combat. The Nazis couldn't get past our isolated outposts. The Panzer Lehr didn't make any headway. The delay that our boys imposed on them denied the Germans entry into Bastogne and gave no ground for the critical road juncture to Hosingen. Stopping them was a stunning setback for the enemy.

"So," I asked, "you're not sure where Bayerlein and his panzers are now?"

"Right. Keep your eyes open."

I laughed. "Are you kidding? The men up there on that observation point have been nervous as it is. I'm sure they'd scream like wounded buffalos if they saw a panzer unit rolling down the road."

"The other factor you must be aware of is that the Nazis are painting their tanks and trucks white. They've started putting their troops in white gear. In weather like this, with the snow still coming down on the snow-packed forest, white makes the enemy nearly invisible. Your boys up there in the observation station need to be conscious of this situation."

"Well, I guess so!" I said. "I'll make sure they know. By the way, Bastogne hasn't fallen yet?"

"No, our soldiers are paying an incredible price. The stories of their heroism would fill a book. This may be the toughest battle of the war."

"What are they calling this skirmish?" I asked.

"The Battle of the Bulge."

18

★ ★ ★

ROLLING ON—REGARDLESS!

My conversation with the lieutenant caused me to think further about this war we were caught up in. We had to be in an important battle with repercussions for the entire war. My unit may have been only a small piece of the action, but I still wanted to know more about what was happening around us. I set out to put the pieces together.

I quickly discovered the complete overview was still hidden in the Allied headquarters, and our job was to do what they told us. End of story. That's just the way the army and warfare work. Still, by talking to a number of people who came by our camp, I began to develop a greater sense of what had happened and what was going on.

Apparently, back on December 16 the VIII Corps was heavily attacked in the Ardennes sector and forced to give ground. Up north, the V Corps abruptly experienced brutal fighting. Because the weather was bad, the Army Air Forces wasn't able to get airplanes in the air. Nevertheless, the Luftwaffe began strafing and bombing the front lines. Our few observation planes that were able to fly over western Germany identified heavy rail and road movements in the areas around Trier, near Luxembourg, and, to the southeast, Homburg. Obviously, something important was going on in the German camps.

The German high commanders under Rundstedt had made a bold and desperate stroke and were knocking on our door big time. The entire 106th Division had been decimated, and the Twenty-Eighth Division battered. The VIII Corps headquartered in Bastogne had been forced to flee, and no one knew where it was. Because the Germans penetrated within a half mile of the First Army command post, the staff had been forced to withdraw its entire operation.

As the situation worsened, a special meeting was held at Verdun, where Supreme Commander Eisenhower and Generals Bradley and Patton reviewed the situation. I was told that Eisenhower asked Patton how many days it would take to bring the Third Army forward into the action. The lieutenant who told me the story said that Patton smiled and said, "Days, hell! We're already on the way!"

Just a few days before Christmas, they found the VIII Corps headquarters in Neufchateau, France. The 110th Infantry Regiment of the Twenty-Eighth Division had held on to the town of Wiltz, in Luxembourg. Unfortunately, the 109th and 112th Infantry Regiments were out of contact. The situation was intense. What was clear was that the Bastogne area had held on at all costs, although two regiments of the 106th Infantry Division were cut off and surrounded. It was feared that they all could have been killed or captured. It appeared that the enemy's effort was focused on Bastogne.

I had no idea what was happening back in the United States, but I believed that the parents of the men were praying night and day for their safety. I kept pulling out my Psalm 91 passage and reading it over and over. The silent words on the paper rang out loudly in my mind: "Though ten thousand are dying around me, the evil will not touch me." I kept praying, "Please, Lord. Make it so."

On Christmas morning, while we were in England loading up for our landing in France, near Saint-Lô, something amazing happened: the official military weatherman said he believed the next seven days would bring clear weather. I was told that the officers laughed because they hadn't seen a clear sky for nearly a month, and it seemed impossible that such a miracle could occur.

The weatherman claimed that an unexpected pattern was to follow. Two high-pressure areas were going to come together right over us. He believed they were of equal force and would bring clear weather until one of the high-pressure systems weakened and gave way.

And that is exactly what happened.

Call it what you will: freak of nature, luck, Providence. At that moment, when it was so critical for our airplanes to fly, the clouds parted, and the sun came bursting through at the exact moment we needed a clear sky the most. For seven days, our air squadrons blasted the Germans from the air, and our infantry battered them on the ground. Supplies were flown in and dropped for our struggling men in Bastogne. Food and ammunition came in daily. A large group of gliders landed with medical supplies and nine doctors. Absolutely amazing! The sky had parted like the Red Sea when Moses and his people needed to escape Egypt. The same salvation followed in Bastogne.

While this struggle was unfolding, the strangest story broke in the American newspapers. Apparently, the Nazi Ardennes offensive had caused a boom in the stock market. People seemed to think that the Germans might prevail in the Battle of the Bulge and make the war go on indefinitely. That would be bad for us, but perhaps good for investors.

On December 27, when we were barely figuring out what was ahead, the big breakthrough occurred. Combat Command Reserve of the Fourth Armored Division, along with soldiers in the Eightieth Infantry Division, broke through German resistance and pressed on toward Bastogne. The beleaguered defenders were overjoyed with the arrival of fresh troops. Trucks loaded with supplies and several ambulances came through on the first night. The only way the road stayed open, however, was through heavy fighting. Even though the end of the battle was now in sight, the struggle wasn't over.

Everyone I talked with told me that the fighting on all fronts continued to be fierce. Luxembourg was bombarded by eleven-inch long-range shells fired from railroad guns. A new type of rocket had also been fired at us and we weren't sure what it was. Casualties had even occurred at headquarter buildings. Nevertheless, we were re-capturing territory that the Germans had overrun. Our army proved just how tough it could be, regardless of the circumstances. Still, the campaign proved costly. At least 4,796 soldiers were killed and 22,109 wounded. The only consolation was that the German losses were worse: 32,000 killed, with total enemy casualties estimated at 143,818.

The town of Treier proved interesting. Like all these picturesque villages, Trier's appearance had been carved out through centuries. Rock-walled houses with slate roofs and smoking chimneys came straight out of a picture book. However, the people of this village didn't know whether to fear us or greet us as friends. The Germans had once occupied them, and the experience had been horrific. The villagers were waiting to see what we would do. They had been treated brutally by the Nazis.

We rolled into town and found most houses empty. Apparently, the owners had fled to the countryside. We started scouting out the village. Mr. Dobson quickly found a vacant two-story house that our unit could use. The house was clean and accommodated us well. The lingering scent of food cooked over decades offered a homespun feeling.

"Put your gear upstairs," Mr. Dobson said to me. "There's two beds up there, and the rest of the crew can bunk on the ground level."

"Sure," I said and started up the stairs. The railing seemed stout enough but had been worn smooth. Each step reflected a thousand footprints.

From the window of our room, I could look down on our encampment and see what the road might bring. The second floor made a good observation deck. I unloaded and came back downstairs.

At thirty-five years of age, Mr. Dobson knew his way around. The rest of us—kids, really—needed his experience. He soon had Al Jackson building a fire in the hearth in the center of the room. Mr. Parker carried in some logs for the fireplace and found several bottles of wine tucked away in the bottom of a kitchen cabinet. We were settling in as if this quaint house were home.

As the sun started to fade, we sat down at a real wooden table. Quite a change from our meals in the snow-packed woods and with icicles virtually hanging from our pants. The men laughed and talked. Everyone was relieved to be out of the cold. Snuffy Smith always came up with a few cornball jokes. No guns roared in the distance, and it almost felt like we were in America again.

"Tell me, Al," Parker said. "You got a girlfriend back in New Jersey?"

"You mean other than Betty Grable? Why, who could want more than Betty?"

"Little hard to be in love with that picture in your pocket, ain't it?"

"Now that you mention it, I do have three others!" Not pictures of Betty Grable. Girlfriends. "One lives in Newark, and another in Union, and the other in Maplewood. Just far enough apart that they never meet. Works better that way, you know."

The men laughed.

"Well, now just how deep do those relationships go?" Parker asked.

"Wouldn't you like to know!" Al quipped.

The men hooted and hollered.

"Now, take Parker over here," Al said. "You notice he never tells us about the women in his life. Come on, Mr. Parker. Tell us your secret."

Mr. Parker stiffened. "I got a girlfriend, you know."

"My, my," Al said. "Do tell."

"She's as pure as the driven snow," Mr. Parker said.

"And I'll bet about as cold!" Al quipped.

Mr. Parker's face blushed.

The men laughed again.

Suddenly an explosion shook the house. We hit the floor. Another discharge rattled the windows and caused the table to slide. The men scrambled across the room to grab their helmets.

Another burst knocked the door open, and freezing air burst across the room. Shells were falling all around us.

A minute seemed like forever; five minutes felt like an eternity. And then it all stopped, and quiet fell over the town again.

"I thought the Germans were out of this area!" Mr. Dobson exclaimed.

"Sounds like they's a-coming back," said Snuffy.

Mr. Parker crawled to the window and looked out. "Don't see no sign of the Nazis out there. No trucks. Tanks. Nothing but a couple of houses that got hit."

"Must be shooting those Panzer IVs at us," Walt said.

"We'd see one of them moving up if it was the tanks," Parker observed. "I think it's more long-range artillery."

Dobson agreed. "A Krupp K5 railway gun fires off big shells from its twenty-one-millimeter-long barrel. The shells could reach up to a distance of around forty miles. They may be shooting from way out there."

We waited awhile and then finally got back up to the table. Nobody was joking anymore. We finished up in a hurry and stationed a sentry by the door.

After the sun had gone down completely, we felt somewhat more secure, but we sure weren't putting any lights in the windows. You didn't have to look out but for a second to realize everyone in the town had the same idea. We wanted to be as invisible as ghosts.

As the evening progressed, we could periodically hear cannons firing. Somewhere out there, the Germans had the village of Trier in their sights. Maybe Mr. Dobson was right. They could be many miles away, but if their capacity to shell us was a fact, we remained in constant danger.

"How about a little poker?" Al suggested, deftly shuffling a deck of cards. "Anybody up for a little distraction?"

Everyone knew what he meant.

"Count me in," Jack Postawaiet said.

"Me, too," Snuffy added.

"We need one more player," Al said.

"Okay," said Parker. "I'm in."

They shuttered the windows so that no light escaped and hunkered down around the wooden table. Al had a flashy, theatrical way of shuffling the deck, and the game was on. I watched for a while but knew I was too tired to waste a good night's sleep in a real bed. After saying "Sleep well," I clumped up the rickety steps. I barely hit the bed before I was far, far away in dreamland. Completely gone for the night.

A soft voice kept whispering something . . . something . . . from far away. I wasn't sure where it was coming from. But it seemed to be calling my name.

"Frank . . . Frank . . . wake up."

I jerked. The voice was in my ear. I looked up. Mr. Dobson's face was inches from my own.

"Don't move," he whispered. "Listen to me."

"What?"

"You must tiptoe out. We've got to get out of the house. Now!" Dobson pointed to the middle of the room. A large round black projectile had lodged halfway through the floor.

I blinked several times and then realized that a 75-millimeter unexploded artillery shell was sticking up in the floor between our two beds. I stared up at the ceiling and could see a hole in the roof where the shell had burst through. I couldn't believe that I had been so tired that I slept through the crash.

As gently as I could walk without shaking the floor, I got through the door and down the stairs like a cat bounding after a rat.

"Get out of here!" I shouted at the men. "There's a shell upstairs about to go off!"

The men tore out of that house and into the street. We stood out there in the freezing weather that was as cold as any other day. This time we didn't notice. We could have all been dead.

19

★ ★ ★

STAYING WARM—AND ALIVE

Nobody had seen a winter like the one we were living through. The cold seemed to go on forever. The thermometer read minus-twenty-two, although we later heard some forecasters said it was even colder. I guess when you get that low, nothing registers right. The snow kept falling like we were at war in the North Pole. Even with the thickest gloves and socks, my hands and feet stayed cold. At first, I thought they'd find my frozen body out there in the trees, but with the passing of the weeks, I somehow adjusted to the reality that it wasn't going to get any warmer for a long time.

Even when the resistance was stiff, we continued to make progress. The Eleventh Armored Division in the west had contacted the Second Armored Division pushing down from the north. Troops of the III Corps had taken the towns of Wiltz and Diekirch—the latter less than ten miles from the German border—as well as cut the main highway in St. Vith, Belgium. This route was extremely important because we were closing in on Germany. The U.S. XIX Tactical Air Force had taken advantage of the now-open skies and really whacked the Germans, dropping 263 tons of bombs in front of our Third Army along the Our River in the Prüm area of Germany. Our bombers knocked out the bridge at Dasburg, giving the retreating enemy no place to cross the Our back into the Third Reich. We were hitting them from the air and pressing them on the ground. The Nazis were getting bottled up, their vehicles piling up near Eisenbach, and we were massacring them. The enemy was on the run. We were bombing them to pieces.

I've got to give the Germans credit, though, for putting up a stubborn resistance. They kept fighting in the north and the south flanks while their troop tried to withdraw. But by January 26, 1945, the III and XII Corps had taken the high ground west of the Clerf River in Luxembourg. Two German divisions were trying desperately to get behind the Siegfried line, Hitler's fortified west wall, away from our advancing troops. With obstacles called "dragon's teeth," this barrier was intended to stop tanks and motored vehicles. Once we took this area, we could look down on all the pillboxes and defenses supporting the Siegfried area without them stopping us.

I believed that when General Patton looked back on the Third Army's involvement in the Ardennes campaign, he would agree that it was the bloodiest fight of the war. Every inch of ground that was taken was bitterly contested. Back and forth we went. The Third Army would take an area and then retreat. The Germans would lose their position and then recapture it. But in the end, we ran over the Nazis. General Fritz Bayerlein's Panzer Lehr Division had roared in like a herd of dragons only to be repelled. The vital highway through Marnach and the critical route to Hosingen remained closed because of the fierce resistance that the Allies put up. U.S. troops denied the German attempts to take control of the Skyline Drive area, the ridge between the Our and Clerf rivers that would have led west to Bastogne. American tankers won the battle with the Lehr Division near Celles, Belgium. The German defeat marked the end of their drive to the Meuse River.

Our unit continued to move up the road. Nothing was slowing our progress. In fact, we often discussed why the Germans didn't throw in the towel and sue for peace. We were knocking on the door of their Fatherland, and at least they could have salvaged something rather than see us go on bombing and strafing across their countryside. We suspected that Hitler might be as crazy as their General Dietrich von Choltitz thought when he refused der Führer's command to destroy Paris.

Rolling on, we came to another town but weren't sure what its name was. The village had probably been pounded already by both sides in the war. Rubble was everywhere, and the streets filled with debris. The trucks of our unit came rolling down the central street. On all sides stood the charred remains of destroyed buildings. Many houses had been blown apart, but one little villa stood untouched: a beautiful chateau with two stories and open windows at the top. Perfect for us.

The men dispersed through the village, looking for places to stay. We left our gear in the truck and decided to explore the house first. Not one villager was in sight, so we could roam around unnoticed. We walked in.

Whoever had lived there had left a clean, well-ordered house when they fled. Much like all the houses, this one had a big downstairs living room with a kitchen and an open hearth at one end. On the other side stood a large fireplace that undoubtedly warmed the entire abode. I followed Mr. Dobson upstairs, where we found a couple of bedrooms. We could only hope that the rest of our unit had found similar facilities. We took off our heavy overcoats and hung them on a coatrack in the hall.

"I think we can go back to the truck and pick up the rest of our gear," Mr. Dobson said.

We carefully shut the door behind us to keep all the heat in the house. The truck we came in was still parked out front. We grabbed our shoulder bags and set them on the ground. Mr. Dobson climbed in to get his last duffel bag.

The electrifying roar of heavy artillery shook the ground. One hundred yards up the road, a detonating shell sent dirt flying. Another mortar fell in the wreckage of an already destroyed house. Pieces of splintered wood and shattered bricks fell around us. Without a second thought, my reflexes sent me diving under the truck. Bombs kept exploding with a deafening roar. I grabbed my helmet and crunched up in a ball. Another eruption pounded the street behind us.

I fumbled around in my shirt pocket until I found that little piece of paper with Psalm 91 on it. I read out loud, "I choose the God above all gods to shelter me." I prayed those words over and over.

The blast sounded like it was only yards away. Fortunately, I'd clapped my hands over my ears, but I still couldn't hear for at least a minute. The roar began to fade, and the rumble of boards hitting the ground and walls cratering slipped away. The bombing stopped.

After a few minutes, I crawled out from under the truck. I stared in disbelief. The entire top floor of our little *la maison* was gone. It had been completely blown away; our heavy overcoats cremated. I stood there staring.

Mr. Dobson hopped out of the truck and shook his head.

"What if we'd been in there?" I said.

Dobson kept shaking his head, saying nothing.

20

★ ★ ★

OUTMANEUVERING
THE ENEMY

General Patton always said that the last great battle would be fought west of the Rhine. His conviction was that if the bulk of the German army could be captured west of the great river—which forms a natural border with part of eastern France but, as you go farther north, slices as much as a hundred miles into western Germany—only isolated military groups would be left to the east, and the rest of the conflict wouldn't prove difficult. He seemed to be out to make his point.

Patton's skill had already been confirmed. Despite everything, German General Hasso von Manteuffel's Fifth Panzer Army was making one last desperate attempt to take Bastogne. The Luftwaffe came blasting in on New Year's Day. Of course, for us New Year's was just another day with no celebrations. Unfortunately for them, Patton's tanks came rolling in and beat back the assault. Patton's sudden, unexpected arrival after having crossed a hundred miles had saved the day and virtually ended the German threat.

Following that encounter, we kept moving our troops back and forth across the battle plain in every possible direction. Our unit had little time to waste as our position seemed to be always on the move. The big guns would aim to the north and then suddenly shift to the east. Just about when the Germans were sure the Third Army was going to hit them in the center, we'd strike at one of their flanks. Back and forth, up and down, the Wehrmacht had no idea when or where we were coming from.

The enemy remained confounded by Patton's strategy. The Nazis would be sure we were going to try an end run around them, only to discover that we came right down the middle. Of course, they couldn't position their reserves correctly, and it left them vulnerable. I'm sure they must have thought they were chasing ghosts in a game that they lost every time.

Our troops broke through directly to the east and covered more than sixty miles, ending up on the edge of the Rhine. General Patton then dispatched two corps through that opening. He immediately regrouped the troops and sent the two corps south. The result again caught the Nazis off guard, and we overran their supply dumps. When the troops reversed course yet again, they cornered the Germans between two giant pincers. We either killed or captured practically all of their troops caught in that ploy. The Nazis were running scared.

By the end of January, elements of the Third Army had crossed the Our River and were inside Germany. We captured the town of Sinz and were facing the Siegfried line. Sinz, however, proved to be somewhat of an ordeal.

The battle went from house to house, with fighting in the streets and through shattered windows. The Nazis kept firing small mortars at us, but our troops didn't retreat. The exchange was intense; men crawled behind any barriers they could find to keep from getting hit. Our boys didn't back down an inch and kept working their way through the back alleys and down the narrow streets. The Germans kept retreating and were eventually pushed out of the town.

With snow everywhere, the world seemed to have turned white. The color of the day had become white, and that realization wasn't lost on the Germans. We had already lived through the infiltration of our lines by Nazis wearing our uniforms and speaking good English. When such a German soldier was caught in one of our outfits, he was shot by a firing squad. The raids were commanded by one scary guy, Otto Skorzeny. The lieutenant colonel had a formidable reputation. A member of the SS, the political assassination arm of Hitler, he had been part of the rescue of Benito Mussolini earlier. Nazis who came strolling in in those albino outfits were walking murder machines.

As the Germans retreated, they left minefields that our soldiers had to uncover and detonate. The work was delicate and took a soldier with trained hands. When they retreated, one could bet that a trail of mines followed them. By this point, the Germans were short of manpower and equipment. They no longer had an effective defense but were compensating with those road mines. We just kept moving.

Crawling through a bombed-out and destroyed town like Sinz and the many other villages we worked our way through left an impression that wasn't going away. The roofs of once quaint houses and buildings were now nothing but craters with timbers sticking out the front like bundles of scattered toothpicks. Windows were empty holes in the remnants of the once-proud stone walls. Pieces of what were once white fences were intermingled with rocks, bricks, and hunks of broken cement. Next to a deserted hovel might stand an ornate building completely untouched. What the propaganda of the U.S. War Department never told anyone was that when those bombs fall, they hit everything and everyone underneath. Sure, they hit enemy installations, but they also destroy innocent lives. That's simply what war does.

Meanwhile, the German propaganda machine resounded with radio voices such as "Axis Sally" telling us that their previous losses were meaningless. Axis Sally was a woman who spoke English as perfectly as if she was from, say, Portland, Maine. Which, we later found out, she was! As we'd speculated, she was betraying her country in service to the Nazi regime as a propaganda-warfare operative. Her real name, it turned out, was Mildred Gillars. In her broadcasts, she kept predicting that a "great secret weapon" was coming that would allow Hitler to wipe us out in one fell swoop. Honestly, after awhile, Sally's little chats became humorous. She was telling us how badly we were getting beaten while we were marching toward her doorstep. Captured after the war and sentenced to prison, she moved to Columbus, Ohio, when released and died there at the age of eighty-seven.

The truth was that many of the German people were struggling to avoid starvation. Food was scarce, and the Nazis carried off what they could find. When the doughboys showed up with chocolate bars, they were mobbed by the citizens—who quickly discovered we were a benevolent crew.

The Germans had camouflaged many of their forts to look like ordinary farmhouses and barns. Behind the wooden barn doors and frame façades stood walls of steel and concrete four to six feet thick. The actual doors were heavy steel that couldn't be opened except with a burst from a bazooka. These fortifications made excellent fronts from which to blast away at us as we poured in. The only way to take these facilities was with hand-to-hand fighting. The Germans always built with accuracy and thoroughness, which made these structures appear to stand forever. You have to hand it to them, the Germans paid attention down to the last detail.

As we moved down these ancient roads, we saw plenty of fallen German soldiers who'd been left behind by their comrades. I saw one

German soldier crumpled up in a depression where a cliff dropped off. He had been shooting an antitank rocket launcher called a *panzerschreck*. Somewhere in the conflict, we had hit him. He couldn't have been dead very long. Not far away, a German machine gunner was lying facedown in the snow. His German MP 38 submachine gun stood in the snowpack beside him. The weapon could fire five hundred rounds per minute. The German looked like he might have ducked to avoid a bullet and got shot anyway. Snow had already begun to blow over his body.

We were sitting in one of those charming, picturesque little houses, keeping our feet and hands warm by the fire in the hearth and waiting for the trucks to arrive to pick us up. As always, Al Jackson had already smoked a cigarette or two and was starting in on the next round.

Snuffy Smith had that silly grin on his face that meant something was whirling around in his brain, but nobody could be sure what it was. He pulled out one of his own cigarettes and looked at Jackson.

"Tell me, Al," Snuffy began. "Have you looked at that Betty Grable picture this morning yet?"

"Of course," Al said. "I always start the day with Betty."

"What's so special about her?" Snuffy asked.

"It's them legs," Al said. "Ain't no woman in the world got legs like Betty Grable."

The men laughed.

Snuffy turned to Walt Brandon. "You're our preacher boy. Actually, Wes, I see you as being like a good luck charm in my pocket. The man upstairs ain't gonna strike us down as long as we got one of his boys traveling with us. Ain't that right?"

Wes looked at him but didn't say anything.

Snuffy shrugged. "Ain't joshing you none. Wes, you're straight as a stick, and I know you got a girl back home. What you got to say about all this?"

I watched Wes because I respected him. He was one good soldier, and in cards he never dealt from the bottom of the deck. He was conscientious and always tried to do the right thing. I wondered what he would say.

Wes rubbed his chin. "I'm not a good luck boy. I'm just like any of the rest of you. But I do know there's a passage in the Bible that I pay attention to and try to follow. 'Blessed is he who comes in the name of the Lord.' That's all that I'm trying to do. In the midst of all this killing and terror, I attempt to come in the name of the Lord. That's my objective."

Silence fell over the room. Nobody said anything for a while.

Finally, Snuffy turned to me. "Well, Frank, you never told us nothing about *your* girlfriend. In fact, you never admitted that you had one. Come on. Come clean with your brothers."

I knew that once you opened a can of worms with these guys, you'd never get 'em back in the can. On the other hand, we could all be dead by tonight. No point in hedging my bets.

"Yeah," I said. "I get letters from her as frequently as the mail comes through. Of course, we haven't seen the mailman lately, but I suspect he'll be around soon. Her name is Alice. Alice Anderson."

"Interesting," Snuffy said. "Tell us about her. She's a good looker?"

"Oh, yeah. Alice and I went to school together from the grade school. She's back there in Weleetka, waiting for me. When I get back, we'll get married."

"Well, I'll be damned," Snuffy said. "You got a genuine romance going on there."

"Sure," I said. "Her letters keep me going."

Again, nobody said anything for a while. Mentioning letters from home pressed some buttons. Some men never received anything from the States, and I know that bothered them. I wondered if Snuffy got answers to whatever was on his mind. I kept hearing the trucks driving up and knew we'd soon be on our way to the next stop. Time to pack it up.

No rest for the weary.

21

★ ★ ★

RAPID RAMPAGE

We started encouraging German soldiers to give up the fight. Most were average guys who had been conscripted into military service and never bought into the Nazi party line. The Wehrmacht was built on rigorous, rigid discipline that dictated blind loyalty to whatever was commanded. They could be a tough, resistant force. However, General Patton's relentless attacks began changing some of their minds. They realized what was ahead. They weren't going to win.

Our airplanes began dropping "safe conduct passes" that allowed the enemy to desert without penalty. In one day, thirty-two German soldiers from the 256th Volksgrenadier Division came across the battle line with their hands up. Though it was a small number, their surrender was encouraging. It was a sign that the Nazis were taking it on the chin. Air reconnaissance reported large columns of vehicles moving in a southerly and southwesterly direction from the German city of Bitburg. We could guess they were attempting to reinforce their front lines because they were being steadily pushed back. Since General Patton launched his late-January attack, the deadly numbers had started to mount. We had knocked out 936 enemy pillboxes, while other corps held similar records. The main obstacle holding us back were the mines and roadblocks that the Nazis left behind.

In mid-February, the weather cleared, and the sky opened. We went after the Luftwaffe. We hit them from every angle, and the score really added up. More than 445 of our bombers hit targets all over Germany. In addition, 770 bombers came up from Italy and attacked targets in southern Germany. The Royal Air Force represented Britain well in these clashes. General Patton stayed there behind the scenes, lending guidance and encouragement at every turn.

One story about him emerged when the army had to cross the Sauer River. Of course, we were still in the dead of winter, and the snow and ice had not dissipated. A newspaper correspondent snapped a picture of General Patton wading into the icy water with the current coming up to his knees. The reporter wrote a story suggesting that the general swam across the river ahead of his troops. Now, the pencil pusher was stretching the truth there, but the old man loved that type of article.

In the North, our troops made it across the Prüm River and fought their way into Bitburg. Even with constant counterattacks, the XX Corps held on. We were beginning to see that the Germans were scraping the bottom of the barrel to find recruits. Their soldiers had only carbines, and many had been thrown into battle only days earlier. On one day alone, the XX Corps gathered seven thousand prisoners. By the time this operation was over, we had captured forty thousand Germans.

We returned to the city of Trier, which was one of the oldest townsites in Europe, dating back to Roman times, when it was called Treves. Snipers had been everywhere. The city would not be easy to take. General Rundstedt had launched his offensive on the Ardennes from there. By the time the attack was over, Trier was a wreck. The area had once been a Roman resort, and oddly enough, this site of the baths wasn't touched by the bombing. However, the equally well-known local hotel was smashed. The population of eighty thousand had been reduced to hardly a thousand, all scrambling to escape starvation.

In the final months of the war especially, the Germans acted like savages. Major General William H. H. Morris, commander of the Tenth Armored Division, had told a story that got back to us. A week or two earlier, an officer commanding one of his battalions had been badly wounded. Two medical corpsmen placed him on a stretcher and prepared to whisk him to the rear and out of the fighting. Abruptly, the Germans counterattacked and overran the defenses. As they rushed in, the Nazis shot the two medics. As the men tumbled to the ground, they dropped the stretcher. Seeing that the officer was still alive, the Germans shot the severely wounded, defenseless soldier. Other men in the battalion saw the murder happen and were outraged. When it was discussed among the unit, a decision was made: they would no longer take *any* German prisoners alive.

When that story reached my guys, it sparked a debate. Jack Postawaiet was adamant that we should shoot every German we saw, regardless. "Listen, those bastards are inhuman!" he hissed. "They are best dead!"

Walt Brandon shook his head. "Look, we're here because we stand for higher values. If we turn into savages, we're no better than them."

Al Jackson took a long draw off his cigarette. "Now, boys, let's face it. War is war. It's all about killing. That's why they sent us over here. We're supposed to be killing the enemy."

"But there must be justice," Walt insisted. "There are three kinds of war," he added thoughtfully. "In a revolutionary war, one side is trying to overthrow the other government. We're not in that type of warfare. Then there's a holy war, where one side or both sides believe

God has called them to strike. They're on a divine mission. Again, our war is not a holy war, but it *is* a war for righteousness. We believe the good is on our side, and the Nazis are evil. That rationale allows us to fight with a clear conscience."

"Look!" Jack barked. "I don't pay attention to philosophical talk. I just know that if we don't kill the Nazis, they are going to kill us. That's good enough for me."

"This isn't a bunch of nonsense," Mr. Parker interjected, siding with Brandon. "Someday we are going home, and then we'll have to think about what happened to us in this war. If we don't want to spend the rest of our lives with a bad conscience, we've got to believe we did the right thing."

Jack shook his head. "Hell, none of us may get home again! Good men are getting killed every day. If we don't protect ourselves, we won't make it off this hunk of land. The way we get to go home is by killing Germans."

"But," Walt broke in, "we can't turn into killing machines without a conscience. We are still called to be righteous, even in war."

"Righteous!" With that, Jack exploded. "Who gives a damn about being 'righteous' when we're running at the enemy with bayonets drawn or dropping mortars on them that blow their heads off. Don't talk to me about being a nice guy. Nice guys get killed." He slapped on his helmet and stalked off.

For a long time, no one said anything.

22

★ ★ ★

CROSSING THE RHINE

As we advanced into the Third Reich, the Germans started digging in along the riverbanks. They knew what was coming and were bracing for our attack. The Eifel Hills, around the river, had steep slopes, and their banks made for good defense. A panzer division and the Sixth SS Mountain Division were among the German reinforcements. General Patton kept pushing and applying pressure, giving the enemy no time to get settled. His armored spearheads were able to advance thirty-five miles in two days and got within twenty miles of the Rhine. A regiment of the Fifth Infantry Division was able to plow another nineteen miles and reach the high ground overlooking the Rhine, just north of Koblenz. Our Third Army spearheads left the Kyll River and made it to the great river, covering fifty-five miles in just fifty-eight hours. For an army to travel at that speed was incredible.

We were still dealing with frigid weather. General Patton wrote later about how we dealt with that problem in rather ingenious ways. Obviously, some of the towns around us had not been occupied yet. Such a situation meant we didn't have houses to sleep in and had to endure the freezing temperatures. Someone came up with the idea of making huge snowballs. One of these snow rolls would be placed on each side of where men would sleep. A third snow roll would be placed in the middle, facing where the wind blew. With covering on three sides, pine branches were placed over the top. Three or four men could sleep in between these huge icy balls of protection to keep out the bad weather. Fighting under these subzero conditions seemed impossible, but our soldiers were tougher than rocks. We found a way *always*. Clever indeed.

The wide, deep Rhine had always been thought of as a formidable barrier that would stop any attacking army. While its dark waters seemed to amble on, any observer would realize immediately that the current was not to be underestimated. In peacetime, the Rhine would make a beautiful site for a cruise, with green forests running down to the banks. In war, the breadth and the current created a fortress. However, the opposition had not considered the speed with which General Patton could move. The Allies made no air attacks or artillery advances that might have alerted Nazi military leaders to where we might hit. The crossing was such a complete tactical achievement that the Germans were caught by total surprise. When they finally realized what had happened, they responded with violent air assaults, weather permitting, but there were few counterattacks.

The weather didn't do us any favors and generally made conditions for flying poor. When the sky cleared, we noticed for the first time the number of jet-propelled planes the Nazis had produced. The Ludendorff Bridge at the town of Remagen, roughly sixty miles inside Germany, was attacked by the first all-jet bombing raid. The four-engine Arado Ar 234 Blitz bomber came swooping out of the clouds escorted by Messerschmitt jet fighters and proved deadly. To the amazement of the Third Army, the bridge withstood the air assault. The Ninth Armored seized the bridge just minutes before demolition charges set by the retreating Nazis were set to detonate. The Rhine had stayed open, but the fighting hadn't slacked off any. Even though the German infantry faced overwhelming odds, its soldiers continued to fight with professionalism long after their defeat had become inevitable. Armed with fully automatic 7.92-millimeter Sturmgewehr 44 rifles, they remained a formidable opponent.

As a boy, I'd hoped to see the Rhine River someday, but I never dreamed I might cross it. Here we were ready to do just that. General Patton's Third Army lined up, prepared to come over. We would be crossing the river twenty-four hours ahead of any other unit. A pontoon bridge had been constructed by the U.S. Army Corps of Engineers, and the vehicles started to move.

I was riding shotgun, with Mr. Parker driving. He always could make the truck work even when the temperature was way south of zero. Our crew walked in front of the vehicle. The bridge made a weird, creaking sound, and I wondered what would happen if one of those pontoons slipped or broke loose. A river with a freezing, icy flow would swallow us before we could swim a foot. I reached in my pocket to find that scrap of paper with Psalm 91 written on it. "I choose the God above all gods to shelter me." I read those words three times and then put it back.

Just as I looked down the river, I recognized an airplane circling. I looked again. One of those new German jets was coming back toward us. Painted completely black, that Nazi aircraft looked like a monster flying up from the deep. It was probably a Messerschmitt Me-262 A. Undoubtedly, the pilot spotted the caravan when flying over and was coming back to knock us off. Maybe to destroy the pontoon bridge as well.

I jumped into the back of the truck and grabbed the mounted .30-caliber gun we kept back there for protection. Then I swung it around and lined up the sights. The jet wasn't slowing. I put my hand on the cocking lever and pulled. It didn't move. I pulled again. The lever simply wouldn't move. We were doomed.

The jet came straight for us, barely feet above the river. The guns on the airplane weren't hitting anything either. I couldn't move. The jet zoomed by the rear of the truck. For a split second, the pilot and I locked eyes. He probably wondered why I hadn't blasted him, while at the same time, I was thinking about how I had survived certain death. In that moment when we passed each other, we were both undoubtedly grateful to still be alive.

As the plane pulled away, the cocking lever unlocked and fell into place, but by then, the jet was gone. How was it that the hand of God made my weapon freeze? At that moment, I realized that if I had hit the German pilot, quite possibly he would have crashed into our convoy and maybe killed all of us. Had the Lord spared us both for some mystical, unknown reason? Who could say, but I sat there with my hands on that .30-caliber gun, bouncing up and down on that pontoon bridge with my teeth chattering.

Man, was I glad when we got to the other side! We rolled on and hit dry ground again. As the truck rumbled down the road, I sat there with my finger virtually frozen on the trigger. Just another one of those close calls.

I'm sure the irrepressible fury of Hitler exploded when the Ludendorff Bridge at Remagen was never destroyed and stood there inviting us to come across. Army engineers started building additional bridges up and down the river from the Remagen bridge. Because the Germans failed to destroy the big bridge, the Luftwaffe was ordered to mount a series of intense bombing raids. We kept two M3 half-track armored personnel carriers with .50-caliber machine guns ready and waiting for them to return. By March, the ice and snow were vanishing, but a heavy drizzle filled the skies, and this brought limited success to the Nazis' flyovers. Eventually the bombing and heavy usage took its toll, though, and exactly one week after our successful crossing, on March 17, the bridge fell sideways into the river, killing twenty-eight U.S. engineers and injuring many more.

The forward push that captured the enemy was like sacking up a batch of marbles into a bag. We soon had more than 150,000 in Allied POW camps. No telling how many had been killed. By the end of March, our front ran from the English Channel to the Swiss border. Hard to believe, but we were only three hundred miles from Berlin.

Mr. Dobson and I stood on the bank of the Rhine and watched the current roll by. The river was broad like the Mississippi and the flow mighty.

"Man, is that something to see!" I remarked.

Dobson shook his head. "For centuries, everything from knights on horseback to blacksmiths have stood on this bank. And now we are here. Remarkable."

A couple of soldiers from another unit came walking up. They nodded, and we responded.

"You boys waiting to cross the river?" I asked.

"Naw, we're with the Army Corps of Engineers," the first man said.

I didn't ask them their names. After you've seen so many men killed, you get to the point where you don't want to know any names.

"Understand we sent a good number of gliders over," Dobson said. "True?"

They told us some of the gliders hadn't done so well. We thought that we had neutralized the flak sites where they were supposed to land. Apparently, we'd missed a significant number of those guns, which opened up on our boys. About a quarter of the glider pilots got hit when they were coming down. Not a good number.

The glider boys that came down in that crossing were able to eventually join up with soldiers that had crossed the Rhine amphibiously, and they took the bridgeheads. The Nazis kept shooting, but our men took care of the problem. Of course, this was all preceded by two divisions of parachute troops that landed first. They delivered a hefty punch. We discovered later that it all worked to our advantage in the end.

"Well, the Germans certainly know where we are," Mr. Dobson said. "Thanks for the info."

The men walked on. Some of the American armies crossed at a more southern portion of the Rhine. Most of them came over south of Mainz between Nierstein and Oppenheim. The first wave was an assault regiment under the command of General Patton. Around midnight, under a brilliant moon, the assault boats started across. Soon the entire Fifth Division crossed the river. During the next few days, crossings were made at Boppard and Saint Goar. By the end of March, Darmstadt and Wiesbaden were ours, and armored columns were on their way to Frankfurt and Aschaffenburg.

A couple of German soldiers in heated rubber suits were caught swimming toward one of our bridges. With large rubber fins, they had on special breathing apparatuses that allowed them to breathe underwater. Equipped with explosives, they were obviously out to blow up our bridge. Fortunately, our soldiers spied them and hauled them in. Another German ploy that failed.

The Fourth Armored Division met only scattered resistance. In some of the little towns, the police and a few citizens with small arms put up opposition, but the real story was the number of prisoners of war we were taking. In one day, we hauled in 18,800 POWs. Nothing was stopping us. We were on the move to Berlin.

Much later, we learned about an argument that occurred in the backroom. England's Twenty-First Army Group was in a position to race forward and take Berlin. However, General Dwight Eisenhower believed the German capital was an easier reach for the Soviet army approaching from the East. President Franklin Delano Roosevelt supported this idea, assuring Ike that in a postwar situation, the Soviets would be cooperative and amenable. Man, oh, man alive! Would Joseph Stalin ever have gotten a laugh out of that idea!

23

★ ★ ★

LETTERS FROM HOME

I hadn't forgotten about my family or Alice Anderson; I just hadn't heard from them in quite a while. The pressure of the war kept my mind elsewhere—particularly on survival. We had just pulled into the little town of Boppard when the mail caught up with us. Boppard is in the German state of Rhineland-Palatinate, lying in the Rhine Gorge. A quaint, beautiful area, the town was a good place to receive mail from home. I had five letters from my mother and four from Alice. Believe you me, the men grabbed their mail and devoured those letters.

Mom's first letter updated me on my brothers and sisters. Since she had seven children, including me, there was plenty to report. Buck and Bob were doing fine with school. Of course, Mildred and Faye were married and gone from the house. Mother said they were all worried about me and prayed every day for me. She said the news from the war front sounded positive and only hoped I was doing fine. I guess she had no idea how cold it had been.

As for my girl, she kept me up on all the doings around school. Sounded like the basketball team was playing all right, although no one in Weleetka got that excited about bouncing a ball in a gymnasium. Alice wrote about her friends and what they were doing, who was going with whom—that sort of thing. Sitting there in the middle of a war where anyone could get killed at any moment, I found most of Alice's report a little childish. But she told me how much she loved me and hoped we'd be back together soon. Alice said she'd love me forever. Her letters always had a faint scent of perfume. I think I reread all four of them at least three times sitting right there in the middle of that little town of Boppard.

"Okay, men!" Sergeant Maddox called out. "We're loading up and moving out. Let's go!"

The soldiers started poking their letters into their gear and moving toward the trucks. Mr. Dobson was already in the driver's seat of the truck carrying spools of wire. I walked toward him. In my shirt pocket, I kept one of Alice's letters handy—the one in which she promised to wait for me forever.

The truck roared to life, and we were on the road again. By this time, the Germans had figured out what we were doing and begun counterattacking. The strikes were relatively small, though. I gathered that they had discovered they no longer ruled the sky, and that we were in their backyard and coming on full steam ahead.

The Fourth Armored Division drove twenty miles, bypassing Darmstadt. However, the Ninetieth Infantry Division came behind it and cleaned out the town. By March 20, all units of the XII Corps had crossed the Rhine and were soon on the doorstep of Frankfurt. The primarily industrial city offered resistance mainly from police, firemen, and air raid wardens, and only a few military troops. It fell quickly to us. At the same time, the Germans were improving their defensive positions on the east bank of the Rhine. When the VIII Corps made a landing in assault boats, its men came under heavy fire but got across successfully. Light artillery fire and mortars didn't really make a dent in their landing. The next day, another beachhead was established at Saint Goar by the Eighty-Ninth Infantry Division. In both of these crossings, fire support came from the Seventy-Sixth Infantry Division on the river's west bank. In the next day or so, we came roaring across both the Rhine and the Main rivers near Mainz. The enemy threw up stiff resistance, but with only moderate artillery support.

Our trucks came to a halt, and Sergeant Maddox appeared at the rear of the unit's truck.

"Okay, men. We're setting up the howitzers right now. We need to get that wire strung up the hill. We've got to blast the Nazis out of their socks. Get up to that hilltop and give us a reading on where we're shooting and what we're hitting."

Mr. Dobson jumped into the smaller truck that hauled the wire for communication. Our unit grabbed its rifles and quickly started stringing wire. Walt Brandon took the lead along with Snuffy Smith. Snipers were always a possibility, so Al Jackson stood guard with his rifle poised. Of course, he had a cigarette hanging out of his mouth. We could hear the artillery and mortars firing closer than was comfortable. No one was wasting time.

Once we got to the top of the hill, with a large rock outcropping, we could look down on the fortifications far in front of us. No question about it! The Nazis were giving us all they got. We began digging in, making a foxhole in case of an attack.

"Look, Corporal," Mr. Parker said to me. "We need only one man up here observing. You're good at it. Why don't the rest of us go down the hill and make sure no one cuts the wire?"

No one argued. Getting off that hill was one good idea. The top was like a perch where a parrot could get his feathers blown off. I hooked up the wire to the transmitter and prepared to make my reports. I could soon see our artillery making adjustments and hitting the enemy more squarely. Abruptly, a Messerschmitt circled overhead and made a swooping dive just above me. I was relieved when the surveillance plane didn't return, but I was sure he'd spotted me.

For the next forty minutes, I kept sending reports down the line. My binoculars told me we were right on target. I could see the enemy soldiers scurrying around. Suddenly an explosion shook the hill. Almost before I could move, another blast exploded just below me. I had become their target.

Mortars began blasting in. No reflection was needed to tell me that the Messerschmitt had reported us, and the enemy decided to blow me off the top of the rise. I made one last call on the line, telling the unit down there with the big guns that I was their new target and was signing off. I held my helmet on tight and dived into the nearest foxhole. I slapped my hands over my ears and hoped I wouldn't go deaf. Huddled up in a prenatal ball, I started praying. Psalm 91 came immediately to mind. I'd looked at it so many times that I didn't need to take it out of my pocket. I just kept repeating the promise "I choose the God above all gods to shelter me."

I could hear trees splintering and falling. I felt the dirt flying through the air and dropping on me like giant raindrops. After what seemed like an eternity, the explosions stopped. I guessed they figured no one was left. Possibly, our howitzers had knocked out their cannons. I didn't know, but I was just glad to still be alive. The German bombing had destroyed my transmitter and blown the wire off the rock outcropping. Nothing was left to do but crawl back down the slope, with my ears ringing.

The men were crouched behind bushes and rocks. Upon spotting me, Jack Postawaiet looked like he'd seen a ghost. Snuffy Smith stared at me too. "We thought maybe they'd blown you off that crest," he said.

"They certainly tried," I answered. "Next time, one of *you* can sit on the perch and see how you like it."

Mr. Parker stood up and surveyed the long field in front of us. "They've stopped firing," he reported. "Not sure what that's a sign of."

"Maybe they're hotfootin' it out of there," Al Jackson suggested.

"I don't know, but we need to go back and see if we can find out who's in charge to tell us what to do next."

"Maybe Sergeant Maddox is down there by the cannons," Mr. Dobson said.

"We'll find him," I said. "Let's go."

We worked our way carefully along the edge of the field and through the brush. The roar of our cannons kept shaking the earth and was loud enough to make one deaf. Once we got back to the road, we could smell the acid of the howitzers still firing. The sergeant came walking up to us.

"Good job, men," he said. "I think we flushed them out. We think they're now in a retreat."

"Excellent," I said.

"You want to watch out, though," he warned. "The enemy is coming at us in a new way. Ever hear of the *Volkssturm*?"

The men shook their heads.

"The *Volkssturm* is apparently a new idea Hitler's come up with. Means 'the people's storm.' It's a national militia established by Nazi Germany. It was *not* set up by the German army, but by the Nazi Party on the direct orders of Adolf Hitler. He's been talking about them protecting the Nazis' rightful gains in war—if you can believe it. I hear they are rounding up everyone from sixteen to sixty who isn't already in the military. They slap a pistol in his hand and tell him to shoot every Yankee he sees. They are also capable of setting off mortars. We now have orders to summarily shoot any civilian caught with a firearm. Propaganda Minister Joseph Goebbels is promoting this wild idea that the Nazis can overcome us by their force of will.

A little on the goofy side with our guns sticking down their throats, but that's about all they've got left."

"Don't they know that their boat is sinking?" Walt Brandon asked.

"I guess if you're gonna drown, doesn't make much difference what you say."

The men laughed.

"What's ahead?" I asked.

"We're still figuring that one out," Maddox replied. "We ought to know soon. You boys sit down and take a smoke. You've earned a breather."

We sat down and started rereading those letters from home once more. Alice's perfumed pages sure smelled good.

24

★ ★ ★

THE SOVIETS

We didn't know the Russians that well until the war was over. In Wel-eetka, Oklahoma, we knew as much about the Soviets as we did about how to make a Swiss watch tick. We knew that they'd had a bloody revolution of some kind twenty-however-many years ago. Sounded like a lot of people got killed. From what we heard on the battlefield, we figured the Nazis had really whacked the Russians hard with an invasion aimed at capturing Moscow and ultimately turning Mother Russia into the Fatherland's personal plantation, with the hated Bol-sheviks as slaves. Picking up the rest of the war story helped us real-ize what a stupid mistake Hitler had made by attacking everybody in sight at the same time, including the Russians. Small countries like the Netherlands, Belgium, and Luxembourg were one thing. The Soviet Union, which he attacked in June 1941, breaking a nonag-gression pact signed less than two years before, proved to be quite another. Overnight, Hitler turned the USSR, with its enormous and ferocious Red Army, from an Axis Powers sympathizer into part of a mighty triad with England and, a short time later, the United States.

Two years earlier, the Germans suffered a humiliating defeat at Stalingrad. The six-month-long conflict had raged on with both sides taking terrible losses. By January 30, 1943, one estimate suggested that the Germans had forty thousand to fifty thousand wounded soldiers without bandages or medications. Field Marshal Friedrich Wilhelm Ernst Paulus directed the Wehrmacht ground attack. Their assault was vicious and without mercy. Day and night, heavy artillery pounded everything in sight. Children suffered greatly. Many were separated from their parents, and a frightening number never found them again. When the unexpected bombing in Russia began in 1941, many families were still out on holidays. Many children had just started in pioneer camps, like Boy and Girl Scouts, where youth learned self-development. The chaos of evacuations caused millions of parents to end up far away from their children, with no way to find them. Often the only hope of the youngsters was to be taken in by strangers. The cry of these native children was "Who will take care of us?" Horses were fed to unsuspecting orphans. The loss of parents ended up a loss of memory. Questions such as "Tell me about the day I was born" could never be answered. The Nazi attack left a mark on multitudes of children that would never be removed.

Overcoming insurmountable odds, the Soviets not only hung on but also outmaneuvered the Nazis. With Soviet troops breaking into the German headquarters, the Germans were forced to surrender ignominiously. German casualties exceeded 150,000—with another 90,000 POWs. Humiliation was showered down on the entire German war effort. The loss stung.

Two years later, on January 12, 1945, the Soviets launched the biggest offensive of the war. Across the Belorussian and Ukrainian fronts, tanks, artillery, and soldiers came rushing at the Nazis. In two days, the Russians made tremendous advances and began to pressure the German defenses in East Prussia. Recognizing the serious assault, Hitler transferred the Panzer Corps four days later with the intention of mounting a flank attack on the Polish city of Poznan. All he accomplished was depriving East Prussia of much-needed defensive manpower.

By January 17, the Soviets' Forty-Seventh Army had encircled Warsaw, the Polish capital. Along with the northern forces, the steady move toward the coastline from Danzig to Königsberg created a new frontier. The Nazis couldn't stop them. Warsaw had witnessed the worst horrors of war. Holed up in the horrifically overcrowded Warsaw ghetto, the city's struggling Jewish population rebelled against the highly armed Nazi soldiers but finally was overwhelmed by the German army. There were just too few of them, with almost no weapons. The Jews had fought valiantly, but the tide had turned. The Soviet army began applying highly forceful pressure, and although the Nazis tried to scramble, the SS's dominance had come to an end. The Soviets liberated Warsaw.

By this time, the Nazis realized they had lost the Battle of the Bulge and started repositioning their forces. Hitler moved the Sixth SS Panzer Army from the Ardennes to Budapest, Hungary. While it wasn't possible for us to know exactly what the Germans were thinking, a realist couldn't help but recognize that these were moves of desperation. A few days later, Hitler began renaming his units. For example, Army Group A became Army Group Centre. Again, such moves appeared to be more out of desperation because of the enormous numbers of troops lost and having to retreat than out of any sort of significant strategic planning.

On February 1 Marshal Georgy Konstantinovich Zhukov, the Soviet general and marshal of the Soviet Union, began the advance toward Berlin. However, his First Belorussian Front, composed of several armies, ran into a determined German resistance at Kustrin. The Germans fully recognized what was at stake and knew they must

stop Zhukov or face horrendous consequences. Zhukov made an un-
expected move and joined up with the forces commanded by Ivan
Koven, waiting on the Oder River—which was all that separated
Poland and the Third Reich. The Russian front now extended from
Zehden, south of Stettin, Pomerania, all the way down to the Czech
border. Pomerania existed in the northeastern part of Germany and
had been in one of those areas that shifted back and forth between
Germany and Poland. The Soviets were pushing hard.

The Germans had seriously underestimated Russia as an opponent. Many of the German soldiers came from tranquil farm com-
munities and were infuriated by the barbaric behavior of Soviet
soldiers. Word spread quickly that the Russians would take revenge
on the Germans in every way possible. When a village fell, surviving German women were raped. Naked women might be nailed to a
barn door and left to die. There was no end to the stories about what
the Soviets would do. The Germans had brutally butchered the Russian citizens, but now the tables were turned.

I came to the conclusion that members of the Roosevelt administration, sitting in their padded chairs on the other side of the world,
never grasped how cruel and crude the Soviets could be. Because
they were allies, I think the truth was soft-pedaled by American propaganda people. In reality, the Soviets came on like a throwback to
the Dark Ages.

General Patton, on the other hand, got it! He let it be known that
he was ready to take on the Russians when we got through with the
Germans. Later, we learned he was warned to keep his mouth shut,
lest his comments start World War III. With all the problems the
Soviets caused after the war, how can anyone deny that Patton had
profound insight?

Near the end of February, the Ukrainian Front took the area

around lower Silesia, and the whole territory fell into Soviet hands. In the middle of March, the Soviet Second and Third Ukrainian Fronts began their assault along the Danube River. The armies pressed their way through Hungary and took Budapest. They were on their way into Austria and Vienna. Of course, after the war was over, Hungary ended up behind the Iron Curtain. The Soviets had driven out the Germans only to leave a dark shadow over the Hungarians that would last for decades.

The battle for Budapest proved to be a horrible confrontation with the Germans. Hitler did not listen to his generals' recommendations and ordered the relief of Budapest, now held by the Red Army. The capture of Budapest gave the Soviets a unique opportunity to quickly advance into the Balkans. When the Russians sent two officers carrying white flags to negotiate a surrender of the Germans, the Nazi garrison shot them dead. The bloody battle continued.

The Germans reached the Budapest airport. Hitler demanded that the army fight to the last man. However, the Soviets formed a special Budapest Group Corps to spearhead their attack. The fighting continued street by street, house by house. The Germans' final attempt to take the city came with the Sixth SS Panzer Army attack. Because the Soviets already held the city, all the Germans could muster was six operational tanks, while the Red Army took back the airport. The truth is that the Germans fought hard. They simply could not overcome the Soviets. The price paid: thirty-five thousand killed and sixty-two thousand captured. In the end, Hitler's insistence on holding Budapest ended up compromising the flanks of the Reich.

The increasingly irrational Führer berated his army for failing to take Budapest. The irony was that the men he attacked were among some of his most loyal followers. After the screaming fit Hitler threw as a reward for their loyalty, the remnants turned west and surrendered to U.S. forces.

By the end of March, the Soviets' front line had cut deeply into Germany. Running from Stettin to Küstrin, they were now only fifty miles from Berlin. Like giant pincers, we were coming from one direction and the Soviets from the other. Hitler was doomed.

25

★ ★ ★

ON THE ROAD

General Patton always said that one should make plans to fit the circumstances, not try to create circumstances to fit the plans. That philosophy helped guide our success. Patton figured out what the Germans thought we were doing and then did the opposite. We all lived with uncertain circumstances.

In his projections, the general was somewhat contemptuous of defensive holdings such as the Siegfried line and the Maginot Line. Not surprisingly, his view was shaped by history, as he pointed to walls that fell, such as the city walls of ancient Troy, the wall of Hadrian that divided Britain and Scotland, the Great Wall of China, and others. He believed that the only effective defense was an offense. Success would always lie with warlike souls doing the fighting.

We were certainly on the offense, cutting through the German lines wherever we found them. As we pressed on, our unit came near the city of Dortmund. Of course, we remained aware of the problem of the *Volkssturm*. No one wanted to get shot in the back by some local hick firing from behind an oak tree.

We were prepared to search anyone that got in our way for weapons.

When we rolled into the city, I discovered that another crew like ours had run into a problem. For some reason or other, the soldier in charge of laying communication wire was out of pocket. They asked me to step in and take his place. Of course, I obliged. Whether I wanted to or not was irrelevant.

We laid the wire, got a transmitter fixed, and put a man in place to handle the situation. While I was finishing this assignment, the other unit leader returned and took my crew out to complete a similar assignment. As always, my men worked diligently. The only difference was that Mr. Parker had come down with a sore throat and left on a sick call. Some other guy had been grabbed to drive the truck. There we were in Dortmund, laying wire with our crews reshuffled.

As my crew finished and prepared to return, the wire-hauling truck hit a land mine. The substitute crew chief was killed, and the driver had his foot blown off. If Parker and I had been with them, that would have been us lying on the ground. Sure made me pull out Psalm 91 and read it again.

In one famous story, General Patton was nearly struck in the head by a shell at a medieval chateau. Driving back, one of the officers with him became emphatic about his religious beliefs. He said, "By God, General, my family have been Catholics for more than three thousand years." Patton looked at him skeptically and grinned. "What, BC Catholics?" The officer retreated sheepishly.

We finished up in the Dortmund area and started the truck back down the road. After hitting the land mine, our vehicle was demolished. We ended up getting a brand-new truck. What a deal, except we'd rather have the old truck back with everybody alive.

Mr. Parker drove as usual. He asked me, "Where are we headed?"

"The sergeant told me that we're on our way to Marburg." Obviously, we'd never been there, but he filled my ear with the story of the city's history. "Said it's a beautiful area."

"Really?" Parker said. "Tell me more."

"It's a university town along the valley of the Lahn River. He guesses maybe around seventy thousand people lived there. I think the former president of Germany Paul von Hindenburg is buried there."

"Interesting. What are we going to find?"

"The sergeant said the war has turned the place into a giant hospital. Every building in sight is being used for the wounded. Apparently, our airplanes have avoided bombing the city because of all the wounded. He thought that our planes hit mainly the railroad tracks."

Mr. Parker nodded and kept driving. We joggled along for some time. Nobody said much. Eventually we came to a crossroads where an MP was directing traffic.

"We've got an assignment in Marburg," Parker said.

"Yeah, we've been expecting you," the MP replied. "They're already setting up the howitzers. I'm supposed to tell you to start stringing wire through that wandering field over there." He pointed over his shoulder. "Up that cliff. The big boys want you to start immediately."

We saluted.

Parker put the truck in low gear and started across the bar ditch at the side of the road. We bounced around but came up the other side in what at some time had been a farmer's planting area. Some distance away, the observation hill stood straight up. We immediately began to string wire. By this time, each man knew exactly what to do. No one fooled around, and the wire began to spin off the spool. It didn't take long to realize that we didn't have enough wire to get to the top of the hill.

"What are we going to do?" Snuffy asked.

For a few moments, the seven of us stood there in silence. Finally, I said, "If we get out of the path we've been following, I think we can cut through yonder field and those trees, and we'd have enough wire left to make it up the hill. All we got to do is cut across and restring."

"I don't like the idea," Mr. Parker said. "Crossing that field is an absolute invitation for walking into a minefield. We've already lost one truck and a life by driving over one of them boogers. I don't like it at all."

I looked at him sternly. "You got a better idea?"

Mr. Parker shrugged. "Don't guess I do."

"Well," I said, "we can't wait around. I'll tell you what: Dobson and I will walk in front of the truck. I'll be on the left and Dobson on the right. We'll walk carefully and watch for any sign of mines. That should give us the protection we need."

Parker shook his head. Everyone could tell he didn't like the idea, but he couldn't do anything about it. The truck backfired, and we started across. We kept our pace slow and easy.

Then I saw it: the nose of an unexploded shell sticking out of the creek bank inches from the front wheel of our truck.

"Stop!" I screamed. "Good God! Don't move!"

Parker ground to a sudden stop.

I ran around to the side of the truck and jumped up on the running board. "When they trained you to drive this truck, did they teach you to back up without moving forward even a smidgeon?"

Parker's eyes widened. "Y-yes, sir."

"Well, if ever in your life you backed up without absolutely no forward thrust, this is the time to do so."

Parker swallowed hard and nodded. "Oh. Okay . . ."

The truck inched backward slowly. Perched on the running board, I felt a tug on my shirt and looked over my shoulder: Dobson was hanging on for dear life. After the truck had driven a safe distance away, Parker stepped out of the truck and gave me one hard look.

"Okay, okay," I said. "My shortcut didn't work. We'll simply have to go back and get more wire. I'll go down there and put out a red flag for the maintenance men to take care of the shell."

The other six nodded and jumped in the back of the truck, which sped off and disappeared along the tree line. Quiet settled in, and it felt good to be by myself for a change. I sprawled out on the ground. A gentle wind blew through the trees, and I started reflecting on what it had been like back in Weleetka, when, say, I walked across the thousand-foot-long train trestle with the stream running far underneath. An image of that old swimming hole where we used to go diving during the hot days of summer floated across my eyes. Oh, to be there once more.

A soul-shaking boom blew off the top of a tree behind me. I jumped up. The Germans must have spotted our truck driving across the area. Another explosion ripped apart a large pine. I grabbed my helmet and tried to decide where to hide. Another blast cut down a tree to my left. Then a hunk of dirt exploded just feet in front of me. I dived into one of the foxholes the Germans had left behind. Suddenly that dormant shell in the creek bed went off, showering the entire area in mud and debris. The spray covered my face with ugly-smelling muck. I crunched up in a ball and started praying.

The idea hit me to use my steel helmet for protection wherever I thought I was vulnerable. The shrapnel kept flying past me from what seemed like every direction. I could hear it striking and bouncing off the trees and logs around me. I grabbed my helmet and put it over my chest to protect my heart. Pieces of metal kept flying by. I kept moving my helmet, trying to decide where I was most likely to get hit. Small tree branches dropped on top of me. And then it stopped.

I lay there in the silence, wondering if the firing would start up again. Five minutes passed. Ten. Nothing. They didn't shoot again. In the quiet, I thought about how the enemy must experience the same terror when we fired on them; when the same red-hot piercing fragments came showering down just like they did on me. With-out a foxhole to jump into, they would be shredded by the hellfire downpour of mortars and shells. No longer did the German soldiers seem like enemies, monsters, but human beings caught up in this god-awful war like the rest of us.

I started to pray, thanking God that I had survived, but also for the Germans when thousands and thousands of rounds fell on them. "Please, God, be with them too. Cause them to surrender and stop this horrible war." Something in me surged upward, and I just wanted the whole terrible campaign of death to end.

"Hey! He's alive!"

I looked up out of the foxhole. Brandon and Jackson were run-ning toward me.

"We thought them Germans had blown you to pieces," Al said.

"Praise God!" Walt shouted. "They blew this entire outpost to pieces."

I climbed out of the hole and brushed the dirt off my clothes. Parker and Dobson came jogging up. The men slapped me on the back. Several hugged me. I kept smiling but didn't say anything. I was glad to have survived, but something deep in me had been touched. I realized we were out there killing one another, and the people on the other side were just as human as we were.

We were all victims of the circumstances.

26

★ ★ ★

RABBITS

General Patton had his own unique way of approaching everything, and as we marched down the road toward the east, I knew his mind would be buzzing with ideas. No matter whether we were crossing a bridge or entering a town, he maneuvered our combined forces uniquely and with amazing dexterity. He would rearrange units back and forth, always leaving the enemy confused about what was coming next. Men often referred to him as the greatest tank strategist ever.

When we'd hit a town or attack the front line, sometimes Patton sent the infantry in first to create a hole in the opposition. Next, the tanks came roaring through the breakthrough and would be firing at the enemy's rear. But the next day, the tanks would go in first and crush the front line of the enemy so that our infantry could charge in through that opening, shooting in every direction and mopping up the residue of the enemy—if any was left.

We were on the move like nothing anyone had ever seen. The Sixth Armored Division pushed rapidly in a northeast direction that extended almost to Kassel. Facing little or almost no resistance, we covered more than a hundred miles in three days—the fastest advance in the entire history of the Third Army. The only hitch came when we did hit Kassel. For three days, we were slowed while battling to take the city. Nevertheless, we soon cleaned out the entire area.

The rest of the encounters proved to be much the same. The Eightieth Infantry Division plowed into the city of Wiesbaden, where they found only disorganized resistance. Determined struggle came from just a few small groups. The prisoners of war turned out to be combined units, which indicated disorganization and a serious reduction in the number of troops opposing us. Some local citizens were laying mines during the night, hoping to catch us unaware. These explosives knocked out two of our vehicles in the town of Germscheid. But overall, such actions were little more than irritants. The German army was falling apart.

At the same time, reconnaissance observed heavy traffic behind enemy lines. Tanks, half-tracks, and even horse-drawn wagons moved in a heavy flow toward the Third Army. Our airplanes also observed heavy rail movement. Our better guess was that the Nazis were moving another division against us. Meanwhile, at the city of Giessen, we joined up with the First Army, now under the command of Omar Bradley's successor, the implacable General Courtney Hodges, a native Georgian. Their efforts had captured a two-thousand-square-mile area between Frankfurt and Giessen. Enemy elements were falling apart while trying to slow our press. Most of the German troops made only token resistance before surrendering.

The history of Germany, and Europe more broadly, was filled with endless wars. Countries had fought with swords, spears, and arrows, but never had they seen what World Wars I and II brought. As the Allies systematically destroyed their means of commerce, I wondered how the average citizen would survive. Eventually the war would leave behind a legacy of starvation.

As our unit kept pressing toward Cologne, I noticed a large number of rabbits in the fields, but we kept moving. The largest German city in the North Rhine–Westphalia area, Cologne (*Köln* in German) was the country's fourth most populous city behind Berlin, Hamburg, and Munich. Just about everyone had heard of the towering, magnificent Cologne Cathedral, the seat of the Roman Catholic archbishop of Cologne. Moreover, the city boasted the University of Cologne, one of Europe's oldest and largest universities. Cologne was founded and established in the first century as the Roman Colonia Claudia Ara Agrippinensium, which was the origin of its name. We picked up all kinds of information as we rolled along.

We knew the Allies had bombed the city heavily. Our best guess was that at least half of Cologne, including the city center, had been destroyed during the 262 air strikes, leaving twenty thousand people dead and another fifty-nine thousand homeless. A massive evacuation of people to rural areas reduced the population by 95 percent.

We started down a street with collapsed buildings on both sides. Roofs were cratered in and storefronts left in shambles. Rubble was piled high with broken bricks and splintered boards everywhere. Glass peppered the streets with piercing shards. The city looked like a wrecked train.

Here and there we could see people peering out from behind empty door frames, clearly hungry. Many survivors were struggling to find food—and to just stay alive. I immediately thought of the rabbits I'd spotted on the way into the city. I had my gun.

Dobson and I turned around and started back the way we came in. At the edge of the city, farmland stretched across a wide expanse. Even some rabbit ears stuck up out of the tall grass in a corner of the field.

My .30 caliber did the trick. I'd shot plenty in Oklahoma. The rabbits never had a chance. We roamed through the field shooting right and left. In short order, we had fifty dead rabbits.

We fired up the truck and were quickly back on a main street. People were standing outside, watching us drive through. We stopped, and I stood up and waved.

"*Deine familie?*" I called out. "How many in your family?"

A white-haired woman wearing a dirty apron held up four fingers. Her hair had been pulled back in a bun, but she looked frazzled. Desperate.

"Hey, my fumbling German seems to be working," I said to Dobson. "She just won the raffle."

I held up two rabbits. "One rabbit for every two people." I pointed to the grandmother. "*Für dich.*" "To you."

She looked at me quizzically and hesitated, like she was afraid.

"*Für dich,*" I repeated.

She dashed into the street and grabbed the two rabbits. The old lady began bowing to me as if I were an emperor. We rolled down the street, and people began appearing out of nowhere, holding out their hands.

"*Deine familie?*" I kept asking.

The Germans began running to the truck. They'd stick up one finger, two, and maybe even four. They kept thanking me and waving. Their previous hostility had turned into gratitude.

"*Danke schön!*" "*Danke schön!*" rang down the street. The citizens began smiling.

Once we had given away all the rabbits, we started back to the field, where we shot another fifty. We stuffed the animals in a large bag we'd brought with us. Back we went to Cologne.

People were already standing on the street, anticipating our return. Hands were held out everywhere. We began to sense that we had broken an invisible barrier. Obviously, Allied bombing had destroyed most of their city. We couldn't tell if they were bona fide Nazis or just everyday folks caught up in a terrible war over which they had no control. But our bringing them food touched something basic and human. They could figure out that our war was with the Nazis, not with them.

27

★ ★ ★

GRUESOME DISCOVERIES

The enemy was a beaten nation of men, women, and children, interspersed with a few fanatical Nazis. We found it perplexing to try figuring out what made these obviously close-minded people tick. Apparently, they had some kind of weird devotion to Hitler and what he stood for. I guess Germany was such a wreck after World War I that his promises sounded like paradise. Of course, at first, Hitler did achieve some important advances that put unemployed people back to work. He built an expansive highway system even though nobody had a car. Then he came out with the Volkswagen ("People's car" in German), and they could all go sailing down that roadway.

We knew World War I had ruined the German economy and turned the once-prosperous nation upside down. I think many of the locals weren't sure they would ever recover. What a mess! Then along came Hitler, with a promise to fix everything. Now, as Patton's Third Army barreled across the Fatherland, they probably were starting to figure out their Führer wasn't so smart after all.

Following the fall of Koblenz and the onward march that the big boys called the Palatinate campaign, many observers, including the Germans, called this the greatest effort of the entire war. In three scant days, twelve of our divisions catapulted south across the Moselle River. Everybody was trying to outdo one another in racing across Germany to come up on the rear areas of the enemy. We were roaring past the Siegfried line to line up with the destruction of two German armies. We captured more than sixty thousand prisoners along with ten thousand square miles of German territory while sustaining only minimal losses. Our air forces pounded the enemy day and night, with the heaviest attacks landing on Berlin proper. Why the Nazis didn't throw up their hands and quit was beyond any of us. There simply wasn't much left of their country.

Along the way, there were some of those "funnies" that we all got a laugh out of. One came from Winston Churchill. Apparently, he'd received some kind of enthusiastic report about how well Field Marshal Montgomery was doing and fired off a letter congratulating him on making the first crossing of the Rhine River. The British prime minister's prerecorded speech was broadcast over the radio by the British Broadcasting Company (BBC). However, the truth was that the Third Army had crossed the Rhine thirty-six hours earlier.

When General Patton and General Manton Eddy, commander of the XII Corps, crossed the Rhine, they stopped on the other side. Old Blood and Guts deliberately spit in the river as if he held some measure of contempt for the area. Patton then picked up a handful of dirt to do just as the Roman general Scipio Africanus Major and William the Conqueror had done centuries earlier. William had said, "I see in my hands the soil of England." Patton said, "I saw in my hands the soil of Germany."

Though Germany was beaten, elements of the German army didn't throw in the towel. Fighting continued to be spotty, but resistance could be strong and heavy. The enemy made a significant counterattack on the north flank, recapturing the town of Struth. The battle raged with as much fury as any in the war. Artillery blasted away, and the fighting went from house to house. However, when it was all over, half the Nazi army of more than a thousand were killed or captured. Nine of their tanks had been destroyed, and Struth was back in our hands.

The Fourth Armored continued plowing ahead. We drove thirty-five miles in one day and came out west of Weimar, the seat of the fallen German republic, which ruled from 1919 to 1933, the year that Hitler and his Nazi Party came to power. The city had lately been the location of a large German headquarters. Much to our shock, it was virtually next door to what was to become one of Germany's infamous concentration camps.

General Patton was with General Otto Weyland, who had focused the XIX Tactical Air Command on the enemy during the Battle of the Bulge, when they discovered one of the horrors of the war. A mile and a half from Weimar, they found the Buchenwald concentration camp, one of the largest inside Germany. Out of nowhere, a man appeared who said he had been an inmate and would give them a guided tour of the facility. They were told 250,000 prisoners had been housed there at one time. SS authorities opened Buchenwald for male prisoners in July 1937. Women were not part of the Buchenwald camp system until late 1943 or early 1944. Prisoners were confined in the northern part of the camp in what was known as the main area, while SS guard barracks and the camp administration compound were located in the southern part. An electrified barbed wire fence, watchtowers, and a chain of sentries outfitted with automatic machine guns surrounded the main camp. The detention area, also known as the bunker, was located at the entrance to the main camp. The SS often shot prisoners in the stables and hanged other prisoners in the crematorium area.

The so-called guide seemed particularly anxious to exhibit some of the means by which prisoners were tortured. He pointed out the gallows where piano wire was placed around the prisoner's neck and then the inmate was dropped so his toes would touch the ground. Consequently, it might take fifteen minutes to choke to death, since the neck wouldn't be broken in such a short drop.

The guide then took them to the whipping table. An observer could see that feet were placed in stocks and the victim stretched over the table. Two guards held him while a third beat him with a stick that still had blood on it. The guide claimed that he had personally received twenty-five blows. On the other side of the whipping table was a pile of forty bodies, most of them naked. All had been shot in the back of the head at short range. Blood was still pooling on the ground. Not far from this area stood a shed with more naked bodies inside. They had been sprinkled with lime to reduce the stench, though the measure proved ineffective. Supposedly, the shed could hold two hundred bodies. Only after it was full were the bodies taken out and buried.

The guide also seemed to know much about medical experiments that had been conducted in the camp. Beginning in 1941, a number of physicians and scientists carried out cruel tests on prisoners at Buchenwald in special barracks in the northern part of the main camp. Medical experiments aimed at investigating the efficacy of vaccines and other treatments against contagious diseases such as typhus, typhoid, cholera, and diphtheria resulted in hundreds of deaths. The Nazis' great experiments killed everyone they toyed with. In 1944 a Danish Nazi physician named Dr. Carl Vaernet began a series of procedures that he claimed would "cure" homosexual inmates through hormonal transplants. Of course, none worked.

When the Nazis realized the Americans were coming, they tried desperately to destroy the evidence. Prisoners were forced to dig up bodies and pile them up on a mammoth griddle, where they attempted to burn them. It was a horrific scene.

Somewhere along the way, one of the Allied generals noticed how well fed their guide was, while the rest of the prisoners were emaciated. Turned out the guide was actually one of the guards trying to sneak by without getting caught. He was handed over to the inmates, who promptly killed him.

As bad as the scene was, the smell was worse. For American boys who had come from farms and small country towns and were observing this, the camp was unimaginable and lingered in our memories, never to be erased. Never could we have conceived such a place. Whatever we thought about the Nazis, now it was evident that we had underestimated their cruelty. I remembered my conversation months earlier with Eli Cohen, the Jewish soldier I'd sat next to in the mess hall in England while we were awaiting deployment. He was the first Jew I'd ever met. Eli had told me about pogroms and enlisting to fight for his people

I didn't really get it when Eli Cohen told me about anti-Semitism. I did now.

The generals decided that as many soldiers as possible should see the camp. If anybody questioned why we were fighting, a walk through Buchenwald would quickly assuage any doubts. Then General Patton ordered that the burgomaster of Weimar (a position similar to mayor or magistrate) and his wife be forced to tour the grounds, along with approximately one thousand of their constituents. Of course, all the Germans protested that they *had no idea* what went on there, just three miles away. After the burgomaster and his wife saw the horrors of Buchenwald, they went home and committed suicide.

Shortly after this, Patton met with General Horace McBride of the Eightieth Infantry. McBride came up with the idea of shooting a projectile filled with leaflets informing the townspeople that if they surrendered, they would be spared the cruelties of war. If they didn't lay down their arms, a full-court press was coming. The burgomaster of Weimer was to come out with a white flag to signal that there were no Nazi troops in the town. Should he not do so, the Allied Air Forces would promptly bomb the town.

The idea worked, and, consequently, many other German towns were spared devastation. The people knew the war was over, and surrender was the only way out. Hitler was deluded, determined to keep the insanity going despite the destruction it brought to the Fatherland, but the locals weren't. They had had enough war for three lifetimes.

28

★ ★ ★

MARCHING ON

The weather had improved greatly. Those bone-rattling days when the bottom dropped out of the thermometer were over, but it was still cold at night. Spring would be on the way soon, and that lifted everybody's spirits. We had not taken a shower or bath in months. You know what that means: stay downwind. We just had to get used to the inconvenience. Eventually we could tell whenever soldiers got a run at the showers. The hot water felt great, of course, but shortly after they dried off, they got hit with the big itch. The blood vessels near the skin had settled in for a winter's nap, but when the hot water woke them up, it felt like ants crawling everywhere. Just one more deal that came with being in the war.

The sun had come up, and the warmth felt good. I could see a group of officers talking over near the clearing. I watched them because I knew they were discussing something that would affect my unit. I could see men waving their arms and pointing in different directions. Probably some new adjustment was in the works. We'd been moving fast enough that the top levels had to reconnoiter and keep an eye on the maps. Finally, the sergeant came running over to me.

"Corporal, the big boys are impressed with the job you been doing. You are now one of the men in charge of communications for the entire battalion."

"Really?"

"Yeah, that's what they sent me to tell you. We're moving at a fast clip, and your unit's been doing a good job. Now, you keep your unit of six men laying wire. Just add this new assignment. Four other men will be involved in communications, like you will be. We got to keep that rolling. Communications may even become more vital as we get closer to Berlin.

"By the way," he added, almost as an afterthought, "you have been promoted to sergeant. Congratulations."

"My gosh! That's unexpected."

"Keep your eyes open. I understand we got some important people coming this way." He winked at me, turned, and took off.

My crew of six was standing around eating Spam out of the can. Wasn't our favorite meal by any stretch of the imagination, but it kept us fed. Al Jackson and Snuffy Smith had been watching me talk with the sergeant. Walt Brandon walked over and joined them.

"Looks like the big boys are talking to you," Al said. "Must be important."

I eyed him for a moment. Al always wanted to make some smart comment and loved to see people get riled up when he poked at them.

"You stickin' your nose in where it don't belong?" I said.

"Oh, no." Al smirked. "Just checking out the situation. Hell, I'm just talking." He blew a smoke ring in the air. "It's all one big puff of smoke."

"Seriously," Snuffy interjected. "Something going on with the big dogs?"

"I'm now one of five battalion leaders in charge of communication," I said. "They're pleased with what we've been doing. Want us to keep it up. Made me a sergeant."

"*W-o-o,*" Jackson cooed. "Big time. We are now under the direct authority of the front office."

Walt Brandon nodded. "Good. That's good. We're doing something worthwhile."

"Old Walt's always looking for the sunny side," Al said. "Mr. Holy Joe. Always reading that little black Bible."

"Listen!" Walt snapped. "I don't have to take your—"

"Okay!" I yelled. "Okay! Let's cut out the horseshit. We got enough going on without this nonsense. Now, everybody settle down."

Al kept that silly grin on his face but didn't say anything further. I watched them out of the corner of my eye. I certainly didn't want any funny business exploding this close to a group of officers.

"Tell me, Walt," Jackson said. "You're going to be a preacher. What do you believe in? I mean, *really* believe in?"

Walt eyed him suspiciously. "What do *you* believe in, Al?"

"I believe in Betty Grable," Jackson quipped. "Yes, sir-e-e-e. She's my religion."

"She going to get you to heaven?" Walt asked.

"Betty Gable *is* heaven!"

The men laughed. Walt didn't smile.

"Now, look at our glorious leader, Mr. Sisson. Corporal—well, for the moment—Frank even wears a cross hooked on his dog tags. He's shoutin' what he believes in."

"You're damn right," I said. "I'm a Christian, and if anything happens to me, I want to go down with that name hooked to my body."

"Ain't nothing wrong with that," Snuffy chimed in. "We all got our own set of beliefs. Parker says the Presbyterians got it, while Jack hangs in there with the Methodists. They're all okay. Just different."

"Oh, I'm all for heaven," Al said. "I want to make sure I ascend that golden stairway into the sky."

"I don't joke about heaven." Walt's voice became low and intense. He wasn't kidding around with Al. "That's too serious an issue. Especially when we could get killed out here on any day of the week."

"Everything is serious to you," Al said. "Let me ask you a real question: I see you reading that little black book all the time. Every day a truckload of men get killed. We're burying our buddies right and left. Sounds like somebody is at fault big-time. Why shouldn't we blame God?"

Walt scratched his head for a moment. "You don't blame God, because God didn't do it," he said at last.

Al frowned. "What do you mean, 'God didn't do it'?"

"God created us to have free will," Walt argued. "Our Creator made us with the ability to make independent decisions. We are responsible for ourselves. The Germans started this war, not God. And we decided to stop them. That's all our decisions. You can't push the killing off on the Almighty. We're the ones that should have done better."

Al stared at Walt and didn't say anything more. The joshing around had turned too serious for him.

After a few minutes, the sergeant came back.

"Mail call!" he shouted.

The men came running. Mr. Dobson stepped right to the front of the line—nobody was going to get in his way. Or Mr. Parker's as well. The rest of the men hovered around, obviously hoping to have a letter from home.

"Jack Postawaiett!" the sergeant called out. "You got a letter."

Jack's hand shot out to grab the white envelope. You would have to have been there to understand. We were hoping to hear from home to remind us why we were here getting shot at every day. A letter lifted us, inspired us, made us feel important and remembered.

"Got three letters here for you, Corporal." The sergeant handed me my mail.

I grabbed them and looked at the return addresses. One was from my mama and one from my sister Ruby. The last one was from Alice Anderson. That was where I started. I tore open the envelope and started to read every word that my girlfriend wrote.

Alice rambled on about happenings at school. Before long, they'd have the big spring prom. I couldn't tell whether she was going to go or not. It kind of left me with the feeling that she wanted to be there and just might go. Alone? Really? Well, there I am sloshing through the mud and bitter cold while she was worried about missing a chance to wear a formal dress to a big dance. Somehow it just didn't feel right. Then again, she wrote how much she missed me and hoped I'd be home soon. That felt good, so I shrugged off the spring prom bit, but at the same time . . .

Ruby's and my mother's letters were obviously meant to cheer me up and encourage me. Mama said she planned to cook my favorite cherry pie when I got home and hoped it would be soon. Ruby let me know how her children were doing, and it sounded like she was happy.

Those letters were like an umbilical cord that kept me hooked to a reality that I needed to remember. When you're jumping in foxholes and hearing mortars whistling overhead, it's hard to remember where you came from. You get so focused on survival that some days it feels like that's all that counts. A letter from home helps you stay connected.

Off in the distance, I heard the muffled roar of what sounded like a jeep coming our way. I looked up from my mama's letter and peered into the dust flying down the dirt road. Flags flying on the front fenders meant a staff car was coming. I watched the officers near the road stiffen and salute.

I couldn't believe my eyes. Here came the supreme Allied commander, General Dwight D. Eisenhower, with General Patton in the backseat. I had seen the two of them together once before. Man alive! Did I ever come to attention and salute! The generals returned the salute and went flying by. Eisenhower seemed to always have a determined look on his face. Not unfriendly. Just serious. Patton grinned.

The last time he came by with Patton, the Germans started blowing apart the trees and the fields. Of course, then the Nazis thought they knew what they were doing. I suspected that now they were just hoping to survive. The enemy probably had no idea where our top man was going. Things were simply not going well for the Germans. Every day, we captured more POWs, Wehrmacht tanks, and equipment.

The Nazis had come up with a mobile armored antitank unit that was cheaper than a new tank, consisting of a Hetzer 75-millimeter gun mounted on the chassis of an old panzer. However, some of our revolutionary Sherman Duplex Drive tanks, outfitted with twin propellers, had even "swum" ashore on the D-Day landing and were now coming on like gangbusters. The tanks of the Third Army were hitting the Wehrmacht right and left, with little resistance. Our Sherman tanks had nearly reached one of the main autobahns that led to Berlin. German traffic was left in a tangled mess. They couldn't stop us, but they certainly weren't going anywhere.

The German POWs often proved to be talkative. A few hardened Nazis turned up, but most of the prisoners were simply farm boys who had been raised to do what they were told. One prisoner of war fessed up that the enemy was preparing poisoned sugar and coffee substitutes, as well as contaminating cigarettes and chocolate, all in hopes of killing us.

The story also came back to us that one of our air support planes bombed a German train loaded with ammunition and explosives.

The airplane swooped low out of the sky and hit the train. The immense explosion destroyed not only the train but also the plane, killing its crew. Tough for our guys, of course, but there's no telling how many lives they saved by knocking out that train.

However, the Nazis weren't quitting. Their resistance in some areas remained strong and tough. Their troops continued to fight, and their artillery continued to be as deadly as ever. The German army had a stiff backbone. The problem for them was that the Third Army couldn't be stopped. The Sixth Armored Division crossed the Fulda River on a treadway bridge—a floating steel structure—and a captured railroad bridge. The drive eastward continued unabated. Nevertheless, the Germans had some advantages when they were holding hilltops. They fought from supply trains and vehicular convoys. At several points, the enemy defense was able to brace itself and respond with counterattacks. The war was not over yet.

We certainly had our share of good luck or divine intervention—call it what you will. When our units were preparing to cross the Moselle River en masse, half of the German Second SS Mountain Division was set up at the point where it seemed like the crossing would occur. But the XX Corps attacked downriver at a different location than expected. The enemy, assuming we were going to cross there, raced down to stop us. Instead, the XX Corps crossed the river at the original point, virtually unopposed.

What can I say? Looked like Al Jackson's cynicism ended up in a ditch. On the other hand, Walt Brandon's faith and convictions had worked out just right.

29

★ ★ ★

CLOSING IN

Being in charge of communications for the entire battalion meant I had to keep my eyes open and make sure the flow of information didn't get interrupted. At the same time, it was necessary to keep my unit of six men working. Because they were all good guys, and we had slugged it out together so well, it wasn't hard to do. By this point in the war, we had strung enough wire that it was just a matter of following procedure. They knew the routine well.

The Third Army remained on the move. Enemy resistance had intensified along the line between the Eder River and the Fulda River, where the Germans had dug in. We discovered from captured enemy documents and reports from POWs that the Germans had constructed a defense line that ran south from Kassel. Their resistance seemed the strongest we had seen since crossing the Rhine. They were blowing bridges right and left. The vital crossing at Heimbold-shausen got knocked out. The enemy was now defending these areas with bazooka teams. They had also hauled in some big assault guns as well as more tanks. We had our hands full responding. Nevertheless, the Sixth Armored Division crossed the Fulda River on a treadway makeshift bridge. A large railroad bridge had not been blown, and that helped us. However, the enemy kept destroying overpasses and underpasses, making it hard to move on the autobahn.

It took house-to-house fighting to finally take Kassel, where the Nazis were pushing new enemy divisions into place. Their defenses definitely stiffened, but we were able to repel three counterattacks. The Germans hadn't quit.

Along the way, we picked up information from other soldiers and units that we contacted as we moved forward. One of the most unusual discoveries was the POW camp for Allied officers inside Colditz Castle, which we liberated. Designated Oflag IV-C, the castle became the prisoner-of-war camp for what the Germans called "incorrigible" Allied officers—those who had escaped repeatedly from other camps. During the early years of the war, prisoners were held from Poland, France, Belgium, the Netherlands, and Canada, but since 1943, the captives were limited to British and American officers. Some of our best officers got hauled into the stronghold.

The castle, towering above Colditz on an imposing hill, looked straight out of a Dracula movie. The little town was situated between Leipzig and Dresden, just east of the Zwickauer Mulde River. The larger outer court had only two exits and contained a large German garrison. Adjacent to the courtyard, a tall building housed the Allied prisoners. It was surrounded by barbed wire, and armed sentries kept a constant watch on them. Every aspect of the huge castle was controlled by the Wehrmacht. Yet even though this was allegedly a high-security prison, Colditz held the record for the most successful escapes.

We were told that Major Reinhold Eggers, a former schoolteacher, was the commandant of the castle. Eggers ran the prison with the expected military status offered to officers. He was not lenient, but neither was he a sadist. The major discovered quickly that he had a houseful of "naughty boys" who would test the tolerance of any schoolmaster.

The stories that we picked up kept us in stitches. One inmate figured out how to dress up like a woman and literally walked past the guards in high heels until one of the security officers asked to see "her" ID. "She" took off running but was caught. The prisoner's entire outfit had been scavenged from bits and pieces found around the castle grounds. Apparently, he must have looked feminine to have gotten so far.

Then there was the glider built right inside the prison. Someone noticed that the attic above the castle's chapel was out of the sentry's line of sight. Anything constructed in that upper level of space would be unknown to them. Consequently, the prisoners snuck into the attic and built a false wall to hide the area above the chapel. In order to construct the barrier, the men had to carefully steal pieces of wood. They could get away with this effort because the Germans were always looking for tunnels but never thought to look up. Still, the Allied builders had their own men staying on lookout and even built an electric alarm system that would go off if the German sentries approached.

To construct the glider, the prisoners used bed slats and even floorboards. They carefully stripped out electrical wiring in areas of the castle where no one was living. As they worked with the best specifications they could muster, the glider eventually reached a thirty-two-foot wingspan. Materials from sleeping bags and cotton cloth became the skin of the plane. The unique flying device slowly came together. All that was left to do was to tear the tile off the roof and break open enough space to put the glider through the hole. The whole time the glider was being constructed, the Germans didn't have a clue. Even though the aircraft had been constructed mathematically, and the Americans were sure it would fly, they never got the chance. The glider remained hidden in the loft.

The prisoners tried every imaginable method of escape. Usually the plans were quashed before they could succeed, but that didn't stop them from trying. My men loved hearing these tales from inside the crypts of Colditz Castle. We were reminded of the courage necessary to endure the struggles of war.

General Patton once told the troops that the average person thought bravery meant having no fear. If that was so, the veteran of two world wars declared, then he had never seen a brave man. Everyone is frightened when he goes into battle. According to Patton, the more intelligent a soldier was, the more frightened he would be. A courageous man pressed on *in spite of* his fear. Afterward, while standing around a small campfire, my unit of six chewed on what the general had said.

"Why, I'm the bravest man any of you ever met!" Snuffy Smith said, laughing.

"How's that?" asked Mr. Dobson.

"'Cause I'm terrified every time I hear the artillery go off! You can pin the coward-of-the-week medal on me."

"You're joking," Jack Postwaiet said. "But it ain't no joke."

"No kidding," Mr. Parker reflected. "I guess part of what makes us tick is that we were raised to do what's right regardless of what it costs. That's what we do every day. We get up and go about our business because we love our country and want to protect our homes."

"You're older than most of us, Parker," Al Jackson said. "How did you get into this dog fight?"

Parker rubbed his chin for a moment. "Well," he began slowly, "we were a poor family. My parents emigrated from England after the end of that war to end all wars. They ended up in Pittsburgh, like so many other immigrants, and went to work in the steel mills. My father did right well, and soon we had our own house. I guess when I heard that the Nazis were bombing London, it did something to me. I thought of those distant relatives having their homes flattened and burned down. I knew somebody had to stop those damn Germans, and I figured that might just be my job. I went down to the office and enlisted."

For several moments, no one said anything. Snuffy turned to Walt Brandon. "You're the religious kind, Walt. What got you over here?"

"I guess if I had gone to a seminary, I might have gotten a defer-ment," he replied. "Somehow that didn't seem right. I tried to sign up as a chaplain's assistant, but that didn't work out. I ended up getting sent down to Fort Sill, Oklahoma, and learned about the big guns and artillery. Just felt like it was the right slot for me. I did pray about it. Prayed a lot. So, I concluded this was the right place for me to be."

"Ain't that a little like throwing the dice?" Al Jackson said cyni-cally. "I mean . . . you could have ended up anywhere."

"But I didn't," Walt said. "I ended up here, and I think God's hand was in it all along."

"Nice to have a faith like that," Mr. Parker said. "Helps you get through those times when the bombs are flying." He turned to me. "Tell me, Sergeant. How do you answer that question about what makes a man brave?"

"I don't know that I have an answer," I said. "I just remember my daddy going to work every day out there in the oil patch. Running those drilling rigs was dangerous business. The irony is that he didn't die pushing towering oil field pipes around. The doctor just waited too long to remove his appendix. He died in a hospital. I guess you figure when your time comes, there's not much you can do about it. So, in the meantime, you keep a steady hand and live your life as best you can." I reached into my shirt pocket and pulled out the piece of paper with Psalm 91 printed on it. "Every now and then when I get a little nervous, I read this: 'For Jehovah is my refuge! I choose the God above all gods to shelter me.' That's the best answer I have."

"Good enough," Walt said.

Al Jackson pursed his lips like he was going to say something cute—but didn't.

"I think anybody who puts on the uniform and goes to war is a brave person," Mr. Dobson said. "I don't care what he does or how often his hands shake. It takes guts to walk into a war." He looked around at each of us standing there. "You are all courageous men in my book."

We started back up the street when a soldier came running toward us.

"Have you heard?"

"Heard what?" I asked.

"President Roosevelt died!"

"What?" we gasped.

"Just got the news! Our president is dead!"

30

★ ★ ★

OBSTINATE

The crazy thing was that the Nazis *still* wouldn't quit.

German citizens were running for their lives as our tanks rumbled through their villages. The Russians were coming one way, and we were coming the other. The Third Reich would soon be crushed like an empty can under a truck's tire. But the Nazis kept fighting, almost fanatically. The best that we could tell was that Nazism had become the equivalent of a fundamentalist religion. Their soldiers must have thought they were on some sort of holy crusade.

The horrendous winter had finally yielded to spring. No one had ever seen what we'd lived through, with snow up to our waists and temperatures below minus-50 degrees, while winds nearly blew down trees. Looking back, I don't know how we survived. Living through a deadly winter with the enemy trying to kill you every day starts to consume your mind. The pressure hangs around your neck like a noose. You almost become a different person. Most of us had entered the war as just kids; in a month's time, we had become old men.

Mail call came. I got two letters from my mother but none from Alice. I wondered if she had gone to the prom after all. Her letters seemed to be thinning out, and it made me worry. My mother filled me in on some of the details of everyday life in Weleetka. My brothers and sister at home were all doing fine, and life went on in a normal fashion. Kids went to school. Mother had a job that brought in some money. The Sisson family apparently was surviving just fine. I wondered what they would think if they could spend just one day with me, going down any road that led to the front. Bodies lying in the bar ditch. Heads with bullet holes in them. Pieces of human beings hanging from trees and strewn over the grass. The ghastly smell that sometimes hung in the air. What would they think? They'd be terrified out of their minds!

I realized we'd probably never tell them what we were seeing right now. American civilians would go about their normal eight-to-five jobs, stop for lunch, and come home at night and read the evening paper before turning on the radio. Everything would float by as just another day. They simply wouldn't get it.

I know that I was beginning to sound depressed, and I was. My mother's letters were always nice and sweet, but the tone contrasted with my world so severely that it didn't sit well. Don't get me wrong: I loved hearing from her and wanted her to keep writing. Still, I could feel the chasm that now existed between us.

And then there was Alice. Always telling me she couldn't live without me and then not writing very often. She seemed to be stuck in a schoolgirl world. When she did write, I realized that our worlds, too, had diverged. I didn't think like a kid anymore. My job was to keep information flowing so that we could kill more people and stay alive another day.

I folded Mom's letter and stuck it in my pocket to read again later. I could tell from the rumbling messages coming into the artillery center that we were about to move again. The Germans were crumbling and offering little resistance. If you wandered around near the front line, though, you could certainly get shot in the head. That was for sure. However, the reality was they were beaten, and any intelligent person knew it. Hitler and Goebbels had to be totally nuts.

A first lieutenant walked by, and I stopped him. "Can you tell me where my men are headed? We string wire from observation points to the big guns to ensure accuracy."

"I don't have the whole story," the officer said, "but we're being put on hold for some reason. We seem to be moving too fast. I think you're going over to Munich for a breather. Of course, we're in the process of occupying the city. Still a bit of work to be done."

"Really? Munich?"

"Yeah, our boys just got through bombing the hell out of the city. They tell me we've already made seventy-four air raids that killed nearly seven thousand people and left a pile of wounded. Munich got hit with four hundred fifty large bombs and who knows how many magnesium incendiary bombs. Our planes were coming in at low level. A new targeting approach. Devastating."

"I guess so," I said.

"I understand that half the city was damaged. One report said eighty-one thousand houses were wiped out, leaving three hundred thousand homeless. At one time, Munich was the fourth largest city in Germany. You can imagine how much damage we did."

"Sure."

"We are now taking the city," he said. "Won't be hard or take much time. I know the Third Infantry and Forty-Second Infantry divisions are on the way, as well as the Forty-Fifth Infantry Division. They may already be on the attack. If so, they are already blowing the resistance apart. The locals aren't going to be happy campers."

"I imagine so," I said. "I don't imagine we'll be too popular with the locals."

The lieutenant laughed. "I wouldn't run for office if I were you. Hard to say what their attitude might be. I imagine after you got your house blown away, you'd be having big second thoughts about Hitler and his Nazis. Rather hard to be enthusiastic about the boys down at the Reichstag in Berlin when they've caused your country to be blown to pieces."

"They might not show their hostility to us?"

He nodded. "Not if they are smart. I think Winston Churchill once said the Huns are either at your throat or your feet. I'd bet on licking your boots regardless of what they think or feel."

"Should prove interesting," I said. "Back when we first rolled into Germany, citizens were planting mines in the streets and running around with pistols. I guess that's fading."

The lieutenant nodded. "But keep your eyes open."

"You bet."

I walked over to my six men, sitting on the ground under some trees. "Looks like we're going to Munich. We'll be moving out quickly."

"Munich!" Al Jackson exclaimed. "They've got that famous Hofbrauhaus beer hall that's supposed to be the biggest beer garden in the world. I understand old Hitler staged the Beer Hall Putsch from there. I think they called it the Bürgerbräukeller then. The Putsch was his attempt to overthrow the government. Can't wait to hit the place."

"I doubt if it's there," I said. "The city was bombed seventy-four times, and the downtown is probably a pile of rubble. We'll have to see."

Al shrugged. "That'd be a nasty blow. Don't you imagine they got prostitutes running around selling at bargain prices?"

I shot him a harsh look. "I wouldn't say that too loud if I were you. I don't know if you're joking or serious. Whatever, keep it to yourself unless you want a military policeman following you around. I don't think General Patton's big on drunkenness or whoring."

Walt Brandon nodded. "I'm sure we'll find plenty of hungry people wandering down the streets. Munich was a great city. It was once the capital of Bavaria when it was a kingdom. I believe it was also the center of the Weimar Republic that Hitler tried to overthrow. I understand the Nazis built the first concentration camp ten miles up the road at Dachau."

"You're just full of info, Walt," Al sneered. "A real walking encyclopedia."

"Don't be such a smart mouth!" Mr. Parker barked at Al. "You might learn something that you don't know."

I glanced at Parker, weighing at least 225 pounds. No matter how big Jackson's mouth was, I didn't think Al would want to mess with him.

"Anybody know any more about Munich?" I asked.

The men shook their heads.

"Okay." I said. "Get your gear together. We're pulling out."

31

★ ★ ★

MUNICH 1945

The final battle for Munich began on April 29, 1945, when four U.S. divisions—the Twentieth Armored, the Third Infantry, the Forty-Second Infantry, and the Forty-Fifth Infantry—converged from the outskirts of the city. Some sectors were well defended against this opening drive. However, the city itself was captured quickly, as the German defenders there offered only light resistance, on April 30.

The troop carrier bounced down the dirt road heading toward the front lines. Dust flew and settled over us. We figured that the back road kept us fairly well concealed from enemy fire except from the air, although our P-51 Mustang fighter planes were doing a good job of keeping the sky clear. As we crawled along, it was obvious that our driver was playing it safe. We soon transferred to our own truck.

Mr. Parker had picked up the pace after some adjustments were made on the truck. We kept traveling a significant distance to the east and then south. Munich was only about seventy miles from Austria, Hitler's birthplace, which Germany had annexed in 1938. Mr. Parker pulled up, and we stopped at a crossroads. The rest of our unit was standing there waiting for us to show.

"You boys looking for a ride?" he called out the window.

"You bet!" Walt Brandon hollered back.

"Hop in," Parker called back. "We're on our way to see the Oz."

The men climbed in, and we were off again. As we got closer to Munich, our unit could see smoke on the horizon. The sound of gunfire carried a long way. We were certainly picking it up like a resounding echo. The truck kept moving until we came to another checkpoint.

"Where you men headed?" the sentinel asked.

"We've been ordered to hunker down in Munich," I said. "We're with Patton's Third Army and were sent to Munich until further orders come through."

"We're finishing up cleaning out any resistance right now," the guard said. "You'll need to go around before you drive straight into Munich. Apparently, they can use some help this side of the city. Take the side road."

We continued down the road. The noise of gunfire grew louder. The results of a recent skirmish became evident. Debris was scattered across the road. A few vehicles were still burning. A German Focke-Wulf 190 had crashed in a field just off the road. The airplane was a capable fighter but must have simply gotten too close to antiaircraft fire. Ahead we could see the outline of a small town. A few clouds of smoke were curling up into the sky, but other than that, everything looked so quiet we guessed the residents had either run for the hills or were hiding in their cellars. One very large building looked like a manufacturing plant of some sort. Could be a center for producing Messerschmitt aircraft. We kept rolling.

Northwest of Munich, we crossed a railroad track that ran along the edge of the town of Dachau. Not far ahead stood a large metal fence and gate. Barbed wire had been strung everywhere. On the top of the entrance, stretching clear across the two lanes, was a sign that read "*Arbeit Macht Frie.*" We pulled to a halt.

"Anybody know enough German to translate?" I called out.

"I'm no German school student," Snuffy Smith said, "but I did study a year of German my first year in college before I joined the army. I think that says, 'Work makes you free.' Not exactly an invitation to a vacation."

A couple of sentinels walked up to our truck. "Headquarters sent you?" the guard asked.

"No, we're on our way to Munich."

"You can't get in there yet," the guard said. "We need some help here. We'll let you in if you can give us a hand."

"Sure," I said.

The guard looked me square in the eye. "Hang on, 'cause you've never seen anything like what's inside this place."

Our truck rolled through the iron gate, and immediately the odor hit us. Death hung in the air like a maleficent fog. We stopped, and the men got out. We could see barracks and buildings. Barbed wire lined the perimeters. On the far side of the camp stood a blackened brick chimney. The crematorium, I realized with horror.

A guard walked up to us. "We need help feeding these prisoners. They are literally starving to death. It ain't a pretty sight."

I nodded. "Where do you want us to go?"

"Walk down the corridor in front of you. At the far end, survivors are standing in line waiting."

We headed toward them. At the end of the first long building, I stopped and stared. At least a dozen bodies were piled up like a cord of wood. Most were naked, with arms and legs sticking out like broken tree limbs. They looked like all the muscle had shrunk away from starvation. I gasped and could hardly move on.

"Oh, my God!" blurted out Mr. Parker. "Never seen nothing like that in my whole life."

I couldn't speak, so I just waved my hand and we continued walking. At the end of the next building, a barbed wire fence held back a crowd of prisoners. They cheered and waved to us.

I looked into their sunken faces and could only blink. Some of their eyes looked empty, like all life was gone. Empty, like they had seen so much death that nothing was left but despair. Their heads were shaved, their cheeks drawn. Some didn't even have pants on— only long, black-and-white-striped prison shirts that hung to their knees. Their thin legs looked like nothing more than skinny poles that could barely support their bodies. Interspersed among them were a few teenage boys. Their faces were dirty and splashed with mud, like they had not washed in two lifetimes.

Still, they kept cheering and waving. Some of them seemed almost hysterical with joy that we had taken the camp. We kept smiling and waving back, but when I glanced at my men, I could tell they were having a hard time digesting what they could not avoid seeing. We were walking through hell itself.

We came to the end of the row, where a line of prisoners were standing, waiting to get a bowl of soup and some bread. An army attachment kitchen had been set up and was distributing food. I walked up to a sergeant overseeing the operation.

"What do you need us to do?" I asked.

"These men are starving," he said. "When they get food, they wolf it down, and that causes serious digestive problems. Actually, it can kill them. They've got to eat slowly and in small amounts. Your men can watch them and make sure they don't damage themselves. Just pick out one of them when they come out with the soup and bread in hand and keep them in low gear."

"Will do," I said.

I looked at my six. "Everybody got it?"

They nodded.

We walked over to the front of the line and waited. A walking skeleton hobbled out with a bowl of soup in one hand and bread in the other. Both hands were shaking. His emotionally wrinkled face looked if he was about to cry. I followed him, and he sat down at a makeshift table. I sat down across from him.

Along the way, I had learned a few German phrases. I wondered if he spoke English. *"Sprich Englisch?"*

He tasted the soup and closed his eyes for a moment. *"Ja, in der tat."* "Yes, as a matter of fact."

"Great. You know some of the language."

The man took a deep breath. *"Ja,"* he said slowly. "I was once a teacher. An English teacher in a gymnasium."

"Eat slow," I said. "You will make yourself sick. Slow down."

He rubbed his mouth and nodded. "Y-y-es. It's been so long since no food," he said with a strong German accent. "So long."

"Why would a schoolteacher be in a concentration camp?" I asked.

"I publicly opposed the Nazi party line," he explained. "I not would teach my class about National Socialism as best ideal. Me, they arrested, and I endured four years here."

"Four years!"

"I believe so . . . Sometime it hard to remember . . . hard to . . ." His voice drifted away.

"Just eat a bite of the bread," I said. "A small bite."

He nibbled at the crust.

"Do you have a family?"

"My wife . . ." He stopped. "I think still alive she is in the town of Küstrin. I don't know. I hope." He grabbed the soup bowl and took a big gulp, then lowered it slowly to the table. "I know," he acknowledged. "Slowly."

"I assumed the prisoners were all Jews," I said.

"Some are. Lots of Roman Catholic priests in here. Some gypsies. Everyday people. Even famous clergyman Martin Niemöller was here. If the Nazis didn't like you, they hauled you into here."

"They made you work?" I asked.

"Constantly," the teacher said. "We cultivate plants in field. Sometimes fall in dirt."

"Horrible!"

The prisoner looked up at me. His lip trembled. "Thank God you come. You save our lives."

I looked around. Everywhere, broken, starving men were gawking at us. Pitiful, sick, emaciated human beings. The only specter that reigned supreme here was death. Ghastly, undignified death.

32

* * *

CATCHING OUR BREATH

Night was falling when we left the Dachau concentration camp. We had helped a multitude of prisoners get fed as well as taken care of others. One never got used to what has to be done in such a ghastly place. Along the way, we met a variety of men who wanted to bow at our feet and treat us like conquerors from the Roman Empire. We tried to reassure them that our only interest was in helping them survive. Just treating us as friends would be fine, we said.

I kept thinking about Eli Cohen and what he'd told me about pogroms and the persecution of the Jews through the centuries. It just didn't compute fully until I spent the afternoon in Dachau. I'd gotten a good sense of the problem when we worked our way through Buchenwald, but this horrible place seemed more personal. I thought I had the full picture earlier, but I didn't. It was incomprehensible.

Near the end of the war, religious leaders of all kinds had been put in one barracks. Roman Catholics, Protestants, priests, and other clergy were bunched together like cabbages piled on top of one another in a grocery store. We learned eventually that one-third of all the Catholic priests in Poland were incarcerated in Dachau. We discovered also that many of the prisoners were forced to work in an adjacent manufacturing plant making Messerschmitt airplanes. Any mistakes on the assembly line were rewarded with a bullet to the head.

Nighttime didn't seem the best moment to enter Munich. With the shooting being so recent, we might make a good target for some rogue sniper still on the loose. Instead, we stayed in the town of Dachau for the night. There were plenty of empty houses around, so we settled in. Most of the town was gone. We guessed people had been scurrying to save their lives. Dobson and I found a nice little villa that looked like it had just been prepared for us to walk in and kick up our heels. There was even a hunk of roast beef in the cooler and a stock of wine bottles. We could grab a good night's rest. Believe you me, we washed our hands about three times that evening.

Around eight o'clock, a lieutenant showed up to reassure us that we could enter Munich in the morning. He believed the streets had been cleared of snipers, but the city was not in good shape. We could see the sights that were left, but there wasn't much going on. Actually, a couple of beer halls had survived the bombing. He couldn't tell whether they'd be friendly or not, but they certainly wouldn't give us any static. The average citizen had decided some time ago that the Nazis were defeated and Germany had lost the war. They were simply facing the facts even if Hitler and his cronies couldn't read the handwriting on the wall.

"Lieutenant, where are you from?" I asked.

He set his helmet on the table. "You probably never heard of the place, but I grew up in an old gold rush town in the mountains of Colorado. Ever hear of Fairplay?"

I shook my head. "Sorry, but I bet you never heard of Weleetka, Oklahoma."

The man laughed. "Man, we ought to get an award for coming from weird places."

"How did a town get a name like Fairplay?"

"Had to do with the gold rush days, when people were stealing one another's claims. Fairplay became the county seat of Park County, high up in the Rocky Mountains."

Mr. Dobson held up a bottle. "Pour you a drink? We found this wine in the basement. It's good stuff."

"Don't mind if I do."

Dobson poured him a glassful. "We've had a grim day. Worked in the concentration camp over there." He pointed over his shoulder.

The lieutenant shook his head. "Ain't nothing more grim than war. At least that's what I always thought until I hit this place. I've had to rethink my ideals. The Nazis have to be the most frightening aberration that ever hatched from a rotten egg. They even did diabolical medical experiments on the bodies of the prisoners. Just cut 'em up." He took a big gulp.

We didn't say anything for a while.

"I heard General Patton speak once," the lieutenant said. "He said that we had three things that led to victory. The first was strong, patriotic men. The 'dogface' GI Joe types that are mentally clever and physically strong. On the other hand, the German soldiers came from a different world. They were certainly obedient enough, but they were rigid and lacked the ingenuity that was natural for our guys. When it came to trading blows with the enemy, we came out on top because we were more innovative."

"Interesting," Dobson said. "What's the second factor?"

"Patton thought the skillful labor and excellent production that we have in America meant that we could deliver the goods to our fighting men overseas without stopping, just as we have in this war. That's no small accomplishment, and Patton applauded what we do at home."

I smiled. "Occasionally we hear about Rosie the Riveter. When I was welding in California before I turned eighteen, I saw women working there just as hard as men. Quite a sight."

"And number three?" Dobson asked.

"General Patton believes in superb leadership that can produce a comprehensive strategy and the kind of field tactics that leave the enemy guessing. Patton is the master of those skills. He left the enemy sitting there staring at the wall without a clue about what would come next. Absolutely amazing! In my book, he'll go down as one of the greatest generals in history."

"The times that I saw him," I said, "he was inspiring. The man literally was walking confidence. When he waved at you, you could tell he was in total control."

"The trouble was that he couldn't keep his mouth shut, and his opinions rattled everyone from the politicians to the top commander," the lieutenant said. "I think Eisenhower has been afraid Patton will pop off and start World War III with the Russians."

"No love lost there," Dobson said. "Anything left to see in Munich?"

"We were there earlier in the day and found the streets deserted. Rather scary situation riding through the city where Hitler got his start. Came in nice and slow because the enemy could be hiding anywhere, waiting for us. We weren't creeping in behind a tank or with dogs to sniff out the city. All we had was our jeeps and rifles. Gave us the creeps."

"How far did you go in?" I asked.

"Got clear to the center of the city. As we got closer to the Marienplatz, the center, we began to see some people. Then when we got to the center, we found a small crowd. Most of them were really old and probably couldn't have gotten into the *Volkssturm,* Hitler's last stupid idea. They clapped like we were their liberators. Those old Germans waved like we were their last hope. I thought that was stupid. Here we were capturing the city where Hitler's movement began, and which had also published the Nazi propaganda newspaper, and they're treating us like heroes? These people probably had it better than just about anybody else in Germany, and they wanted us to think we had set them free? Who were they kidding?"

"I imagine they were scared to death," Dobson said.

"Probably," the lieutenant replied. "Amazing how these supposedly fierce enemies could quickly fall into line when they knew they were finished. One of our guys told me that they found a police station and figured soldiers or officers might be in there, ready for a fight to the death. The soldiers knew they had to confiscate any weapons that were on these Germans. They cautiously walked in with their rifles ready to fire. To the soldiers' surprise, the police gave them a military salute. They had already boxed up their guns. Each pistol had two tags. One was the number of the weapon and the other the name of the officer who had been issued the weapon. Our boys just couldn't believe it. All their weapons were in a box on the table. I think all that's left is some sort of final skirmish out there around the Munich Airport. Other than that, you should have no problems."

"Thanks for the update," I said. "Appreciate the insights. We'll be going in tomorrow morning."

The lieutenant stood up and put his helmet back on. "Enjoy your stay. The city is all yours. Compliments of Mr. Hitler."

33

★ ★ ★

R&R

The sun broke through the window and woke me. As it swept across my face, I felt like it was washing away some measure of the agony and unspeakable memories from the day before. But then suddenly I was back in somebody else's bed simply trying not to remember those shrunken faces and emaciated bodies strung across the ground. We knew the war couldn't last much longer, and for some reason we didn't understand, we were supposed to enjoy ourselves in a bombed-out city where a huge number of the population had disappeared.

For once, we weren't in a hurry. I got out of bed more leisurely than usual. I had seen enough destroyed cities and beautiful ornate buildings reduced to a pile of dust that I wasn't in any more of a hurry to get to Munich. The city couldn't be ten miles away at the most, but I wanted to take it easy. Mr. Dobson had stayed across the hall and probably wasn't in any more of a hurry than I was.

I walked into the kitchen and discovered that I was the first one up. I sat down at the wooden table that had obviously been handmade. Its worn surface must have fed who knows how many people over the years. The kitchen had a charm that felt almost like home. I found some cheese and a small, round loaf of bread tucked away in a cupboard. The cheese had a different smell to it, and I had no idea what kind it was, but the taste was on the mild side. I sat there in the quiet, enjoying the absence of cannons blasting and rifles firing.

I lit a cigarette and thought about what it might be like to go back home again. Would the town be any different? Would the people be the same? Perhaps life in Weleetka had rolled along like a train leaving town, and I would be left in the station alone as it roared away. Hard to say. But I knew the war had made everything different whether I liked it or not.

Mr. Dobson came in and sat down across from me. "I see you ate everything in the house," he said with a grin.

"Would I betray you?"

"Yeah, you would!" Dobson laughed. "Anything left?"

"Try that cupboard over there. I think you'll find something better than those army rations."

We sat there lost in our own thoughts. Finally, I spoke.

"Thinking about home?"

Dobson looked down at the table for a few moments. "Yeah. Seems like it's a chapter of a book that I once read, but now the book is lost. I'm somewhere else."

"Know what you mean." I blew a puff of smoke overhead. "You can certainly disappear in this strange land called Germany. Never seen anything like it. The buildings are different. The streets twist and turn without any rhyme or reason. Never heard people speak German before like they do every day of the week here. I miss that Oklahoma twang. Really different."

"Know what you mean." Dobson looked away. Of course, he was

A portrait of me in uniform. *(Courtesy of the author)*

The Kaiser Shipyards in California, where I welded ships for the war effort before my draft number was called. *(Imperial War Museum)*

An aerial view of Camp Bowie, where we trained before deploying to Europe. *(Brown County Museum of History)*

Me and the boys at Camp Bowie. *(Courtesy of the author)*

Leaning against an army vehicle. *(Courtesy of the author)*

Before he was one of
the greatest generals of
World War II, George
Patton was a cadet
at Virginia Military
Institute, where he is
shown here in 1907.
*(Virginia Military
Institute Museum)*

Generals Patton and Eisenhower in Tunisia discussing the war in March 1943. (*U.S. Army*)

Patton atop an M3 Scout Car, in a scene not unlike that first day I encountered him. (*U.S. Army*)

A photograph I sent to Mom. *(Courtesy of the author)*

We all admired that General Patton wasn't afraid to stick his own neck out on the front lines. Here he watches ongoing operations in Sicily, alongside his staff. *(Imperial War Museum)*

Patton's scowl here is a look we knew well. He was never afraid to speak his mind. *(U.S. Army)*

Patton smoking a pipe as he watches maneuvers in 1941. *(U.S. Army)*

Sitting on a bench with Snuffy Smith, one of my closest friends from the Third Army. *(Courtesy of the author)*

In a rare moment of levity, I posed here on the barrel of a
destroyed German cannon. *(Courtesy of the author)*

An aerial shot of Saint-Lô, France, in 1944, before the devastation. (*U.S. Army*)

The famed Normandy hedgerows, in what General Omar Bradley called "the damndest country I've seen." (*U.S. Army*)

The Church of Notre-Dame in Saint-Lô, surrounded by rubble. *(National Archives)*

A battlefield outside Saint-Lô. (*Courtesy of the author*)

Snuffy Smith and I sit amid the ruins of Saint-Lô. (*Courtesy of the author*)

The watchtower at Dachau concentration camp, 1945. *(National Archives)*

The liberation of Dachau in April 1945. I will never forget what we witnessed there. *(U.S. Army)*

When General Patton passed away suddenly on December 21, 1945, I felt as though I had lost a second father. Here pallbearers carry his casket. *(National Archives)*

Patton's funeral was held at Christ Church in Heidelberg, Germany. He was buried at the Third Army Cemetery in Luxembourg.

Even seventy-five years after his death, General Patton looms larger than life. Here the Patton Monument at West Point stands guard over a new generation of soldiers. *(Ahodges7)*

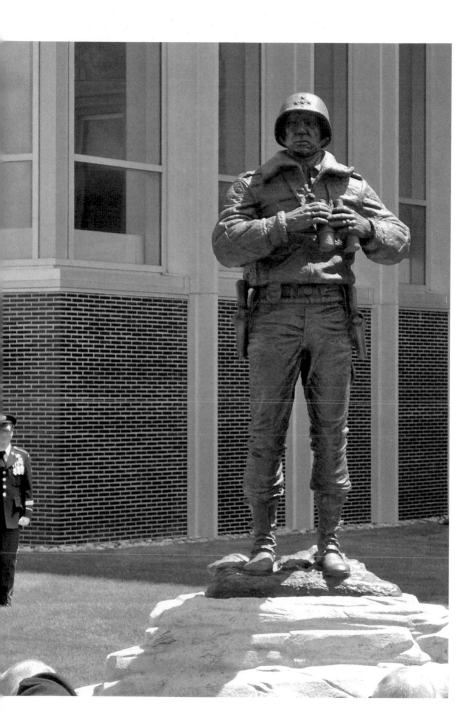

Placing a stone upon a monument in Kerpen, Germany, dedicated to the residents of that town who died in the Holocaust. (*Courtesy of the author*)

At Dachau. There isn't a day goes by that I don't think about the war. (*Courtesy of the author*)

older, but something had touched a nerve, and he didn't want to talk about it.

I finished my bread and cheese. Put out the cigarette. "I guess I'll go pack my gear, so I'll be ready to go when everybody else is."

Mr. Dobson nodded but didn't say anything.

An hour later, the six of us were sitting on the curb waiting for Dobson to pick us up. Nobody was saying much. The concentration camp experience had affected everybody in much the same way. We didn't want to talk about it.

Our truck rolled up in front of us. Everyone picked up his gear and climbed in. We rode back to the highway that took us into Munich proper. The smoke had cleared, and there were no sounds of shooting. Military trucks loaded with soldiers were going in the opposite direction, probably, I would realize later, on their way to the final battle at the airport. We passed a cart loaded with home furnishings of some sort being pulled by a man and a woman, with another woman in back helping to push the cart forward. They were dressed like poor people in the 1920s looked, with shawls wrapped around them and bedraggled coats.

We turned into the city. It was clear that Munich had been as badly bombed as we'd heard. Everywhere we looked, the evidence of explosions littered the streets. Splintered boards and scattered glass were strewn over the sidewalks. Roofs cratered. Windows and doors gone. Hunks of concrete piled up. Church steeples destroyed. Devastation everywhere.

Not until we were halfway into the city did we finally see anyone: an old lady walking a dog on a leash turned a corner just ahead of us. Her scarf was pulled down, nearly covering her face, so she didn't have to look up. The woman didn't glance at us as we roared past.

Since we seemed to be the only vehicle within miles, we got the picture. Her avoidance meant "Go to hell."

As we got nearer the Marienplatz, an American guard stepped into the street and held up his hand to have us stop.

"Where you men headed?" he asked.

"Believe it or not, we're here for a little R&R. Doesn't look like much of a place for a little vacation, though," I said.

"You got that right," the guard said. "You need to check in so they'll know where to find you. Straight ahead is a bombed-out hotel. You'll see the sign. Aloft Munchen. Headquarters is in the basement."

The only habitable area in many of these bombed buildings was the basement.

"Okay," I said and saluted.

The guard returned the salute, and we drove off. A block away, the Aloft Munchen sign hung precariously at an angle like it was ready to fall off. We walked inside—made easier by the fact that the front doors were gone—stepping over broken glass. One look around, and we spotted the stairs that led down. We walked up to a sergeant sitting behind a desk.

"We're here to sign in," I announced. "We're with the Six-Sixty-Seventh Field Artillery Battalion. We were sent here for a little relaxation. Where in the hell can you put up your feet in this blown-up city?"

He laughed. "Now, that's a challenge, but you'll find a number of places the bombers missed. Just come back after you settle in and let us know where we can find you."

"Will do," I said.

Each of the men registered, and we walked out. Back on the street, we glanced around. A huge cathedral looked like it had been hit but was still standing. Inside a tall tower, a huge clock with moving figures grabbed anyone's attention that walked by. The bombers missed it, but the magnificent clock no longer ticked.

"Maybe we ought to find a hotel or some housing facility," Al Jackson suggested. "Possibly there are some empty houses around."

"Okay," I said. "Let us see what we can turn up."

34

★ ★ ★

ROUGHING IT

By nightfall, we'd found one hotel near the center of town that was semifunctional. They seemed overjoyed to see anyone, much less seven of us. We quickly found our rooms. To do nothing more than relax seemed heavenly. A real change of pace. Other soldiers began to roll into Munich as the occupation developed. The surrounding small towns became sites where houses were commandeered. The owners were allowed to stay there without any disruption to their kitchen or facilities. The commander explained that bedding was needed only for a night or two, and then they'd be moving on.

Word spread quickly that the vast majority of local citizens actually did see us as their liberators. They had not only not supported the Nazis, but many had been abused by them. Hitler had become a hated symbol of tyranny. These German natives now recognized us as their deliverers. We found quickly that they wanted our friendship. Of course, that was smart on their part.

We strolled the streets to see anything that was still worth seeing. On one corner, we found a large concrete swastika statue with an eagle attached on the top. Wouldn't be long before someone tore that down. We found shrines and some statues that had survived. Actually, Munich proved to be a fascinating city even with all the destruction. The medieval touches of the distant past remained in much of what we saw.

That evening we hunted for a nightclub still standing. The infamous Hofbrauhaus of Bürgerbräukeller, where Hitler started out in the basement, had been destroyed, so that beer garden was out. Someone told us about a place called Kulbtiaabrik, but we couldn't find it. Another nightspot, the Strom, operating out of a cellar in the center of the city, seemed to fit our needs best, so we sauntered over.

We were met at the door by a maître d' who was almost out of his mind with joy that U.S. soldiers had walked in. He immediately showed us to a table next to the dance floor and brought us a complimentary bottle of wine. You would have thought we were royalty. The food selection was skimpy, but we understood; they were lucky to still be in business.

I noticed a small group of women walk in and start looking us over. I imagined they hadn't seen too many GIs up close and wondered what made us tick. We had just about finished eating when two of them came over to our table.

"*Tanzen?*" the first girl said, beaming. "Dance?" She was tall and kind of skinny, with a pretty face.

"*Der Tanz?*" the second one added. "Do you dance?" Much shorter, she had a knockout figure.

"Sorry," I said. "No *sprechen*. Only English."

The girls giggled. One said, "Swing? Jitterbug?"

"Hot dog!" Al Jackson jumped up. "You're on!" He held out his hand, and the tall one took it.

I noticed a waiter pushing a record player onto the edge of the dance floor. He held up a 78 single record and studied it for a moment. Then he put the black platter on the turntable and set down the needle. Suddenly the infectious rhythm of clarinetist Benny Goodman and his orchestra echoed around the room. Jackson was out there in the middle of it, having the time of his life. The woman that he kept swinging around seemed to know the steps like a pro. While the Nazis abhorred swing music as degenerate, and, of course, hated bandleader Goodman, who was Jewish, somehow these girls had smuggled the records in under the door. She was following Al like an American dance queen.

"You dance?" Snuffy Smith asked me.

"Not worth a hoot."

Snuffy laughed. "Well, here's your chance. I see one of those girls over there eyeing you."

"Get serious," I said.

"Here she comes!"

I looked up to see blond hair framing a beautiful face. *"Tanzen?"* She appeared to force a smile. Even though she was poured into a dress on the suggestive side, and wore fire-engine-red lipstick that was almost fluorescent and too much rouge, under it all, this young woman certainly looked to be on the naïve and unsophisticated side. *"Tanzen?"* she repeated.

I glanced around at the men, knowing my face was turning red. They were laughing. The young woman kept grinning.

"No *sprechen* German." I shrugged.

"Okay, American boy," she said with only a slight accent. "I teach you." She laughed.

"I'm not good at dancing," I replied.

"Okay, American boy, you can learn." She reached for my hand.

The next thing I knew, I was on the dance floor, probably looking more like a clown than a dancer. She kept moving her feet to the music and swinging her hips with the beat. I tried to imitate whatever she did.

"How'd you learn to speak English?" I shouted over the music.

"Study in school it." She kept grinning.

"And your name?"

"Am called Greta. Greta Hirsch."

"Well, Greta, my dancing isn't very good."

"Oh, fine." She kept moving her feet back and forth to the music.

I kept doing whatever turns and twists that she did. I didn't have to talk while dancing, so that made it easier. When the song stopped, Greta didn't let go of my hand. She pulled me over to an empty table away from the rest of the guys.

"We talk here nice," Greta said. "What your name, American boy?"

"Frank. Frank Sisson."

"Oh, nice name."

"How old are you, Greta?"

"I am twenty-seven years."

I laughed. "Don't kid me. How old are you really?"

Greta blushed slightly. "Seventeen."

"Ah, just about what I thought. You like a cigarette?"

"Sure."

I pulled a pack out of my pocket and gave her one. I lit it for her.

"Keep the pack," I said.

Her eyes lit up. "Oh, thank you. Thank you." She quickly slipped it into her purse. "You have . . . I think you say . . . girlfriend?"

"I do. In the United States. Her name is Alice."

"Sorry," Greta said. "I make you nice girlfriend."

I smiled. She didn't.

"You would, Greta. But I'll be here only a couple of days, and then I'm gone."

The waiter came prancing over immediately and bowed slightly. "Bottle of wine for you, Herr soldier?"

I had a sense where this might be going, and I didn't want to hop aboard that train. "*One* glass for the lady."

"Of course, Herr soldier." The waiter hurried away.

"You escaped danger during the war, the fighting?" I asked.

Her smile disappeared, and she straightened in her chair. "This is difficult to talk about. Unpleasant. Why you ask?"

"I would like to know about your experience. Your struggle."

"Maybe we can talk of something else. Like discuss swing music. The sound. The beat."

"The past few weeks have been hard for all of us. Has been for me. I'm sure it has been for you. Your city was bombed. I've walked down the streets and seen the rubble everywhere."

"Pleasant it has not been." She swallowed hard.

"Tell me some of the details. What happened?"

Greta looked at me for several seconds as if struggling to decide whether or not she should speak of her experience. Her jaw tightened. "My friends been killed. Our house bombed. Very dark time."

I studied her face for a clue. All flirtatiousness had disappeared. Her eyes looked haunted. I had touched something painful that had been lurking just below the surface. It had taken only a second to peel back a scab on a throbbing hurt. Abruptly, it seemed as if a different person was sitting in front of me.

"I find it hard the war to talk about. Please, can we change subject?"

For a moment, I studied her eyes again. Sadness had surfaced. "You are a nice person," I said sincerely. "A good girl."

Greta nodded but didn't say anything. She stared at me. Not hard. Not angry. But as if I had stripped her of a façade she had not expected to reveal on this night.

The waiter slipped a glass of wine in front of her, smiled perfunctorily, and handed me a bill. I paid it.

"No more hard questions," I said. "Do you come here to dance with men often?"

Greta shook her head. "Before never."

"Just want to have some fun?"

She shrugged and looked away.

"The Nazis made it hard for you?"

"Hitler made big promises, and then everybody got pushed into army." She stopped. "My brother never came back."

"I'm sorry, so sorry."

Silence fell between us. I watched the crowd on the dance floor, swinging away. Al Jackson looked like he was a monkey going out of his mind. Even Parker was jumping around like a toad on a hot plate.

"You are kind man," Greta said eventually. "Your soothing words good to hear. Important for me tonight."

"You must be cautious, Greta. Most American soldiers are good folks; some aren't. Don't make yourself vulnerable to the bad boys."

"Vulnerable?" Greta shook her head. "Don't know this word."

"Means don't let anybody talk you into doing something that will degrade you, demean you," I explained.

"Oh!" She blinked several times. "Understand. Yes . . . understand."

"You are a good person," I repeated.

Greta nodded soberly. "Understand." She managed a weak smile. "Thank you for your kind thoughts. They help. Tonight . . . a hard time for me . . . yes, hard." She scooted back in her chair and stood up. "Thank you for cigarettes. Thank you, Frank American boy. Thank you."

I watched Greta bypass the girls she'd come in with, press her way through the crowd, and disappear out the door. Meanwhile, the swing sound kept pumping and the GIs hopping. The rest of her group was out hoofing it with the guys. Quite a sight.

I never saw her again.

35

★ ★ ★

THE RUSSIANS

The next morning, Walt Brandon, Jack Postawaiet, and I started out again to see what remained of Munich. Snuffy and Al stayed behind, as did Dobson and Parker. Even with all the destruction, the city retained some of its glory. When we walked down Gumpendorfer-strasse, we passed the huge concrete tower that had been built to combat World War II air raids. We came back around to St. Stephan's Church. The ancient building had been hit at least twice but came off better than most of the downtown and remained awe-inspiring.

We found an open outdoor corner coffee shop and sat down. The waiter smiled pleasantly.

"What can I get for you gentlemen?"

"You speak excellent English," I said.

"I can speak English, French, German, and Italian," he said. "In Munich, one learns to be versatile."

"You're way ahead of America," I said.

"How about strudel?" Walt said. "Got any?"

"Of course. Strudel is our specialty. Coffee as well?"

"Sure."

We talked while we sat there waiting for our order. We knew the

Russians had already hit Vienna, Austria, and that the struggle had been fierce. The waiter returned carrying a large tray with our strudel and coffee. His balancing act could not have been easy.

"Sit down," I said. "You are working too hard."

The waiter laughed. "I am happy to be here at all. Yes, today hard work makes me feel good."

"Have a question for you. Do you know anything about Vienna?"

The waiter nodded his head gravely. "Of course. I have a cousin who lives there."

Walt leaned forward. "We heard the battle to take Vienna proved to be tough."

The waiter shook his head. "You are Americans. Civilized. You have come to set Munich free, but the Russians always had other ideas. They hate the Germans, and the Austrians are too much related to us. The Russians were savage."

"We've heard such reports before," Walt said.

The waiter's eyes narrowed. And he told us of his cousin's experience. He was living in an apartment on a side street. As the Russians approached, German soldiers started shooting from the roof. When the exchange stopped, the Russians ordered everybody out of the building and lined them up in front of the apartment building. Apparently, they thought somebody in the apartment building had been firing at them. The Russians prepared to kill every one of those people. A man was standing there with his infant grandson and realized they were all about to die. He suddenly tossed the baby to one of the Russian soldiers. The Russian looked puzzled, but he realized the man was doing everything he could to save the child. Suddenly the Germans started shooting from another building they had moved to. The Russian soldier tossed the baby back to the man and started shooting at the Nazis on the other roof. If the Wehrmacht hadn't started shooting again, the Russians would have killed every one of those people.

Walt stared, but didn't say anything. The waiter walked away.

"We will hear many appalling stories," Jack said. "I just don't understand why we are sitting here doing nothing."

"Me neither," Walt added.

The strudel was as good as promised. Other soldiers walked by. We waved. It wasn't clear who was on vacation and who was part of the occupation. Eventually we saw one of the lieutenants from the 667th Field Artillery Battalion.

"Hey! Lieutenant!" Jack yelled. "Come over and grab a coffee."

We knew Lieutenant Meacham from our trek across Europe. I talked with him frequently while handling communications.

"My, my, look who they let out of the cage," he joked.

"Fancy meeting you here in the streets of Munich," I said.

"Beats trying to walk down the street in Berlin today," he said and sat down.

"We got a question for you," Jack said. "You're an insider. Why in the hell are we sitting it out in Munich instead of racing toward Berlin to end this war?"

Meacham stretched out his legs. "Yeah, there's a story behind it all. I picked up bits and pieces along the way. Reflects a difference of opinion between General Patton and Supreme Commander Eisenhower. Patton never trusted the Russians and thought we'd be going to war with them next. However, someone higher up had a different idea."

"Higher up the line?" I said. "Why, that couldn't be anybody but President Roosevelt."

The lieutenant grinned. "Don't you suppose? Unfortunately, General Patton disagreed but was overruled."

"There's got to be more to this story," I said.

"General Eisenhower had halted his troops on the Elbe River and forbid them to go across," Meacham said. "He wanted to keep the Russians on the other side. We're here because we're part of Ike's decision to allow the Russians to take Berlin. He had three reasons. First of all, Ike's army was already well beyond the line of the western occupation zone. Why go farther when the area would later have to be turned over to the Russians?

"Ike saw Berlin as a political objective and a nonmilitary goal. Of course, Churchill didn't agree with that and thought the general was overstepping his boundaries. Churchill wanted us to beat the Russians to the punch. However, Eisenhower knew the Russians were barreling toward them, and he wanted a river between the two armies. He feared the Russians were unpredictable, and there might be an accidental explosion. Allowing them to enter Berlin first minimized that risk."

"You did get the inside story," Walt said. "There's more?"

"I understand that General Omar Bradley thought taking Berlin could cost a hundred thousand casualties, and that had to be a factor in Ike's thinking. Let the Russians take the risk if they're so damn anxious to sack Berlin."

I quietly considered what he was saying, but something was missing. "I think there's more you haven't told us yet."

Meacham grinned. "My, my, aren't you the perceptive one! What we're hearing is that at Yalta, President Roosevelt promised Berlin and Prague to Stalin in addition to planning the reorganization of Germany. That's the bottom line."

We looked at one another, but nobody said anything.

"I understand General Patton's Third Army is on the doorstep of Czechoslovakia. Of course, it would be all right with Patton to punch the Russians in the nose. Eisenhower doesn't think that way."

"So, we'll be sitting here until the Russians take Berlin?" I said.

"Looks like it," the lieutenant said.

"We don't hear much about the Russians," Walt said. "Mostly

get rumors that make them sound like barbarians. How come we hear so little?"

"We're all in a war together," Meacham said. "Headquarters doesn't want to blast a partner in the battle. Moreover, the stories are so bad, it's a little hard to put them out."

"I don't understand," I said. "Give me some examples."

The lieutenant leaned back in his chair and looked at us harshly. "You boys understand that you're not going to quote me. Right?

"The Russians had a bad history to start with. In 1939 they were kicked out of the League of Nations for invading Finland. Their bad behavior never stopped. We knew some of the murderous acts of the Red Army were committed under orders from Joseph Stalin. During this current war, there have been summary executions, murders of prisoners of war, and mass rapes by their soldiers. Back in 1940, Estonia was illegally annexed by the Soviet Union. One-third of the Estonian population were either deported, arrested, or executed. After the Soviet takeover, at least two hundred thousand were lost permanently. One could see that the Soviets don't come off as your friendly next-door neighbor types.

"So, I can see why General Patton didn't trust them and believed a war with the Soviets was unavoidable.

"When a country fell under their control," he went on, "the Red Army exercised harsh treatment of the local citizens and had strong elements of ethnic cleansing. Torture was a common tool of the Soviets. Female inmates had their breasts cut off, and victims were bound together with barbed wire. You get the picture."

"Not exactly a picture of a friend at summer camp that you write home about," I said.

Walt's interest had become intense. I could see it in his eyes. "Sounds like an army of sadists."

"I think we can conclude that the NKVD, the Soviet secret police, systematically tortures prisoners and puts people to death. Happens every day. You men worked at the Dachau concentration camp and saw the horrors with your own eyes. The Nazis are savage, but the Russians aren't any better. Maybe worse."

Walt stared and didn't speak.

"It's estimated that at least a hundred thousand Polish women were raped," Meacham added. "Nobody knows what the actual numbers are, but Western estimates are that as many as two million women were raped. We're talking about a pattern of behavior happening over and over again everywhere."

"Will any of this criminal activity ever come out?" I asked.

"Hard to say. Probably depends on what they do after the war. For example, we do know about such killings as happened in the massacre of Feodosia. The Wehrmacht retreated from the Crimean city of Feodosia, leaving behind about a hundred fifty wounded men. When Soviet personnel took the city, they raided the hospital, shooting and bludgeoning to death every patient they could find. Some of the wounded were thrown out of windows after being drenched with freezing water so they'd die of hypothermia."

"I've heard enough," Walt said. "How could anyone doubt General Patton's judgment of the Russians? We're not in some modern war. This conflict is a throwback to the most barbaric times that ever existed. How can the generals avoid knowing?"

"They can't," Meacham said. "If I found out this much about the facts, you think they don't know more? Sure. People in charge simply don't want this info out there because of the impact it would have. Well, boys. Got to get on my way. Take care."

We watched the lieutenant walk away. Nobody spoke for a while. Finally, I said, "I'm not sure I wanted that much of an answer about the Russians. I can see why General Eisenhower wanted to keep a river between us and them. I bet the German citizens are running for their lives to get away from the Russian advance."

Snuffy Smith came walking up. "Hey, I just got the word from the registry officers that the party is over. They want us to be the overseers for a load of POWs that are coming in. The Germans are folding right and left. I understand they want us to capture them rather than let the Russians take them."

"Yeah, we understand that now," Walt said.

"Apparently there's some delay in getting the roads repaired, and they are holding these prisoners here. Doesn't sound like any big problems. Just keep them rounded up and quiet."

"Party was nice while it lasted," Jack said with a sigh. "I knew it was too good to be true."

"Maybe we'd better go down to that basement headquarters and see where they want us to go," Walt said.

36

★ ★ ★

CHANGE

Of course, most of the soldiers were shocked by President Franklin D. Roosevelt's death. Some were keeping it together fairly well. But for others, it was as personal as if their own father had died. During early 1941, with war raging in Europe, FDR had pushed to have the United States' factories become an "arsenal of democracy" for beleaguered Britain and France. As Americans learned more about the war's atrocities, isolationist sentiment diminished. Regardless of public sentiment, FDR maintained a steady course.

Roosevelt, the thirty-second president, had been in office since 1933—longer than anyone in U.S. history. He had just begun his fourth term, and for many of us young soldiers, he'd been commander in chief for as long as we could remember. He was a fixture in our lives whom we expected would always be there. Now most of the men had little idea who our new president, Harry Truman, was: after all, the former senator from Missouri had been vice president for less than three months before succeeding the country's fallen leader. But, truthfully, we were too consumed by the war to worry much about Truman. And we figured the conflict was almost over anyway.

"It's a big deal," Mr. Dobson insisted. "I know how bad the

Depression was. Regardless of your politics, you've got to give him credit. Roosevelt pulled us out of the fire."

"I'm not sure I like the decisions he made about this war," Al Jackson said. "I think Stalin snookered him."

"They should have listened to Patton," Snuffy Smith insisted. "I think he knew more than all of them."

"That's a little wild," Jack Postawaiet said. "Hindsight is always twenty-twenty. We got to live with what's here right now."

"Yeah," I said, "and that means getting out there where those POWs are and corralling them. That's what counts today."

"What are we supposed to do?" Walt Brandon asked.

"I think just keep order," I said. "They won't be looking for trouble. They've already surrendered, so they've quit. All they want to do is go home."

"You know, we haven't had a haircut in a long time," Snuffy threw in. "Here we are taking a breather, making it a perfect time for a trim. Jack, you're the man with the magic scissors. Why don't you give us a trim while we're waiting for the truck to pick us up?"

"Sure," Jack said. "Line up, and I'll start lowering your ears."

Jack Postawaiet hadn't been a professional barber before the war, but he could have been. He carried a comb and some sharpened scissors in his carry-on bag, along with a barber cloth he tied around our necks. In short order, the unit went from the shabby side to looking right smart. We sat around smoking, laughing, telling stories, and enjoying the morning sunlight. The warmth of spring was most welcome.

One of the stories that came back to us during this time was that Supreme Commander Eisenhower came to General Patton's headquarters and met with the staff. During the meeting, Ike gave one of the highest compliments that could be offered. He said that General Patton and the staff had not made one mistake since Patton had taken over the Third Army. Such a high affirmation made the staff smile and certainly must have pleased Patton.

By this time, we all thought of Patton as a fearless man who inspired confidence wherever he went. Not that he was foolhardy, but he didn't seem to be bothered in the least when the mortars were flying and the bombs going off. He had a remarkable way of showing up unexpectedly and encouraging the soldiers. Regardless of where the artillery was firing or a counterattack was unfolding, he had a way of appearing and encouraging the men. During a surprise assault or when the firing got the heaviest, the old man would be there right in the midst of it.

The last man was sheared, and Jack put away the tools of his unofficial trade. The truck pulled up, and we were off to be the sheepdogs guarding a herd of prisoners of war. We bumped along through the city and around piles of broken cement. When we got to the edge of Munich, we saw what appeared to be about a thousand enemy troops sitting on the side of a hill, doing nothing. Our troops were standing around holding rifles, but nothing was going on. The truck came to a halt and I jumped out.

A soldier came up to me. "Are you the relief unit?"

"I'm with the Six-Sixty-Seventh Field Artillery Battalion," I said. "These six are my men."

"Fine," he said. "We're still trying to repair the road. Won't be long and they'll be done. We can move all these prisoners then."

"Okay, you want us to simply do guard duty? Just stand around with our rifles loaded and wait for further word to come down?"

"You got it," the solider said. "Good luck."

I turned to my men and gave them instructions. I suggested they just spread out and watch the enemy. If there was any funny business, they were to respond. Other than that, it should be a walk in the park. I gave the German soldiers the once-over and could tell most were just everyday guys not looking for trouble. The assignment should be routine.

My men scattered around and stood in front of the Germans. Nobody seemed to pay much attention to the guards. I noticed a worn lawn chair in the shade of a large tree. As sergeant of the guard, surely I had a right to take it easy and watch the scenery go by. I set my rifle down against a tree across the way and stretched out in the lawn chair like I was taking a nap.

"Sir." One of the supervisors of the German prisoners came over and bent down to speak to me. "Please do not leave your rifle where a prisoner could grab it."

Almost by reflex, I grabbed a single-blade axe leaning against the base of my chair. I came out of that chair like a bazooka shell going off, spun around, and slung the axe at the tree. It stuck next to the barrel of my rifle.

"Is that what you are talking about?" I asked.

The supervisor stood there with his mouth open. Then he walked away.

I sat back down and left the rifle where it was with the axe sticking out of the tree. In a few minutes, another sergeant came over.

"You got excellent reflexes," he said. "Put that axe right on the money."

I grinned. "Oh, we used to throw axes back in Oklahoma, where I grew up."

"I guess so! What's your name?"

"Sisson. Sergeant Frank Sisson."

"Glad to know you, Sergeant Sisson. We'll be talking to you. We're looking for men who respond quickly and have manual skills. You obviously have the physical ability and reflexes we're seeking."

I had no idea what he meant, but that lawn chair felt just fine.

By noon, tin cans of C-rations were passed out to the prisoners.

Most of us hated those damn C-rations, which were most of what we had to eat out there in the field. But the Germans, looking surprised to be getting something so substantial to eat, dived in. We knew they were being fed far better than our poor soldiers that they captured. They should be grateful. The Russians would probably have shot them by now.

By midafternoon, an officer came over to me.

"Sergeant Sisson?"

"Yes, sir." I saluted.

"There was a mix-up. You were supposed to have a personal leave. You are to take a rest in Paris. Your unit will be looked after by another officer."

"You're flying me to Paris!" I nearly leaped across the grass.

"General Patton appreciates his men, and you have been through some tough experiences. He wants you to relax and have a restful time. Are you ready to go?"

"Right now?"

"Yes, sir."

"I'm on my way!" I grabbed my carry-on and my rifle, and we took off. I left the axe sticking in the tree.

37

★ ★ ★

PARIS

To walk the streets of Paris was a dream come true. I had always wanted to stroll down the Champs-Élysées and gaze at the Arc de Triomphe. Although I knew nothing about art, I'd heard of the Louvre museum. I wandered down its long halls, overwhelmed by its paintings. Across the river was the Musée d'Orsay display of modern art. For a twenty-year-old hometown boy from Weleetka, Oklahoma, Paris was almost incomprehensible. I was swimming in culture after spending months wallowing through a garbage dump.

Parisians, now nine months removed from the brutal years of Nazi occupation, seemed relieved the war was almost over; the sidewalk cafés hummed with business. I sat down at an outdoor table to see if I could find one of those local pastries that were always described as beyond delicious. A glass of wine would top it off.

"What can I get for you, monsieur?" the waiter asked.

"A nice sweet roll," I said, "and a glass of chardonnay. Say, can you tell me anything about this particular area of Paris?"

It turned out that I was sitting very close to the subterranean bunker that was important in the city's liberation. An underground tunnel led to the command post of the French Resistance. Colonel

Henri Rol-Tanguy, the leader of the French Forces of the Interior, had a special telephone exchange down there that allowed him to access 250 other phones around Paris without the Nazis having a clue that he could not be tapped by them.

"They even had a bicycle attached to a generator," the waiter told me. "They could pedal and create their own electricity in case of a power outage."

"Amazing," I said.

The French had known that General George Patton and his Third Army were coming. During the night of August 24, Major General Jacques-Philippe Leclerc's Second French Armored Division crept into Paris. The next morning, the bulk of his division and the American Fourth Infantry Division poured in. The Nazis knew they were in trouble, and the commander of the German garrison surrendered. Shortly after that, General Charles de Gaulle led the French army into the city to take control. The Provisional Government of the French Republic had taken back the city.

"Must have been quite an experience," I said.

"Was indeed," he said happily. "The Ninth Company broke into the center of Paris by the Porte d'Italie. They entered the town hall square and fired the first rounds at a large group of Germans with machine guns. The Nazis must have known it was over. Civilians were out on the streets singing 'La Marseillaise,' the French national anthem, and cheering."

While all of this was unfolding, the leader of the Ninth Company, Raymond Dronne, had gone to the command of the German general Dietrich von Choltitz and requested they surrender. The U.S. Fourth Infantry Division also entered through the Porte d'Italie in the early hours the next day. The American regiments covered the right flank of the French Second Armored, turned eastward at the square known as the Place de la Bastille, and then made their way along Avenue Daumesnil, heading toward the sprawling park Bois de Vincennes.

"I'm sorry I missed the show," I said.

The waiter had become animated and obviously enjoyed relating this story. He continued to tell me how that same afternoon, the British Thirtieth Assault Unit entered the Porte d'Orléans, one of the seventeen gates into Paris, and then searched buildings for vital intelligence. They captured the Château de la Muette, the former headquarters of German admiral Karl Dönitz. Then the Ninth Company moved on the H tel Majestic, the Chamber of Deputies, and the Place de la Concorde. At three thirty on the afternoon of August 25, the German garrison surrendered, and the Allies took Choltitz prisoner. Other French units streamed into the capital.

"So, I am sitting here in the midst of a great historic location," I said.

"Absolutely, monsieur." He turned and went back to the kitchen.

The pastry proved to be as delicious as I had hoped. When I finished, I continued my walking tour of the city. I jumped on a tourist bus and settled back to see the sights. The Eiffel Tower zoomed past but lingered in my mind. We passed the famous Moulin Rouge cabaret, with its bright-red windmill on top. But when we came to the Notre-Dame Cathedral, I got off. For as long as I could remember, I had wondered what it would be like to see the inside of this great building. Well, its splendor and sanctity were more than I could have expected. I felt like I had walked into the private abode of God Himself. I sat on one of the benches and almost wanted to cry.

When I finished, I walked outside and sat on a park bench. Another American soldier sat down next to me.

"Corporal Dale Jones," he said, offering his hand. "From Chicago."

"Sergeant Frank Sisson," I said. "From Weleetka, Oklahoma."

The corporal blinked several times. "You got to be kidding."

"No, Weleetka is five miles beyond nowhere."

Jones started laughing.

I knew that corporal might have updates on how the Russians were coming with their march to Berlin. From his insignia, I could tell that he worked in intelligence and should know some inside information. He said that Marshal Georgy Zhukov was leading the Second Belorussian Front in a race with Marshall Ivan Konev's Fourth Ukrainian Front to see who could get there first. "I understood that they were on the edge of Berlin, but I did not have that confirmed. Hard to tell what the facts were, but I was sure it was a bloody battle, for sure."

Corporal Jones had heard that the Soviets were in a rush to take the entire area because they wanted to capture the German nuclear research program in the Kaiser Wilhelm Institute before the Americans could get it.

"Don't really know anything about the nuclear business," I said. "I understand it's some kind of gadget for the future."

"Oh, much more, I hear," Jones said. "They say Hitler was depending on some sort of secret weapon or bomb that could change everything."

"Hmm, interesting. My understanding is that General Patton agreed with Churchill that Marshal Montgomery should go after Berlin. I think he was only three days away. I guess that plan was overruled by the 'big boys.'"

Jones believed that if the Germans were smart, they would throw in the towel, and that Hitler was an idiot. They had tried to kill him a dozen times. It was too bad they didn't because he was going to be piling up German corpses while his army turned and ran to us and the Brits to escape being taken by the Russians. The Russians would rape every woman they found in Berlin.

"I feel a little guilty sitting here in this beautiful city while the last days of the bloody struggle are played out," I said. "But I'll get over it in about five minutes."

The corporal laughed. "Me too. Hopefully, we'll hear before long that the Russians have taken Berlin, and the war is over. Everyone is holding their breath, waiting for it to stop."

"Thanks for the update, Corporal. Best to you."

He walked away.

Seemed like a good time to check in with the office to make sure my assignment was still in order. The situation was moving so fast that it was possible for all sorts of rearrangements to occur. I found the registration office and walked in.

"Any communiqués for Sergeant Frank Sisson?" I asked.

"Just a moment." The officer began riffling through his papers and file index. "No, but a letter was shuffled to you from Munich." He handed me an envelope.

I quickly glanced at the return address. Alice.

I hurried out of the office and sat down outside on a bench. I was surprised at how excited I was to finally hear from her. I guess I'd worried about our relationship more than I realized.

It seemed she'd been tuning in to the radio a lot. Some station down there in Del Rio, Texas, was blasting all over the United States. It was either in South Texas or on the other side of the Rio Grande, in Mexico, I guess. Alice said she'd been listening to lots of country music. A Virginia woman named "Mother" Maybelle Carter and her family sang songs they had written. The voice of one of Maybelle's daughters, June Carter, singing "Keep on the Sunny Side" caught Alice's ear. Then there was some guy named Roy Acuff that Alice also thought was the greatest. Apparently, it was all country music and war songs. Most of her letter was about listening to the radio. She wrote that on Sunday evenings, she tuned in to hear comedians and performers such as ventriloquist Edgar Bergen and his dummy sidekick, Charlie McCarthy.

Alice had a line or two about missing me, but that was it. She was applying for a new job in Wetumka, not far from Weleetka. She'd be doing secretarial work for a lawyer. She hoped it would provide some income for her family. She closed by saying she missed me and hoped I'd be home soon.

I folded the letter and put it back in the envelope. I started thinking about my time in Paris. Change was certainly in the air. Paris was recovering. Berlin was falling. And Alice was talking about a new job. Change everywhere.

38

* * *

CELEBRATION

The news kept trickling in about the final hours left to the Wehrmacht. The Russians were hammering their way into Berlin and apparently blowing the city to pieces. On May 3 a rumor floated through Paris that Hitler was dead. Confirming these stories was impossible, but the people around me were hopeful that the war was almost over. I did learn that General Patton's Third Army had crossed the Inn River and was moving rapidly on Salzburg, Austria, and nearby Berchtesgaden, just inside the German border, the site of Hitler's alpine mountain-top compound. Other units in Patton's army were almost to Linz, the third largest city in Austria. The word was that the enemy was disintegrating everywhere. The Nazis' most famous unit, the Eleventh Panzer Division, surrendered intact. On May 7 the Third Army received orders to establish a restraining line. All units were to halt.

On Sunday I went back to the Notre-Dame Cathedral to pray that all fighting would stop. The church was packed with others doing the same. People kept nodding to me, some saying, *"Merci,"* over and over again. Surrounded by the awesome, towering walls of one of the world's greatest structures, I said my thank-yous to the Almighty.

I didn't know it at the time, but Grand Admiral Dönitz, picked by Hitler to succeed him as Führer, had sent the sad-faced General Admiral Hans George von Friedeburg to negotiate the surrender of Germany in the north with Field Marshal Montgomery.

Once the final negotiations began at Eisenhower's headquarters in Reims, France, it became clear that Friedeburg couldn't offer an unconditional surrender. Colonel General Alfred Jodl, the new chief of staff of the German army, was dispatched to finish the bargaining. Jodl pleaded and argued through the night over terms for a settlement. Early Monday morning, he stopped arguing and accepted the unconditional surrender. After thirty-three hours of negotiating, General Eisenhower's chief of staff, Lieutenant General Walter Bedell Smith, along with British, French, and Russian representatives, prevailed. The Russian representative, General Ivan Susloparov, eyed the Germans with a baleful, sinister stare.

It was all over.

I awoke on Tuesday, May 8, to sunshine beaming through the window of my hotel room. I stretched and tried to get my wits about me. After a few moments, I could hear noise outside. People were rushing up and down the street, singing, clapping, shouting for joy. Some were hollering who knows what over and over. All of Paris seemed to be in an uproar. I switched on the Armed Forces Radio Service, and at nine o'clock American time, I picked up a speech by President Harry Truman. He was saying that the fighting wouldn't be over until the Japanese suffered, but the Allied armies, through sacrifice and devotion with God's help, had brought Germany to an unconditional surrender.

A few minutes later, Prime Minister Winston Churchill announced that the hostilities would officially end across Europe at 12:01 a.m., Wednesday, May 9. Actually, that would be 1:01 Central European Time. Churchill ended with, "Advance Britannia! Long live the cause of freedom! God save the king!"

I leaped out of bed. My most fervent prayers had been answered. I wanted to be part of the celebration outside. I rushed downstairs and into the street. Some people were singing "La Marseillaise" and cheering. One old lady was kneeling beside a large building and praying, tears running down her face. A man was dancing in the street, holding a bottle of champagne above his head. He would periodically stop and take a big swig out of the bottle and then start dancing again. Everywhere, people were hugging one another and dancing. Hundreds of thousands filled the streets of Paris in an emotional orgy of joy. Air raid sirens screamed for three minutes, and airplanes flew over dropping flares. Fireworks exploded everywhere. I shouted along with the crowd as if I were a Parisian. Two women grabbed and kissed me like we were getting married. Men hugged me and proclaimed that I had liberated them. Then they'd go dancing off with someone else they'd never met before. The party seemed like it would last forever.

Somewhere in the midst of it all, the government announced it would issue an extra ration of wine, potatoes, butter, salt, and canned goods. Once more the people burst into ecstasy. I danced along with them. Children found their way into the crowd and were celebrating with equal joy. The little ones kept clapping their hands. I had no idea what they were saying, but I couldn't miss that they were as happy as everyone in the street.

I kept hoofing it down the streets as if I were a real dancer. And then I was in front of Notre-Dame—again. I looked up at those magnificent spires rising into the sky. The carvings all over the entrance seemed to beckon me inside.

The awe-inspiring chancel was filled with people. The little side chapels were crowded with men and women kneeling on the floor in prayer. The overwhelming sound of the organ playing a triumphant hymn sent chills through my body. Down near the front, I found an empty space and sat down next to a young woman. Her head was bent over as she leaned on the back of the chair in front of us. Her body shook slightly, and I knew she was crying. Since I couldn't speak French, there was no way to communicate. Perhaps she had lost someone in the war. A husband. Lover. Relative. Friend. One of the many who had died.

We had lost so many soldiers in these past months. By the grace of God, my unit had been spared, while others had been wiped out. I had seen the enemy dead, sprawled in ditches, German soldiers frozen in ponds or turned into cakes of ice by the subzero snow and ice. At times, I didn't believe I would survive the winter. How I did, I'll never know.

The organ stopped, and a holy hush descended over the massive congregation. No one was talking. Everyone bowed in prayer. In an unexpected way, the silence was more emotional than the loud rejoicing in the streets. Waves of sentiment swept over me. I became more aware than I had ever been that the hand of God had sustained and guided me through a thousand pitfalls. Bullets had whizzed by, missing my head by only inches. Mortars had exploded, sending shrapnel flying past me, yet never breaking the skin.

I had survived.

I reached in my chest pocket, and that piece of paper was still there. Psalm 91 had carried me through the worst of times. The verse that I had seldom referenced when I read these lines during the fighting had become strangely appropriate: "I will see how the wicked are punished." Now fulfilled today! The first verse had promised, "Though a thousand fall at my side, though ten thousand are dying around me, the evil will not touch me." So it had been.

I folded my hands and knelt on the pad on the floor in front of me. Like a thousand others, tears began running down my cheeks. Raw emotion hidden during a hundred escapes erupted, and I began thanking God over and over for His protection. I don't know how long I prayed, but I seemed to drift into another world, another dimension, another realm of blessing. I finally got back up and settled into the chair. The woman who had been next to me was gone, but the cathedral remained filled with people.

I don't know why I survived when others didn't. They were equally good men. Better than me. They would forever remain beneath the soil of Europe, while I would return home. Why? I had no idea. I was simply grateful that the killing and the conflict had come to an end. In the midst of the worst war the world has ever known, God had prevailed.

I got up and walked toward the exit. Warm afternoon sunlight streamed through the clerestory windows far overhead. I headed out into the street. The celebration hadn't waned a notch, with revelers still singing "La Marseillaise" and dancing. Perhaps the party would go on late into the night. But I no longer wanted to make noise. The quiet of the cathedral lingered in my soul.

39

★ ★ ★

A NEW WIND BLOWING

The next two days were filled with excitement and jubilation. People chattered with me in French and broken English. I laughed and nodded as if I understood, and then someone else would come along, and we'd do it all over again. Waiters passed out free wine. Paris continued in what felt like an endless celebration of survival and life. I laughed and laughed and enjoyed every minute.

I knew that my unit had to be equally thrilled. I could see Al Jackson or Snuffy Smith jumping up and down like jackrabbits. Mr. Dobson would be beside himself thinking about the possibility of going home. He was no longer apprehensive about returning. They had lived through daily threats of death and were now liberated from fear. Only someone who has lived with such consternation and dread can understand what that means in the depths of your soul.

But what would they do now? Stringing wire for communication in a war was over. Something called the walkie-talkie had come in late in the war and now made stringing wire obsolete. All in all, my men were out of a job with the army. I'm sure that was fine with them. I imagined that when I rejoined them in Germany, they'd have some interesting observations for me to consider.

After what seemed like a forever holiday, I had only one day left. I went back to the Allied headquarters to get my next assignment. There was already a line of GIs there doing the same thing. If there was one skill you learned in the military, it was to hurry up and wait. After a few long minutes, I moved to the front of the line.

"Sergeant Frank Sisson, Six-Sixty-Seventh Field Artillery Battalion." I saluted.

The sergeant looked up at me with a keen eye. "Ah, one of Patton's boys. We been looking for you."

I frowned. "What are you talking about?"

"You've been reassigned," he said. "You ain't goin' back to them wire pullers."

"What?"

"Says here that someone saw you throwin' an axe like a wild Indian, and you got excellent reflexes. They want to make a policeman out of you."

"They *what*?"

"The big boys are sending you to the police academy, where they'll turn you into a military police investigator. How's them apples?"

That was about the last thing I expected to hear that morning. I was flabbergasted.

"Your days pullin' wire are over, friend. Probably won't see that unit again." He handed me a packet with the orders inside. "You is to leave tomorrow mornin' at the crack of dawn. So, have a big rip-roarin' night before you turn into a cop."

I walked out in a daze. I would have liked to have said good-bye to Mr. Dobson and Walt Brandon. Mr. Parker, too, had been a good friend, as had Jack Postawaiet and Snuffy Smith. I'm sure Al Jackson would be standing there smoking a cigarette. During the fighting, we had formed relationships that we never spoke of but that meant everything to me. Not saying a final word to them seemed impossible.

I started reading my orders. A troop carrier would pick me up and take me to the police academy in Berlin in the morning. Whether I liked it or not, I was on my way to a completely different assignment. That's what I got for throwing the axe with such accuracy. Apparently accuracy and quick reflexes were what they were looking for.

With my leave coming to an abrupt end, I spent the rest of the day taking it easy and packing. When the sun came up again, I was ready to go.

The academy turned out to have special training in the martial arts. I did get some insight into the law and procedures, but mostly I got really good at disarming aggressive prisoners. As part of the process, we were updated on some of the recent intelligence that was coming in. By this time, Berlin had been divided into four sectors. The Russians had the largest, in the east; France laid claim to a small piece in the north; and Britain, a middle section. As for America, we controlled a good-sized southern portion. My job was to keep order there. Didn't sound too bad.

Was I ever wrong!

We were warned about what the Russians might do. Their violent and volatile history was bad enough, but appearances were indicating already that they would not be cooperative, and we should be alert to possible trouble. The stories began to pour in that the Russians were raping every German woman in sight from eight to eighty. Apparently, this criminal behavior had begun as soon as they reached Germany. Later, we were to learn that the estimates of rape in Berlin alone ran from ninety thousand to a hundred thousand victims. The Soviets were taking revenge on the Germans beyond what any American could imagine. Suddenly, being a police inspector did not sound like such an easy job.

Another dimension of French life had begun to surface. Everywhere we went, the French presented themselves as having resisted the Nazis even though they only lasted six and a half weeks when the invasion came. They had maintained the ideals of the French Revolution: Liberty, Equality, Fraternity. Everyone had been part of the resistance. Or so they claimed.

But American intelligence had already been digging up the actual facts, and they did not reflect well upon our ally. The truth was that even before the war, the French police kept amazingly detailed records of refugees fleeing Germany as it fell more and more under Nazi control. The French police harbored a right-wing, nationalist bent—not to mention significant anti-Semitic sentiment. When the Nazis took Paris, the police already had detailed information on where their conquerors could find Jews, and in many cases assisted in placing them in concentration camps.

During what became known as the Vél d'Hiv roundup, in 1942, thirteen thousand non-French Jews were herded into a small, stifling indoor sports arena and left without bathroom facilities, water, and anything more than stadium seats. People were forced to defecate in public against the walls of the stadium. The French police witnessed the entire debacle and did nothing to stop the chaos. They did *nothing* to intervene or provide assistance to the helpless. Ultimately, the Jews were hauled off to a concentration or death camp.

Yes, many French men and women resisted the Nazis and, in the end, helped drive them out of Paris. But many of their countrymen did not withstand and oppose but, rather, complied with the Nazis and were part of France's tragic scourge of anti-Semitism. While it was not my job to deal with this issue—after all, my area of supervision was not France, but Germany—I needed to know it was out there. I felt the French had not defended the Jews and that didn't leave a good feeling in my stomach.

What would I find in Berlin? Frankly, the idea was frightening.

40

★ ★ ★

POLICE INSPECTOR
ON DUTY

The trip down Berlin's crumpled streets fairly well said it all. Boulevards were piled high with broken bricks and rubble. Splintered boards were scattered everywhere. Tall buildings were empty shells of a burned-out past. Structures were pockmarked with bullet holes. Here and there, women had formed conveyor systems and were handing bricks or small pieces of concrete up the line to a dump on the other side of the piled remains of a destroyed building. The entire city had been leveled. We drove slowly through the endless destruction. Hitler's grandiose vision of a glorious thousand-year Reich had been turned into a garbage heap in just a dozen years.

I had no idea where General Patton might be, but I was sure he was angry at not having been allowed to take Berlin. He did what he was told by his superior officers, but he would have been *furious* that the Russians got here first. He knew trouble lay ahead.

Near the center of the city, my driver came to a stop. I got out and walked into an office that had become the headquarters of the military police. A sergeant was sitting behind an old, worn desk. Through an open door behind him, I could see jail cells stretching down a long hall. This place obviously meant business.

"Sergeant Frank Sisson, Six-Sixty-Seventh Field Artillery Battalion, now trained as a military police investigator." I saluted.

The sergeant looked up and returned the salute. "Been expecting you, Sergeant Sisson. We need all the help we can get. MPs are about the only thing that keeps order around here. Sit down."

I pulled up a chair that looked like it had survived two wars.

I was told that we had to keep an eye on public drunkenness. Bad behavior kept popping up in the evening. The Russian soldiers were crazy; they would shoot at you just for the sport of it. There were no boundaries or checkpoints set up in the city yet. But I learned that Allied police officers worked only in the American occupation zone. If I picked up a soldier from one of the other sectors, I was to call over and have him picked up.

"Got it. When do I start?"

The sergeant looked at me and laughed. "You've already started!"

"Okay. I guess I get a jeep and a driver?"

"Sure."

"How about an interpreter? English is all I speak. I need somebody who can jabber German, Russian, and probably French. I need someone who knows the city."

"My, my, aren't you the choosy one. When you come here in the morning, I'll have one waiting for you."

I saluted and went back outside. Across the street sat a destroyed Nazi half-track, its body marked with bullet scrapes. Apparently, they had picked up the bodies of the crew earlier, but helmets and a couple of satchels were in the street. The pavement was covered with dust and debris from destroyed buildings. The fronts of these buildings looked better than many but were still desolate. At the end of the block, half of a building had been blown away. Only one lane of traffic could make it down the street. I got back in the jeep that had brought me here.

"Ain't exactly what you'd expect of the capital of a nation," the private said and grinned.

I didn't feel like grinning. I said nothing.

When I showed up the next morning, the same sergeant was sitting behind the ancient desk. In the opposite corner of the room, a woman in a professional-looking gray suit sat in a stiff, military posture. Her blond hair had been pulled back in a bun. She had a pretty face—blue eyes, fair complexion—but looked strained. I greeted her with a nod.

"Ah, our military police investigator has come back reporting for duty." He saluted.

I returned the salute. "What can I say? I'm ready for whatever."

"You're going to need to keep an eye on speeders," the sergeant said. "The military is getting crews out to clear the major streets, but nails and broken glass are everywhere. We've got to sit on these drivers that speed around like it's a racetrack. Give you any trouble, and we'll cool them off in one of those cells back there." He gestured over his shoulder.

"Yes, sir."

"You come with a high recommendation. They think you'll be one of our better MPs, so don't let us down."

I only nodded. He seemed to be enjoying dishing out the instructions. I had a feeling that he must be extremely proud of himself.

"You said you needed an interpreter and a guide. I want you to meet Edda Muller."

The woman stood immediately at attention and looked straight ahead like an infantryman. Her suit added to her almost military bearing.

"Frau Muller speaks French, German, and some Russian," the sergeant said. "She knows Berlin like the back of her hand. Frau Edda, please meet Sergeant Frank Sisson."

Almost mechanically, she stuck her hand out and waited for me to shake it. I did.

"Frau Edda will ride with you in the jeep. Whatever you need, just ask her."

"Thank you." I smiled and watched her eyes. A hint of fear lingered. "I will look forward to having you help me," I said politely.

She managed a faint smile.

"Okay, MP Sergeant Sisson," the sergeant said. "Here's your first assignment: you are to go into the Russian zone and pick up a GI who got bombed last night and went to sleep on the curb. You are to pick him up and bring him back here. Got it?"

We walked outside, and I suggested that we talk a bit and get acquainted. I immediately launched into a description of Weleetka, Oklahoma, and the Indians that had once lived there. Edda began to smile slightly.

I asked her how she got the job as my interpreter. Edda explained that she had applied for a desk job soon after the city was divided, and the U.S. Army, noting her language skills, had sent her here. She had always lived in Berlin, she said, and then let slip something that momentarily stunned me: she had been in the Hitler Youth.

She seemed worried that I would no longer want her as a translator, but I was interested to hear more about her experience.

"We were taught that Hitler was going to save the nation," she told me. "They instructed us that we could be part of reconstructing Germany. We were building a better tomorrow. I believed that idea."

I nodded. "Who wouldn't?"

I asked her if her mind had been changed by the war.

Her countenance shifted, and she looked sad. She told me she was thirty-one, no longer a child. Looking up and down the street before us, she saw nothing but devastation. Hitler, she told me, had destroyed the entire country.

"These last months must have been extremely difficult," I said sympathetically. But I was thinking, "I am twenty-one, and here I've landed this gal ten years older than I am." This certainly was my lucky day.

Edda nodded her head. "When the bombing of Berlin started, I knew the end would not be very far away. I have a younger sister, Ulrike. We started hiding in the basement of the apartment building where we live. We found a tunnel that led from the back of the furnace to send heat through the building. When the Russians invaded, we hid in that tunnel. We were Catholics and prayed constantly that they would not find us." She became silent for several moments. "They never did."

After a while, I said, "You will find most Americans to be kind. You will not have to be afraid of us."

"That is what I am told. Run from Russians. Run to Americans."

"Was it like that as Berlin was falling?"

Edda nodded. "People knew to run if they could, but the battle lines made it increasingly difficult to get anywhere. Then some of the fanatics kept saying, 'Hitler will save us. Don't worry.' We had to keep our mouths shut, or no telling what might happen."

"Edda, do you smoke?"

"Of course."

"May I offer you a cigarette?"

She smiled broadly for the first time. "Why, yes. Yes. That would be wonderful."

I flipped open a pack and pushed out one cigarette. She took it, and I gave her a light.

"I can get you a carton at our canteen."

Her blue eyes lit up. "Marvelous! Wonderful!"

"Don't worry, Edda. We will take care of you. You have nothing to fear from the Americans."

For a moment, tears filled her eyes. Finally, she said, "Thank you. Much thank you."

"Well, we have a job to do," I said. "Got to go pick up a naughty boy and bring him back. You ready to go?"

She wiped the corners of her eyes and looked at me with a different expression from any that I'd seen earlier. Kind. Appreciative.

"You are a good man. Thank you."

41

★ ★ ★

ON THE BEAT

We took off for the Soviet sector. Since we were going into a zone that the sergeant considered sensitive, I decided to drive and let Edda direct me. She and I sat in the front seat of the military jeep and left the backseat for the soldier we were to pick up. Edda certainly knew her way, directing me to turn left here and right there. We began to see more Soviet troops walking down the street.

I waved; a few waved back. Many simply stared impassively. We kept going until we came to a large building that looked like it had avoided the bombing. Three Russian guards stood outside the door. They eyed us suspiciously, but I saluted as we walked in. They stared.

Edda explained quickly in Russian that I was a U.S. military police inspector and that we had come to pick up a drunken American soldier from their jail.

The Soviet soldier nodded and then shouted something over his shoulder.

"They are calling the guards to bring our man out," Edda explained.

"Good," I said. "I don't want to stay any longer than we have to."

"The Russian asked what unit you are in," Edda said.

"Tell him Six-Sixty-Seventh Field Artillery."

He looked at me critically for a few moments. Before he could respond, the door behind him opened, and the guards brought in the American soldier. The guy looked like he'd been sleeping in his clothes for a year. His hair was uncombed, and his bloodshot eyes looked like a road map. He fixed me with a pitiful grin.

The Russian in charge rattled off something. Edda said that he wanted me to sign some sort of paper. As I was completing the form, he asked Edda a question.

"The man wants to know if your unit is part of General Patton's Third Army," Edda said.

"Tell him yes."

The Russian stiffened and rattled off something.

"He says that General Patton does not like the Soviet army," she translated.

The man's lip had turned down, and his eyes hardened like someone about to hit you in the face.

"*Nyet! Nyet!*" I shouted—about the only Russian word I knew. "Patton loves the Russians!"

Edda quickly said something, but I had no idea what. They exchanged a couple of sentences before the Russian began swinging his arm, gesturing for us to get out.

I grabbed the American soldier's arm and pulled him toward the door. I wanted to get us out of there as quickly as possible. Without stopping, I pushed the GI into the jeep and told him to stay in the backseat. One of the Russian guards at the door abruptly went back inside.

I fired up the jeep and swung it back around. In the rearview mirror, I saw the Russian guard come back out and start pointing at us. Just as I put the jeep in gear, he fired his pistol.

"Hit the floor!" I screamed at Edda and the soldier in back.

Three guards were shooting at us. One bullet shattered the right side of the windshield. I hit the pedal as hard as I could. The jeep heaved forward, but the Russians kept shooting with everything they had.

Without Edda to guide me, I had no clue how to get out of the Russian zone. Bullets clanged against the metal rim of the jeep tire. On the right side, I saw a string of burned-out shop windows that looked hollow and completely empty. If nothing else, those storefronts would provide a shield from the bullets. I jerked to the left and smashed through the broken front of one. I abruptly turned to the left and crashed through the remains of a broken wall. I could see that most of the walls were already gone, and down at the far end was an opening out of the building. Since the jeep was still running, the Russians hadn't hit a tire or part of the engine, so we had nothing to lose by plowing straight ahead.

The jeep lurched sideways but kept persevering through the wrecked buildings. When we reached the last storefront, I smashed through what was left of a brick wall. The windshield crumpled forward, and only the steering wheel kept it from falling in on me. I realized I was now in an alley. I roared down to the end and turned onto a boulevard. I came to a shrieking halt, still trying to figure out where I was. Were the Russians still chasing me?

Two jeeps with big white stars painted on the side drove by. I looked again. We had come out in the American zone! My hands had clamped down on the steering wheel like steel braces. I slowly released my grip and settled back in the seat.

"You can get up now," I told Edda and the soldier.

"Holy shit!" the soldier exclaimed. "I thought I was dead."

"You nearly were," I said.

Edda slipped back into the seat. Her fair skin had turned white as a sheet of paper. She looked at me with consternation in her eyes and kept blinking.

I turned and looked at the soldier. "Son, next time you decide to throw a drunk, I hope you remember what it took to get you out of a Soviet jail."

"Honest, sir. I meant no harm. I wandered into the Russian area looking for a bar that was open. Three Russian soldiers started acting like they were my best friends and began pouring me vodka out of a big bottle. We were laughing and acting silly." He stopped and put his head in his hands. "That's all I remember until I woke up in a Russian jail sick as a dog."

"Next time you throw a bender, you might want to try something other than vodka," I suggested.

The three of us walked into the military police office. The same sergeant was sitting behind the battered desk, reading a newspaper. He looked up and frowned. "That man should be in handcuffs!"

"Let's not get legalistic," I said. "The Russians have scared him so bad that he'll gladly go jump in a cell if it makes you happy. By the way, that jeep needs to be looked at. It's been rather shot up."

"What?" The sergeant leaped up and ran to the window to look out. "Why, the back of that jeep looks like it was turned into a shooting gallery!"

"You're getting the picture," I said. "The Russians used us for target practice."

"Sh-shooting at you?"

"You were right," I said. "I have no idea what was going on in their empty heads. Scare us? Drunk? Just don't know. They certainly don't have much of a sense of humor."

42

★ ★ ★

RUNNING THE STREETS

Word began to get around that the Soviets were not your friendly next-door-neighbor types. All boundaries were fluid, and crossing from one sector into another was a matter of just crossing the street. The French and British were our buddies, but we knew better than to mess with the Russians. Of course, we continued to celebrate the end of the war and the defeat of the Nazis. Most of us were just farm boys used to milking the cows and didn't want any trouble. But it seemed like the Russians were ready to do just that. Fight! We knew they came from a different world, but their ideas and values seemed to be from four centuries back, when wars were fought with savage intent. As best we could tell, the Russians had little regard for human life.

We kept making the rounds to keep our sector on the up-and-up. The soldiers liked to hit the bars at any time of day, but the business really picked up in the evening. By ten o'clock, the American boozers and rum bums were going at it full tilt, and we had to haul them in and put the fun boys in the slammer. By this time, I had turned twenty-one years old, and many of the men were younger than me. They were particularly vulnerable to a walk down alcohol alley.

Something happens to you when you fight a war and are gone for a couple of years. You forget those values that everybody had when you lived in small-town America. People tried to kill you, and you tried to kill them. You ate dirt when bombs went off, and you tried not to cry when your friends got killed. Stuffing the grotesque down as far as you could didn't stop the horrors from coming up again. After a while, you felt like you were twenty going on fifty. It was strange: part of you felt like an ancient warrior, and part of you wanted to cry like a baby because of the gruesome images that lingered in your mind.

Fall was approaching, and it was getting colder, which promised further hardship for Berliners. I could tell that the children were having a rough time. One afternoon I watched a group of boys playing soccer in the street. On all sides were piles of rubble, and their ball was nearly destroyed. The boys were thin. I thought to myself: "Here I am, standing around with money in my pocket while these kids are barely eating." They needed help.

I remembered a hamburger stand up the way. I went back up the war-torn street and ordered $40 worth of hamburgers. (That's about the equivalent of $573 in 2020.) The proprietor couldn't believe his ears but went to work flipping those hamburgers as fast as he could turn them. His wife was slicing buns right and left. They finally piled them in three sacks for me, and I started back up the street. The kids were still playing soccer, so I set down the sacks on the remnant of what once must have been a nice outdoor cement bench.

"Hey, guys!" I shouted. "Anybody want a hamburger?"

The boys looked at one another like they were trying to translate my words.

"A hamburger!" I shouted.

"Humbager?" one of the boys called out.

I held up one of the paper-covered hamburgers. "For you!"

The boys looked at one another in astonishment and then came running toward me. When I handed out one, a boy grabbed it like a starving fish going for the bait. They climbed over one another toward me. Some of the boys yelled something I couldn't understand, and then children began to appear like magic. Little girls pushed aside some of the boys. They wolfed down those burgers like they hadn't eaten in months. Immediately, their little hands were extended just in case there was anything more in my sack. Of course, $40 buys a lot of hamburgers.

Danke schön! Danke schön! Smiles everywhere. One little girl hopped up on the park bench and tugged on my sleeve. I bent down to see what she wanted, and the child kissed me on the cheek. She scampered down and disappeared up the street. For a long time, I stood there and watched them return to whatever they had been doing. I thought to myself, "*That's* what we ought to be doing: feeding the little ones until they smile."

Most of the time, Edda Muller rode with us in case we ran into a situation that needed translation. I was able to go to our supply depot and find grocery items that she needed. Help with the groceries made a huge difference for her. I could tell how much she appreciated what I was able to give her.

That military stiffness Edda carried when I first met her disappeared, and she began to laugh at many turns in the road. Even though she was some ten years older than me, the age difference, too, vanished, and she seemed like a contemporary. When we ran into trouble on the streets, Edda didn't back away from wading in to translate and stand with us.

One evening around nine o'clock, we wandered into a bar to make sure there were no problems. She smiled at me and suggested, "Why don't we have a glass of wine?"

"While I am on duty, I'm not supposed to drink. Got to be completely sober. But *you* can. Let me buy you something."

"That would be nice," Edda said.

"Waiter!" I called out. "A glass of chardonnay, please."

Edda's countenance took on a serious look. "During the fighting, stories circulated through Berlin about what was really happening out there.

"Joseph Goebbels controlled the media, and we knew he was constantly printing propaganda, but no one dared speak of it," she explained. "Nevertheless, the war stories circulated. We kept hearing reports about General George Patton. They said no one could stop his Third Army. He seemed to push relentlessly across the countryside."

I chuckled. "No one could stop Patton."

"What made him so invincible?"

I thought for a moment. Patton was a big man, tall, strong. I knew that he'd competed in the first modern pentathlon in the 1912 Summer Olympics, held in Stockholm, Sweden. He finished fifth behind four Swedes in running. Patton was an aggressive fencer and defeated the internationally known French fencer who lost to no one but Patton. The world viewed him as an outstanding athlete.

"What made Patton the man was more psychological," I said. "We heard stories constantly about his fearlessness. Of course, Patton took reasonable precautions, but he seemed unmoved by anything going on around him as the bombs fell and mortars exploded. No matter what the weather, freezing wind or tropical sun, Patton appeared to care less. When a fierce battle was going on, we all ran for cover. You could get killed by a stray bullet coming out of nowhere. Patton remained unfazed by such obvious dangers. He would come up the road riding in his jeep, with the top down and one gunner on the rear. The general's flag would be flying, and he would come riding in like it was Christmas while shrapnel was flying around him."

Edda laughed. "Most interesting."

"One of the stories came out of our breakthrough out of Normandy at Avranches. The Germans were fighting like hell to close an eight-mile gap in the line. They were sending in continuous air strikes night and day. Our soldiers were running right and left to avoid bomb splinters. The bombing was heavy everywhere. An officer came running in with a secret message for Patton that was in a specially sealed envelope and needed to be put directly in his hands. The officer was looking everywhere for Patton. He finally found him sitting in a deck chair, smoking a big cigar while watching the sky.

"'What are you doing, sir?' the officer asked. Patton took a puff off the cigar and kept watching the Nazi aircraft fly directly overhead. The officer with the secret letter looked up at the ominous fleet and worried that a bomb would drop on them. Patton shook his fist at the sky and shouted, 'Those bastards! Those rotten sons of bitches! We'll get them! We'll get them!' The soldier decided that if Patton wasn't afraid of the German bombers, he wouldn't be either."

Edda laughed.

"He inspired us to not be afraid. With a general like that, we were bound to win."

"Such was his philosophy?" Edda asked.

"Patton hated war, but he knew that if the fight was unavoidable, the only alternative was to win, and that's what he went for. Absolute victory. He wanted as few casualties as possible and expected the officers under him to maintain the same standard. If a leader lost too many men, he was replaced immediately. That was his philosophy."

The waiter set my companion's wine on the table. *"Donku schoan,"* I said in my broken German.

"Were the soldiers around you happy?" Edda asked.

"A war is no damn party," I replied. "However, we kept our spirits up and had many good experiences. Patton's view of morale was that we had to keep moving forward. He believed that once we dug in, we were sitting ducks for German artillery. In his view, the quickest way to get killed was to hunker down. Consequently, staying on the move tended to keep us in a good mood."

Edda sipped the wine and looked up at the sky. "Night is coming," she said thoughtfully. "You must understand that the German people have been through a dark night. Many, many people had hoped that Hitler would do great things for this country. Of course, a great number of people believed in his idea of German supremacy. They wanted to feel superior again. Because of this feeling, they ignored what the Nazis did to the Jews. They just looked the other way." She drifted back into her private thoughts.

I waited a considerable time. Finally, I asked, "Were you like that?"

"Of course!" Edda snapped. "We all were. It took me a long time to realize we had been deceived. When the army failed in Russia, many people began to suspect something was seriously wrong. The cold realization of defeat settled like a fine dust on the windowsill. Probably the vast majority of German people ignored this reality. Hitler kept saying he had a secret weapon that would destroy all our enemies." After a long pause, she said, "Our enemies destroyed us."

We sat there and said nothing. Edda's eyes glazed over, and for a while she seemed to be a different person. "You are a nice person, Frank. I believe I can be honest." She took a deep breath. "Defeat is bitter."

43

★ ★ ★

BERLIN AT NIGHT

I knew Edda's questions about General Patton were prompted by more than inquisitive interest. The word floating around Berlin was that Patton's intense dislike of the Russians and his penchant for off-the-cuff comments could start World War III. The general had never trusted the Soviets and believed that trouble was inevitable. He had always been an astute student of whoever the enemy might be. Because he read Rommel's book on warfare, Patton knew exactly what to expect when he confronted the German general's tanks in North Africa. In a similar vein, he carefully observed the ideas, actions, and brutal treatment the Soviets dished out to the Germans. He knew they weren't from our world and would do the same to us if a conflict erupted.

The rumors suggested that General Eisenhower as well as others worried that if Patton were unleashed, he might light the fuse that would end up in a gigantic explosion. There were many reasons to fear such a confrontation. Americans had been through a horrendous war that was still going on in the Pacific. The Japanese were finished. Moreover, the war across Europe had created catastrophic conditions that left many people struggling to stay alive. Famine remained a frightening possibility for masses of Europeans. Displaced persons, or DPs, were everywhere, seeking shelter and food. I could see all around me in Berlin how many people were close to the edge. A continuing war with the Soviets would push such people over the cliff.

I was sure Edda worried about the prospect of another conflict in Berlin. She'd had enough of war to last three lifetimes and didn't want to do it all over again. I imagine the gossip caused her to think about General Patton as the logical general to stop the Russians. I tried to assure her that Patton had no intention of starting another war. I told her he loved battle and confrontations, but he was also a prudent person.

Edda stayed with us on our night trips through the American sector. I usually had a driver who was also a military policeman. The three of us roamed the backstreets and alleys making sure nothing was amiss and none of our men were being bad boys. We picked up the usual count of men who'd had one too many beers or still wanted to fight someone and got their teeth knocked out. Just the usual nonsense that the young and stupid got into.

One day, Edda invited me to her apartment for a home-cooked supper. I put on a clean shirt, slicked down my hair, and even buffed my boots. My driver dropped me off at the address she had given me.

Her side of the street was still intact, but across the cluttered thoroughfare, the buildings were smashed. Some looked like a mortar shell had knocked out all the windows and doors; others had clearly been hit by bombs. The sidewalks on Edda's side of the street were clear, but many of the windows were boarded up, and the results of war were obvious. I started up the steps that led to the second floor. No artificial light clarified where the steps were, so I reached for the banister. Unfortunately, the wooden railing had been broken and the splintered pieces hung loosely against the wall. I kept walking, cautiously.

The second floor didn't appear to have any working lights either, but I found the door with her number on it. I knocked. The door quickly opened.

"Ah, the American Army has arrived!" Edda exclaimed.

I walked in and gave the place a quick look. It appeared there was only one small bedroom, while the couch in the living room was also a foldaway bed. In some spots, strips of torn wallpaper hung down. A rug on the floor looked like the Russian army had marched over it. But she'd covered the small, round dining table in the middle of the room with a tablecloth, and two candles threw a soft glow across the room. To say the place was third rate was a compliment.

"I see you have placed candles on the table," I said. "Very nice."

"They are among the few items we saved when the Russians came bursting in. Some of my mother's china endured, but most was stolen." Edda sighed. "We have to make do with what is left." Her sister lived with her, but she was gone for the evening and would not be back until late. Very late. Edda suggested that I sit down at the table and let her pour me a glass of wine. "Somehow this bottle was overlooked by the raiders and is a nice wine." She poured me a glass.

"You have lived here long?" I asked.

Edda shook her head. "No, we had a nice house near the edge of Berlin. Unfortunately, it was bombed and completely destroyed. We felt lucky to settle into this apartment before someone else grabbed it. Right now, Berlin is caught up in great confusion about who owns what and who can collect rent. We hope the mess will be cleared up soon."

"Of course," I said. "I'm sure your job with us helps in this struggle."

"Saved my life," Edda said. "We are grateful to the army for this position."

"You do a great job. No problems there."

She smiled broadly. "As you know, food items are hard to come by. But with you and the army store's help, I have been able to prepare for you a genuine German supper."

Edda opened the door on the small oven and brought out a steaming bowl of red cabbage. The aroma swept me away.

"Oh, my gosh!" I exclaimed. "My favorite! I love red cabbage."

"I think you'll particularly like the way I prepared it. From your store, you bought me the spareribs that give the cabbage flavor. I believe you'll find it acceptable."

"Far beyond acceptable," I said. "Thank you for preparing such a generous supper. I deeply appreciate it all."

She sat down and lifted her glass. "Let us make a toast to better days."

Our glasses clinked.

Edda proved to be an excellent cook indeed. The meal was delicious. We laughed, talked, and had a great evening. For the first time in years, I felt like I was home again. Wolfing down C-rations while standing in the freezing cold definitely dulls your taste buds. Edda had certainly touched my sensitivities.

As we were finishing, she reached over and placed her hand on top of mine. "You know . . . I don't mind being ten years older than you. You have lived through the worst there is, and it has matured you. Ten years is nothing."

I glanced at Edda's hand. Her fingers were long and tapered. They had an elegant grace. I could feel her warmth. I knew where this was going.

"Do you have a girl back in America?" she asked.

I forced a kind smile. "Yes, I do."

"Oh!" she said with a touch of disappointment in her voice. "What is her name?"

"Alice. Alice Anderson."

She didn't remove her hand. "I suppose you will go back to her?"

"I guess so." Because the letters had become so sparse, I wasn't sure exactly how to answer and didn't want to explain.

"Guess?" Edda smiled. "Perhaps you'd like to have a girl in Germany? In Berlin?"

I wasn't sure what to say, so I sat there in silence.

"You know that I made mistakes about Hitler and the Nazis," she said. "That was yesterday. That past is gone forever, and we are here today. We must live in the present, in this moment. Is that not right?"

"I was planning on marrying Alice when I get back. I still have that understanding. I have to be faithful to her. That's how I'm put together. I try to be a person of my word. I can't go back on my relationship with Alice. I just can't."

Edda started drawing her hand back. "I see," she said slowly. "I wasn't thinking of marriage as much as . . . maybe . . . our having a good time together. I can be your German girlfriend. Wouldn't you like that?"

"Edda, one of these days I'll get my papers telling me to come home. My assignment will be finished, and I'll be gone. I might not even have the time or the occasion to say good-bye to you. That's how my life is. In a moment, I'd be finished. You don't want that, that kind of relationship. It wouldn't be good for either of us."

Edda looked down at the tablecloth and shook her head. "I guess not," she said hesitantly. "I guess not." She forced a twisted smile. "Looks like the Germans have lost again."

44

★ ★ ★

A LITTLE
MARRIAGE COUNSELING
ON THE SIDE

Edda accepted that I wasn't looking for a German girlfriend and played my assignments straight up. She remained warm and considerate, but the romantic overtures were finished. She knew that I would continue to treat her well and gladly buy items for her at our depot supply sources.

Rumors that the Soviets were looking for trouble were borne out. The reports kept coming back that they were confrontational and belligerent. I'd already had my encounter with their marksmen and didn't want to try for another round. We weren't going to bend to them, but we weren't looking for trouble, either. The political talk among the politicians from Washington didn't sound promising, either. There seemed to be indecision about what to do next. Who knew what was going to come next?

During the summer, we'd heard that General Patton had requested a command fighting the Japanese in the Pacific but had been turned down. We heard the stories of his return to the United States and his speaking to thousands of people there. As usual, he sparked a controversy that made the newspapers. In speaking to a group of wounded soldiers as well as civilians, he said that a man who dies in battle is "frequently a fool." All the Gold Star Mothers, the mothers who had lost sons, went off like fireworks. Finally, Secretary of War Henry Stimson announced that General Patton would not be going to the Pacific but returning to Germany to assist in the occupational effort.

As the fall progressed, we learned that the general had been appointed the military governor of Bavaria and would be involved in the denazification program. School-age children would learn about the evils of Hitler's National Socialism. For a blood-and-guts warrior, the assignment sounded bland and passive. Somewhere along the way, it was also rumored that he would be writing a book about the war effort. Turned out that he did. The Third Army people kept an ear to the ground because Patton remained our hero in spite of some of those blunders he made in speeches. When the soldiers got together and Patton's name came up, they always defended him and everything he did. As unusual as it sounds, no one had a bad word for him.

My job keeping law and order stayed fairly routine. German civilians tried to clear the streets and sidewalks. You'd see lines of women passing bricks and small pieces of concrete from one person to the next, helping clear the debris. The same work system was repeated everywhere. They never looked happy and were usually dressed in shabby clothing. They were probably the working class, but Germany had been so destroyed that they could have been anybody.

Of course, the military police as well as the rest of the Allies wanted to know what was going to happen to the Nazi leaders who had caused so many deaths. The stories of the concentration camp atrocities continued to unfold, and justice was demanded. It seemed like a century ago that I had met Eli Cohen and first learned of anti-Semitism. Wherever he was, I knew he would be intensely interested in what happened next.

Hordes of displaced persons flooded across Europe. A high number of the DPs were Jewish survivors of the death camps. Many looked like walking skeletons, and all were struggling. The bulk of the German population tried to ignore them and kept their doors locked when the starving DPs came by seeking food. The situation remained awful into the fall, and it looked like they would be there into the winter. Many of them had returned to their former homes only to find that somebody else had claimed their property. Often the survivors that escaped the camps left for some other country, leaving behind relatives desperate to find any remaining family connections. The shtetls, the little farming villages where so many Jews had lived for centuries, were gone, never to return. An entire way of life had been destroyed.

And the cause of all the suffering remained clear. Most of the German citizens claimed they'd known nothing about any of the persecution and displacement. They would throw up their hands and declare, "How could we know?" We usually didn't respond with what we were surely thinking: "How could you *not* know?"

When I asked Edda about the contradictions, she obviously didn't want to talk about the facts. Reluctantly, she admitted to having heard rumors and confessed to some of the "slogans" that had sprung up in German homes. A naughty child might be threatened: if you do such and such again, you'll *go up the chimney*. One could tell that the subject was painful for her—and it should have been.

Of course, Hitler's regime was ultimately responsible. Everyone knew that a huge chunk of the Nazi leadership were criminals. Many had perished, but those still around needed to be held accountable. On November 20, 1945, the first phase of Nazi war crimes trials would be getting under way in the Palace of Justice in the now-ruined city of Nuremberg—selected partly because it had been the site of the Nazi Party's immense propaganda rallies. Twenty-four of the Third Reich's most significant leaders would face justice. But not all. Adolf Hitler and Joseph Goebbels had committed suicide as Berlin fell. Heinrich Himmler had done the same, by cyanide capsule, after having been captured by the Allies in late May. Josef Terboven, the ruthless Reichskommissar of Norway, had killed himself with a blast of dynamite. Two of the worst conspirators, Martin Bormann and Robert Ley, were dead just before the trial started.

But others were alive. Hermann Göring would go on trial. Göring ended up committing suicide the night before his execution by taking a cyanide capsule. The rumor was that Adolf Eichmann had escaped twice and eventually fled to South America somewhere out in the trees. We hoped for justice at Nuremburg.

I was walking down the street thinking about these problems when I realized that somebody had been following me for several blocks. I ducked into a storefront entrance to see who walked by. I could hear the footsteps coming closer. I unhooked my holster. With all the people that I had arrested, one might just be coming back to get a piece of me.

Three men jumped in the front of the entrance. "Surprise!" they yelled. "Your old buddies!"

I nearly fell over. Snuffy Smith, Walt Brandon, and Al Jackson stood there laughing at me.

"Hey, Sisson, when they made you the sheriff of Dodge City, they didn't mean for you to shoot us," Snuffy jabbed.

I started laughing so hard I was nearly crying. I rushed over to hug them all.

We found an outdoor café more than ready to serve American GIs, and I bought them all a drink. We sat there and talked for a couple of hours, remembering our war stories, the ups and downs that we had experienced together. Just like a family reunion.

"And where are the other men?" I asked. "Dobson and Parker? . . . Jack Postawaiet?"

"They got shipped out to other assignments, and we lost track of them," Walt explained. "We were sorry, but everything happened so fast that they were gone before we knew. Many have gone back to the States by now."

"Where are you fellows going?" I asked.

Walt grinned. "Back to New York. I'm going to enroll in a seminary as soon as I hit the shore. I've got a lifetime of stories to put in sermons."

"No, you don't," Snuffy scoffed. "The truth is, none of us wants to talk to anybody who wasn't here about what we've seen. If anything, we'd like to forget it." After a long pause, he added, "But we can't."

For some time, we sat there quietly thinking about what he said. As always, Al Jackson lit up a cigarette. Finally, Al said, "I dream about houses being blown up. People getting killed. Those camps . . . children starving."

"You're right," Snuffy said. "It'll be decades before we even mention what happened to us. People simply wouldn't understand what we've walked through."

Walt nodded his head. "You're certainly right about that."

We talked for a while longer and then tried to keep a stiff upper lip as we said good-bye. I watched them walk down the street, stop, and turn around again for one last wave. We had lived through so much together that seeing them and then having them leave was something like another death in my family.

I never saw them again.

One afternoon a woman showed up at the offices of the army's military police. Berit Hirsch looked like a typical Berliner: blond and blue-eyed, with that square German jaw that so many carried. A tall woman, she looked strong, but her eyes betrayed the fact that Berit was terrified. Her case was assigned to me.

"He is coming home," Berit said in almost a whine. "Coming from the South, maybe from the region closer to Vienna. I don't know exactly."

"Who?" I asked. "Who are you talking about?"

"My husband," she said. "Helmut was a Nazi officer and worked in one of the camps."

Sometimes, she went on, he beat her. She had the look of a woman who feared for her life. I asked her when he was arriving, and she said he would be at the train station in less than an hour. I didn't need to think; I hustled her into the jeep.

We zoomed through the streets of Berlin on our way to the train station. I instructed Berit that when he arrived, she was to greet him with a kiss like old times. I would be behind him and, from the rear, take him into custody. We wanted no hassle in a crowded train station, but I would be prepared if he resisted. She understood.

The Berlin Central Station had been badly damaged, but rail service had been restored to a limited degree. The old building looked like it would eventually have to be torn down and a new one built, but for now, trains were coming and going on a daily basis. The jeep pulled up, and we got out. My driver stayed with the jeep out front.

"Remember," I whispered, "don't act afraid. Be natural."

"I try," Berit said.

We walked through the terminal hall, which still looked rather ragged, and found our way out to the platform where the train would arrive. People were walking every which way, with no end to the flow of traffic. I looked around but saw no other police in sight.

"He come right here," Berit said. "Yeah, here."

"Okay, I'm going to stand over there by that steel support beam.

I'll be somewhat behind it, where you won't see me easily. Do just as I told you. Don't worry. I will protect you."

The woman nodded but looked extremely worried.

"Smile," I said. "Get the frown off your face."

She blinked several times. "I try."

"You are really afraid of this Helmut?" I said.

Her face immediately clouded. "Oh, yeah!"

"Well, don't worry. I'll handle him."

She forced a smile.

The train came roaring in almost exactly on time. The side doors opened, and the passengers began pouring out. Of course, I had not seen a picture of Helmut Hirsch, but I had a fairly good idea of what to expect. A large man swung out of the passenger car carrying a duffel bag. He had on a trench coat covering his broad shoulders. His hair had been nearly shaved up the side of his head, leaving a heavy, black clump on just the top. It was the style of many Nazi officers, reflecting a no-nonsense attitude of rigid discipline. He looked like my target.

The man kept looking up and down the platform as if trying to spot somebody. I saw Berit wave to him and took out my .45-caliber pistol, dropping the gun to my side. He saw her and immediately started toward Berit. No question about it. I had Helmut Hirsch in sight.

Berit held her arms out to hug her husband, and he wrapped his arms around her. I jumped out from behind the post and with long strides came up behind him. I stuck the .45 in his back.

"Don't move! *Halt!*"

His body stiffened. He might be stupid enough to try to elbow me, in which case I'd have to shoot him, and that wouldn't be good. I jabbed the pistol harder. "Don't even move."

Helmut Hirsch slowly raised his hands.

"Put your hands behind your back," I growled. "Your hands!"

His arms started to fall, and finally he brought both hands behind his back. I immediately clicked the handcuffs on him. While he stood at rigid attention, his wife started backing away.

"Don't leave!" I called to Berit. "I need your help."

She nodded her compliance.

"I speak English," Hirsch said. "Did this woman betray me?"

"No," I said. "You betrayed yourself."

For the first time, I looked around and realized that passersby had stopped walking. Some backed away, but a small number watched intently. For a moment, I thought about how these German pedestrians could easily overwhelm me if they decided to line up with old Helmut standing there in handcuffs. Of course, we had become the authorities, the new enforcers, and messing with us could seriously cost anyone dearly who got out of line. However, I wasn't going to stand around to test my theory.

"Okay, Hirsch. Move it." I poked him even harder in the back with the barrel. He started walking.

We quickly cruised through the remnants of the lobby and out the front door while everyone continued staring. I put Hirsch in the front seat and snapped an additional handcuff on his ankle that secured him to the jeep, so he wasn't going to be jumping out and running down the street. Hirsch kept looking straight ahead, with a dark intensity. My driver pulled away, and we started back to the station house.

I got Hirsch out, and his wife followed us in. I marched him in front of the supervisor's desk. "Here's another officer straight from running a concentration camp. I'm sure we got all kinds of people who want to talk to him."

Hirsch fixed his gaze on the wall, affecting a resolute indifference. For a moment, though, he turned and stared at his wife. Seldom had I seen the hate that radiated from his eyes. The look reflected a man who had killed and could kill again in an instant. If there had been any doubt about what his wife was saying, that one look clarified everything.

"You're quite a guy with women," I said to him. "I bet you could beat the hell out of any of 'em."

He frowned as if struggling to make sure he understood what I said.

"Well, partner, where you're going, you won't have a chance to hurt any women for maybe fifty years. That is, if we don't hang you first."

One of the guards came out of the long corridor behind the desk. He took Hirsch by the arm and started pulling him toward the door. By this time, the man's hair had dropped down over his eyes, and he looked like a rumpled mess from off the streets.

"Don't worry, Helmut!" I called after him. "You won't be here long. We've got a much larger prison just waiting for you to show up."

45

★ ★ ★

LEFT TO DIE

A cold wind blew in from the north, and it was clear that winter would soon be descending on Berlin. Of course, the nightly frolics weren't slowed by a little cold weather. The boozers hit it up every night of the week, although the pace definitely slowed. We kept making our nightly rounds. By this time, the Berliners knew who the MPs were and generally kept out of our way. Usually, they avoided eye contact and would only look down at the sidewalk. We had few problems with the locals.

Edda stayed with us and maintained her warmth and friendly disposition. Periodically, she fixed me one of her home-cooked meals, which I loved dearly. However, we never saw her sister. She said her name was Ulrike Muller and she was always busy. Apparently, she didn't seem to ever be there in the evenings. On Friday night, I pushed the subject.

"I never see your sister, Ulrike," I said.

"Oh, she's quite busy," Edda said casually. "Would you like a glass of wine? You got this for me at your army store."

"Exactly what does she do?"

"Many things. Helps people. You know . . . an assistant."

I told Edda that I *didn't* know. Assistants didn't usually work at night. I asked her to level with me.

She stopped and took a deep breath. "I thought you would have found out by now, but you haven't. Being a policeman, you would probably know eventually." Edda sat down at the table across from me. "You must understand, this has nothing to do with me."

"Yes," I said slowly. Her face had become hard, with a worried look. "I am open to whatever you tell me."

"I hope this will not affect my job with you."

"Edda, give me the facts."

Resoluteness returned to her eyes. "Ulrike has become a prostitute and walks the streets at night. This was her decision, but the money sustains us."

"A prostitute?" My mouth dropped open.

"No one in my family has ever done such a thing, but everybody was killed and our house destroyed. We had nothing. Nothing! Ulrike became particularly bitter and didn't care about anything anymore. She could immediately make money to keep us alive. Once Ulrike made up her mind, nothing could stop her. Yes, Frank, night after night, Ulrike is on the streets doing whatever money buys."

I leaned back in my chair. I would never have suspected this story, but it immediately made sense. A quick, easy source of money had kept these two sisters above the poverty line. In a city of nearly starving people, they had maintained more than mere survival. Actually, what her sister did was none of my business anyway.

"I know you will think we are terrible, but we are Catholics and go to church all the time. My sister goes to confession and does what the priest tells her to do. We have always been religious people, but . . ." Her voice trailed away. "People all over Berlin are struggling just to stay alive. Everywhere, good people maybe eat only one meal a day . . . two at best. You would not understand how hard life is." She stared at the floor. "We must do what we must do."

"I make no judgments," I said. "I will not ask about her again."

"Thank you," Edda said and looked away. After a moment, she turned back around. "Thank you for understanding."

I changed the subject and asked her how she had prepared to-night's supper. Edda immediately went into great detail. The subject of her sister never came up again.

The next morning, I worked the early detail. By this time, I knew most of the soldiers in the military police operation and had seen the jail inside out. Life had become rather routine, and I hoped I'd receive notice to return home soon. Putting those thoughts behind me, I reported for work and saluted the captain.

A nasty assignment had just come in. A Russian truck hit a woman and took off without stopping. No point in us trying to run him down; the Soviets would just protect him anyway. They needed me to go over with the ambulance, pick up the body, and deliver it to their version of a funeral home and morgue. The captain wanted me to get pictures of the entire scene.

"I wouldn't take that woman who works with you on this one," he said.

"Why?"

The captain handed me a sheet of instructions and raised an eye-brow. "You'll see."

I told my driver that I might need his help.

The Russians had a way of buzzing through our sector like they owned the entire town. No telling what had occurred. In ten min-utes, we arrived at the scene of the accident. A crowd had gathered around for a look. I noticed many of the observers turn away quickly.

A couple of American soldiers were standing there. After making sure my MP armband was in place, I walked up to one.

"What's the situation, Corporal?"

"Bad news," he said. "You aren't going to believe it, but here's the situation. A German woman dashed across the street and jumped up on the sidewalk. Apparently, her foot slipped, and she fell backward. About that time, this Commie nutcase came barreling around the same corner. The German woman tumbled under the front tire. Wacked her head right off."

"God almighty!"

"Yeah, you'll remember this one for a long time."

I pushed my way through the crowd, my driver behind me. I heard him gasp.

The woman's legs were still partially on the sidewalk; her arms sprawled on the street in a strange, haphazard design. She was wearing a dress that was lifted up to her midthighs. Lying on her back on the street added to the bizarre scene. Her head was gone.

I spotted it three feet from the curb, with the eyes still wide open. Her trachea—the windpipe—hung down from the remnant of her neck like a grotesque Halloween mask.

My driver leaned over my shoulder and stared at the head. I heard him gag, turn, and push through the crowd. On the other side of the street, he started to vomit. Not having any combat experience left him as green as grass.

The sound of a siren filled the air, and one of our ambulances pulled up. A couple more MPs were with the medics.

"Everybody out of the way!" the ambulance attendant yelled. "Officers! Clear the area so we can work."

Two medics carrying a stretcher pushed in and stopped. The face of one of them turned white.

"God help us," the other man groaned.

"Look," the other attendant said to me. "You will need to go with us to the funeral home and sign this situation in with them. They tell me that a Russian hit the woman and took off."

"That appears to be the case," I said. "I'm sure we won't catch the guy, and if we did, the Commies would protect him. By the way, I'm also taking pictures."

The attendant nodded. "Sure." He turned to the other medic. "Let's get the body on the stretcher. We'll have to take the head in a bucket."

His buddy groaned again.

The two men got the lifeless form belted down on the stretcher and covered with a blanket. By now, the crowd had become a small army, but the other two policemen who came with them kept everybody back. They loaded the body into the ambulance and put the head in a bucket as they prepared to leave.

"You can follow us," the driver said.

I looked at my driver, who still appeared shaken.

"Give me a minute to make sure my man is ready to go. He's been a little shook up."

The driver nodded.

"You okay?" I asked my driver.

He nodded for a minute. "Yeah, I'm more than ready to get out of here." He glanced over his shoulder. "What about all that blood?"

"Are you kidding? Berlin is still floating in blood. Forget it. Time will take care of the problem."

I could tell he didn't agree with my answer, but then again, his lack of combat experience had left his finer senses intact. He shrugged.

I waved to the ambulance driver. "Okay, let's roll." Our little caravan took off.

We wound down the worn streets. In the last several months, they had made real progress in clearing up debris, and it had become easier to get around. The ambulance driver appeared to know exactly where to go, and we soon pulled up in front of the funeral home. Katzbachstrasse looked like most streets in Berlin. However, the Funeria Schmidt establishment appeared to have survived most of the war damage. Possibly, the Russians were superstitious and left the place alone. The funeral home was now also serving as a morgue. The ambulance pulled into a side entrance and began to unload. I followed them in.

The owner had the same professional demeanor of every funeral director I'd ever seen: that sweet, distant, "Can we help you?" smile that seemed far too nice under the circumstances. But he took one look under the blanket and recoiled like everybody else.

"I'm with the army," I said. "I need to take pictures and will be making the report. I will need to follow the body in." One of the other MPs came in behind me carrying the covered bucket. "We're all together."

The director nodded, and we proceeded down the hall. We turned a corner and found ourselves in a large room that looked almost like an operating theater. I photographed the entire establishment as well as the corpse lying on the table. An adjoining room, much cooler, was ringed with heavy doors on what looked like giant refrigerators. I couldn't help but wonder what was inside. Nobody was watching me, so I opened the door to one and looked in.

To my surprise, I found trays of what appeared to be steaks, as if prepared for the grill. I looked again. From my time on the battlefield, I had seen the bodies of dead men lying in all kinds of positions, with the skin peeled away. I knew human tissue when I saw it. Those steaks weren't from any cows. Somebody had been cutting up humans.

I slammed the door shut and thought about what I'd seen. No one had to tell me what those cuts of meat meant. Starving people would eat *anything*. If I reported this place directly to the authorities, all hell would break loose. I knew an investigation could keep me in Germany long after I was scheduled to leave. But I felt I had to do something.

When I got back to the station house, I reported the entire incident to the lieutenant. He listened attentively and kept nodding. He said he would run it up the flagpole but would allow me to leave Berlin once my appointment was up.

Relieved, I saluted and left.

Interestingly enough, a couple of months after I returned to America, I picked up a copy of the army newspaper. The *Stars and Stripes* always kept the soldiers up on what was happening in the occupation. To my surprise, I found a story reporting that the military police and the U.S. Central Intelligence Agency had uncovered the crime of cannibalism in a morgue in Berlin. My, my! Who would have thought such a thing!

46

★ ★ ★

THE CURTAIN FALLS

Winter arrived with a bang—or, I should say, a blizzard. Huge flakes of snow swirled and settled down on the sidewalks and streets, covering them with a beautiful, sparkling white coat. The debris and destroyed buildings looked newly hopeful. Maybe with the coming of Christmas, things were looking up for Berlin.

During the storm, I was sitting in the army's dining hall. The GIs' kitchen was manned by chefs disguised as soldiers. These guys really knew how to cook. The smell of a Christmas feast of roasted turkey, cranberry sauce, spice-flavored dressing, and mince pie tickled my nose. Seated around a huge table, I dug into the best dinner I could have imagined. Almost made the entire trip to Europe worthwhile. Well, not quite.

Taking a break from eating, I went to the window to see how much snow had collected in the street. I was stunned to see children standing in the snowbanks peering back at me. The smell of our dinner had drawn them there. Here I was living like royalty, and those hungry-eyed children standing in the cold would have been satisfied with a crust of bread. I remembered feeding kids hamburgers earlier and knew what I had to do.

My hunger slipped away.

I hurried to the PX (post exchange) and asked the cook to fix as many hamburgers as he could stuff into two large paper sacks. He was to call me when they were ready. I simply couldn't let those little kids stand out there with nothing. In short order, the cook came in with a sack in each arm.

"Don't know what you're going to do with all these hamburgers while you got turkey sitting in front of you," he said quizzically. "But here are the sacks."

"Watch and see." I grabbed them and headed for the door.

Outside, I brushed the snow off the curb and sat down with my sacks. The hot, alluring aroma of a cooked hamburger drifted through the air. I figured the children would catch on in a hurry. And here they came: kids of all sizes bounding through the snow. Most looked fairly ragged. One youngster had been bundled up with a bath towel around his neck. Their hands were extended, even without gloves on.

"Now, don't run off," I said. "Stay here to eat." I didn't want parents taking the hamburgers away from any of these kids. I started handing out the burgers. "Eat slow. C'mon, take it easy. One bite at a time." They ignored me and wolfed down the meal.

Before long, I was surrounded by a dozen children. They began to smile, laugh, and even cheer. I laughed with them as they ate. Everyone wanted seconds. I kept handing out burgers until the two sacks were empty. They hugged me, thanked me, and hugged me again.

Soldiers began to spill out of the dining hall. Captains, majors, and even a company commander walked by. Each smiled and saluted me. To my surprise, the hamburger handout outside in the snow tasted better than that turkey inside the hall.

On December 9, 1945, the front-page story got through to us. The day before, Major General Hobart "Hap" Gay had invited General

Patton to go pheasant hunting with him near the German town of Speyer, on the Rhine. Apparently, Patton had been feeling depressed about the results of the war. His request to go to the Pacific had been rejected, and he ended up with what he considered a mere desk job. As they were coming back from the pheasant hunt, Patton was lamenting how bad war was. He had just talked about how war was such a waste of life and property when their car collided head-on with an American army truck abruptly crossing the road.

The other passengers in the car were only slightly injured, but General Patton hit his head on the glass partition in the backseat. A gash in his head sent blood running down his shirt. Patton complained that he felt paralyzed from the neck down and was struggling to breathe. He was brought to a hospital in nearby Heidelberg, where the doctors diagnosed him with a broken neck and cervical spinal cord injury. He would be paralyzed from the neck down.

The report left all of us in shock. How could it be?

Patton would spend the next twelve days in spinal traction, as his medical team tried to reduce the pressure on his spine. I imagine he must have been devastated. He knew he would never again live a normal life. Someone else would have to attend to all of his needs.

He began to decline, day by day. His wife, Beatrice, flew in to be with him. After a career spent dodging flying bullets and exploding bombs, Patton had been laid low by a simple car wreck. It just didn't fit the man.

The rumors began to fly immediately. Every soldier claimed to have inside secrets about what *really* happened. Some men thought that Allied secret intelligence believed Patton would reveal American collusion with the Russians that cost U.S. lives. The spy chiefs wanted him dead before he exposed those details.

Another claim that popped up was that Patton had actually been recovering from his serious injuries and was on the verge of being flown home. The story was that the chief of the recently disbanded U.S. Office of Strategic Services (OSS), the forerunner of the CIA, General William "Wild Bill" Donovan, ordered a skilled marksman named Douglas Bazata to silence Patton. Supposedly, Bazata arranged for the truck to come rolling into Patton's path. Bazata then shot a low-velocity projectile that broke Patton's neck, leaving the other passengers in the car unharmed. Rather far out, but that was some of the hearsay.

Douglas Bazata made statements that only added to the confusion. He claimed American officials looked away while the NKVD (the People's Commissariat for Internal Affairs, the forerunner of the KGB) actually poisoned General Patton. Supposedly, Patton was also on Stalin's hit list. Of course, it was no secret that Patton and the Russians hated each other. So, the gossip claimed, the Russians finished him off. A decade later, Bazata would assert that all of this was true by giving the story to a journalist. Bazata supposedly claimed all of this happened at the command of General Donovan, a highly decorated World War I hero.

Douglas Bazata had been part of an elite unit that parachuted into France to help organize the resistance before D-Day occurred. During his career, he was awarded four purple hearts and a Distinguished Service Cross as well as the French Croix de Guerre medal. With significant artistic talent, he was to become a friend of Salvador Dalí, who painted him as Don Quixote. Later, Bazata was also rumored to enjoy the patronage of Princess Grace of Monaco as well as the Duke and Duchess of Windsor. Near the end of his career, Bazata was an aide to U.S. president Ronald Reagan.

Another report stated that the driver of the truck that hit Patton was immediately transferred to London before he could be questioned. As part of this story was the claim that Patton's body was never autopsied. Never was a general's death surrounded by more intrigue and mystery. Once a conspiracy gets started, the results become like a landslide, with everyone tossing on another boulder. Long after the dust settles, people still have their own ideas, which are often bizarre, while the truth remains simple.

I heard it all and wondered if there hadn't been a conspiracy of some sort, but I could see how various individuals promoted themselves through fables about their involvement in Patton's death. On December 21, 1945, at six in the evening, General Patton died in his sleep. Pulmonary edema and congestive heart failure were given as the cause.

When the news came in over the radio, we discussed it among ourselves. We had been sitting around a table finishing supper. Of course, the report stopped all of us, no matter what we had been doing. The general opinion was that the collision was no accident. Somebody all the way from Stalin to the top of the American command wanted General Patton out of the way. We knew they considered him too dangerous.

We all grieved.

47

★ ★ ★

ALL GOOD THINGS
COME TO ...

General Patton's death really cut. I found myself walking around virtually talking to myself. Other soldiers appeared to be in the same fog. I admired his skills and loved him as a person. Having lost my own father, I had come to see Patton as a sort of father figure. I just couldn't get away from thinking about it. He had been an invisible force that guided me through the days of danger and struggle. General Patton had embodied what our ideals of Americanism were.

The weather stayed cold, and the snow hung on. The nightly raids got a little easier, and we didn't see nearly as many fistfights break out that required us to haul in somebody. The drunks kept on being drunks but usually weren't difficult to handle. My daily rounds became more routine.

On the other hand, Edda started giving me the big eye again. Maybe she thought I'd change my mind, but I just kept on being a nice guy who maintained a polite distance. Her invitations for a home-cooked meal became more frequent, and I had a hard time turning them down. Edda certainly knew how to cook, and the conversations were always interesting. Periodically she would give me a kiss on the cheek or reach for my hand, but I didn't allow the gestures to go anywhere. I tried to keep everything casual.

Winters in Berlin were cold enough, but nothing like we experienced during the fighting when the bottom dropped out of the thermometer. Of course, the army provided us with more than adequate coats, gloves, and whatever was needed. Even in the cold weather, the Germans were certainly industrious enough. Often working only by hand, they cleared the streets and began rebuilding the bombed-out buildings. Traffic picked up, and we could see that life was moving back toward a normal pace. However, nothing got better with the Soviets. The Russians continued to be difficult as well as aggressive.

As usual, I walked into our military police office for the morning assignments. The clerk looked up and grinned. "Ah, Sergeant Sisson," he said. "We've been expecting you."

I laughed. "Really, what did I do now?"

"The big man wants to talk to you. Lieutenant Franks is waiting."

"Franks!" I swallowed hard. "What's going on?"

"Don't ask me. I only run the front desk."

Lieutenant Franks was well known. He had been born and raised in Berlin. Though his parents were American, his German had the accent of a native, and he knew the city well. When the occupation forces were setting up their offices in Berlin, Franks was a natural to run any important facility. He became the head of all military police. Going to see him was talking to the top dog.

I walked in and saluted. "Sergeant Sisson reporting for duty."

"Sit down, Sergeant," Franks said. "I have some important information for you." He picked up a sheet of paper. "This memo just came in today. Your work in Berlin is finished. In two weeks, you will return to the United States and become a civilian."

I gasped. "Praise God!" I exclaimed and then retreated. "I mean . . . yes, sir."

Franks smiled. "Of course you're delighted. Who wouldn't want to get out of this war-torn city? You've done a good job and deserve a trip home. You will return by ship to the Houston, Texas, area and then take the bus to Camp Chaffee. They'll process you out so you can return home."

"Thank you, sir!" I saluted.

Out in the hall, I let out a whoopee holler and could hear men laughing. I was going home.

I figured that I might get home before the mail from Europe arrived, so there was no point in writing to either Alice or my mother. I'd simply surprise them and knew they'd be thrilled that I had come back in one piece.

I didn't have much time to prepare for my departure. Earlier, I had told Edda Muller that I might have to leave without even saying good-bye, but now I could at least thank her for all she had done. I wanted to take her to a nice restaurant to break the news. A public place would be better than in her apartment. She agreed to meet me at Max und Moritz, famous for its traditional German foods, such as pork, sauerkraut, and wieners. I was told that the restaurant had been around since 1902. I knew she hadn't been anyplace that nice since before the war began. I made reservations for us.

The evening proved to be cold, so I had my usual jeep driver drop me off in front of Max und Moritz. The restaurant's façade had survived the bombing, and the building appeared to be in good shape. With a high ceiling, large arching doorways, and expensive antique furniture, this would certainly please Edda.

I walked in, and the maître d' greeted me immediately.

"Could you be Sergeant Sisson?" he asked.

"Why, yes," I said, surprised. "Yes."

"Fraulein Edda is already here. Please follow me."

I thought I had beaten Edda there but was no match for her German punctuality. I spotted her immediately. She was wearing a dress that I had never seen before. The low-cut top accentuated her ample figure and was stunning. Edda definitely wanted to impress me.

We made casual conversation and ordered sauerbraten and *käsespätzle*—the buttery, cheesy egg noodles that traditionally accompany the marinated beef. Both were marvelous. A couple of glasses of wine made what I had to say easier. Near the end of the meal, I turned to the difficult subject.

"Edda, I have something important to tell you."

"I know. I have already heard."

"What?"

"News has a way of traveling," she said. "Everyone in the station house likes you, and so information spread quickly. You are going back to America."

I nodded. "Yes, that's so."

"I thought about this change all day." Edda reached for my hand once more, and this time she squeezed it. "You have become a part of me. I see you every day. It can't end like this." She leaned forward and looked straight in my eyes. "I want to go with you. I want to live in America."

"Edda, we've talked about this relationship before."

"Yes, but now everything is different. You *really* are going back. I will do whatever you ask of me. I want to be with you." She squeezed my hand again.

"Edda, you have been wonderful, but as I said in the beginning, I have a girl waiting for me in Oklahoma. Alice and I have a bond. I must go back to her."

Edda stared at the floor. One last time, she pressed my hand even more tightly. "I was afraid of that possibility." Her hand slipped away, and she sat silent for a while. "All right. If you don't want me to be your . . . your . . . whatever, will you simply take me with you to America?"

"I can't do that, Edda. I'm sorry, it's just not possible."

She took a deep breath and began to nod her head. "You told me earlier, but I thought you might change your mind." She shrugged. "You didn't. Facing the facts has been difficult because I have come to truly care about you . . . to love you, Frank. You are a good man and have been gracious to me. I know I would make you a good wife." She looked away. "I must face the fact that this is not to be."

I didn't know what to say. No matter what I felt, I couldn't allow myself to entertain what she was saying and had to keep a proper distance. If I didn't, the complications would turn into an avalanche of confusion. I knew a disaster would follow.

"I have already made the decision that should this impossibility be the case, Ulrike and I would move to the British Zone. There's a little town on the north edge, where we once lived. We know the area. Hopefully, we will find people we've known. Maybe not. But Ulrike can practice her—shall we say—trade with the British. I will see if my time with the American army helps me obtain a similar position."

"I would help you in any way that I can. Unfortunately, I'll be gone in a week."

Edda took a big drink of the wine sitting in front of her. "I will miss you," she said. "Miss you terribly." With the corner of her napkin, she wiped her eyes. "Terribly," she repeated.

I sat there unsure of what to say. I could only look down.

"I think it is best that I go." Edda pushed back from the table. "God bless you. Good-bye, Frank."

I sat there long after she was gone. Maybe I'd made the biggest mistake of my life. But I knew that when I let my emotions settle,

I would know I had done the right thing. I was virtually a boy when I'd crossed the English Channel and began to fight in more of a war than I had any idea could even exist. I had lived two lifetimes in these few short years. My second father, General Patton, had died; his death certainly continued to touch me deeply. I wasn't sure how the battles had changed me, but they had.

One thing was clear: I needed to get back home. I knew returning to Weleetka would be clarifying. Once more I wanted to walk through the main street and down the railroad track. I wanted to see if the old swimming hole was still there. Were any of my high school buddies still around, or had they all gone to war as well? Many probably never came back.

Most of all, I wanted to know if Alice was still waiting.

48

★ ★ ★

GOING HOME

I had come to Europe on a luxury liner. In May 1946 I was going back on an old ship like the ones that I'd once welded in California. Of course, I had been a good welder, but I hoped my ride wasn't one I had worked on—I guess that was just superstition. Nevertheless, to be sailing across the Atlantic like an aristocrat certainly felt like a just reward for the efforts I'd made in Europe. I got up in the morning when I liked and ate like a horse.

Our return trip took us around Florida and up the Gulf of Mexico to a port near Houston. We came marching off like proud winners, but there wasn't much of a crowd. Too many soldiers had returned already. A year had passed since I started working in Berlin, and Americans had become familiar with soldiers returning. Thus, most of the people on the dock were relatives of the returnees. Nevertheless, we waved to everyone and marched down the gangplank with renewed energy that came naturally with being back on American soil.

Buses were waiting, and we were quickly on our way to Camp Chaffee. The training center was just outside Fort Smith, Arkansas, which was only about a hundred miles from Weleetka. This particular base had been a prisoner-of-war and refugee camp as well as an army training camp. The journey felt surreal because I was just over the hill from my hometown. After years fighting a war in a foreign land, I almost felt like I was cruising through a dream. I was *really* coming home again.

The soldiers tasked with processing at Camp Chaffee understood that every last one of us was anxious to get on a bus that would take us to our final destination. We didn't want any fooling around with army procedure, although some formalities were necessary.

"Okay, Sergeant Sisson," the officer said. "You are officially discharged from the United States Army and will no longer be required to wear a uniform. Of course, you will be listed in the reserves for a time and then be completely released from all obligations with your country. You have served well and will receive an honorary discharge certificate. Welcome home, Franklin Sisson."

For a moment, I felt an unexpected surge of emotion. The meaning of his words left me almost speechless. I had begun this journey as a fifteen-year old boy struggling to help his family. In a span of a little more than six years, I had been transformed into a grown man who had looked death in the eye and walked away. The weight of such a realization bore down on me, but I certainly didn't want to show it.

"Thank you, sir." I saluted.

"Here are your bus tickets that will take you to Henryetta, Oklahoma, where you change buses and go straight to Weleetka. God bless you and good luck." He saluted back.

I walked out into the sunlight and lined up to get on the bus. We would be zooming through the magnificent forests of scrub oaks and the thick, tall grass of eastern Oklahoma. This part of the state had wonderful lakes, like Tenkiller and Eufaula. Each mile seemed to be welcoming me. I was in the home stretch.

The bus rolled down the highway and pulled into the station in Henryetta. At first, I thought about calling my mother, but then decided that I would just surprise her. So many people rode the buses back then that the station hummed with passengers making various connections all over the state. With the Great Depression being what it was, many people still didn't have automobiles and depended on the Greyhound bus service. Fortunately, the wait took only forty-five minutes before we were pulling out. By late afternoon, we rolled into my hometown.

Because Weleetka was small, there wasn't a big station—just a street corner where the bus pulled up in front of a ticket office with one window. I got off and looked around. There weren't many cars going down the street, and most of them looked old. I knew that automobile manufacturers had turned their attention to tanks, jeeps, artillery, and so forth for a while now. Just never realized that nobody had bought a new car for years. Even a Model A Ford came chugging down the street. All the stores were still there and open, just like they should be. Only a few people were walking down the sidewalks. I stood there and watched for several minutes. I was really home.

An older woman walked by and stopped. Then she turned around. "Why, are you Elmer Franklin Sisson?"

"Yes, ma'am."

"You are Myrtle Sisson's son?"

I remembered her faintly as one of the town's leading gossips. Her gray hair had turned a tad whiter, but she looked about the same, just older.

"Yes." Her name slowly came to mind: Hayes . . . Olivia Hayes.

"Oh, my! God bless you, child!" She hugged me. "Back from the war!" She started shaking my hand. "Thank you for what you've done for America. Yes, sir-e-e-e. Thank you with all my heart." She started walking away. "Keep up the good work," she called. "You're a fine young man."

I thought I'd better get home quickly before old Olivia Hayes called my mother and alerted her and the rest of the town that I was home. The familiar path down Main Street with a turn to the right and two blocks down led to our house. I quickened my pace.

I stopped at the front gate. Everything about the house and the yard looked the same. Actually, the front of the house could have used a coat of paint, and the porch looked a little more worn. Nevertheless, this little abode was where I grew up. Just the same.

"Maybe," I thought, "I should knock on the front door rather than just walk in."

The door opened slowly. "Yes?" a quiet voice said.

"Mom, it's me."

Myrtle Sisson swung the door wide and leaped out. "Son! Oh, my God! Frank!" She threw her arms around my neck and hugged me fiercely. "Oh, God help us! You've come back! You're home! Home, at last!"

Mother started crying, and tears ran down my cheeks, too. Neither of us could stop. My return was simply too overwhelming for both of us. She kept hugging me and thanking God that I was alive.

"Come in," Mom said. "Come in and sit down. Oh, Frank! You're taller, and you've filled out like a man. Just look at you in that uniform! You look so handsome!"

We sat down, and she immediately began telling me about my family. My sister Fern had married while I was gone. Both Buck and Bob had graduated from high school and had jobs. Now that I was back, all seven of the children were doing fine. Mother kept talking about Mildred and Faye and their families. She loved talking about all the grandchildren. Finally, she caught her breath and stopped.

"Tell me about the war, son."

I clenched my teeth nervously. "I think General Sherman once said, 'War is hell.' Well, he was right. You really don't want to know more than that. Just know that by God's grace, I survived it." I pulled the smudged paper out of my shirt pocket. "Every day of the war, I carried this passage from Psalm 91 with me. These words guided my footsteps: 'Though a thousand fall at my side, though ten thousand are dying around me, the evil will not touch me. I will see how the wicked are punished, but I will not share it. For Jehovah is my refuge! I choose the God above all gods to shelter me.' Mom, that's what sustained me."

"Thank you, son." She wiped her eyes. "That's probably enough for me to know. At least for now. The hand of the Lord protected you, and that is enough. I must call everyone! All the kids, the neighbors. We'll have a great reunion tonight. Everyone will come. Yes, I must start calling."

"Before you do all that phoning, I need to see if I can find Alice. I owe her a visit first."

Myrtle Sisson blinked several times. "Son, you've been gone a long time. You sent us money, and you kept our family alive. But you know . . . things change. I'm not sure what the situation is with Alice Anderson. We haven't seen or heard from her in a long time."

"I understand she took a job in Wetumka. Is that so?"

Mom nodded. "Yes, I guess. I heard that, but I also understand she's back in town right now. Had some kind of medical procedure that's put her in bed for a spell."

"Then she'd be at her house?"

Mom raised her eyebrow. "I suppose so."

"I think I'll run over there right now while you call people. Okay?"

"You're a grown man, and what you do is your decision. The days are past when I tell you what to do. I just . . . I just . . . want you to be careful."

"Sure, Mom," I said. "No problem."

She looked at me solemnly. "I hope not."

49

★ ★ ★

WAKING UP

I had tried to push my personal problems out of my mind. The fact that Alice's letters arrived less and less had bothered me. Sometimes I felt angry. Here I was putting my life on the line and staying faithful to her, and she couldn't write? Really? Then I'd push it all down and tell myself that the mail probably got delayed or maybe lost. On other days, I thought that maybe she'd wandered off. Regardless, I had kept my promise for more than six years, including the time I'd been working in California. Did Alice do the same?

My mother's hesitation seemed like a veiled warning. I could tell she knew more than she was saying, but I had to know the truth. Apparently Alice had some little medical problem, so she must still be home. The walk to her house was only a few blocks.

Alice's house looked a lot like mine. In fact, almost all the houses were the same. Relatively small. Maybe two or three bedrooms. Straightforward. Simple.

I walked up the front steps onto the small porch and knocked on the door. Alice opened the door and froze.

"Frank!"

"Hi," I said.

"You're back!" She hugged me. "Come in!"

The living room looked exactly the same, just like the last time I was there six years earlier.

"Sit down." Alice pointed to a chair. "Sit down and tell me all about the war."

Alice, too, had grown up. Her hair, all swooped up on top, made her look like one of the Andrews Sisters. She had filled out, no longer a thin high school girl. She didn't have any makeup on, but her face had gotten longer. Alice was still a good-looker, but her entire appearance was older. Today her eyes had dark circles underneath. She didn't seem particularly warm.

"You really don't want to hear my battle stories. They are awful, and the fighting was terrible."

Alice studied me carefully. "You've changed, Frank. I think you're taller than when I saw you last. Heavens, that was years ago."

"You look good as ever, Alice."

"Not today. I'm still feeling a little tired." She looked away. "Well, let's talk about something more pleasant. I guess you know that Weleetka's having a good basketball season this year. Winning many games." Her voice sounded more distant than I expected.

"No, I didn't know. I'm afraid I'm out of touch with high school basketball. I've been living in Berlin."

"Berlin? Oh, my. I'm sure that was exciting." She managed a smile. "Must have been different from our boring little town."

"It was just my job. I was sent there as a military policeman."

"Now, *that* is exciting. Catching all the bad guys."

Alice seemed formal. She continued to be distant.

"A little different from that." I knew my voice had gone flat. "I understand you took a job in Wetumka."

"Went to work with a lawyer," Alice said. "Nice guy—or so I thought," she added ruefully.

"It turned out okay?"

"Not really."

"Alice, we had something going before I left. Are we still on?" I couldn't stand the distance any longer. I wanted to know why she seemed so remote. "You still have feelings for me?"

She looked at the floor. "Look, Frank. You've been gone for years. Life around here goes on. I waited for a long time, and then I had my own life to live. Things just changed."

I didn't say anything for some time. Alice sat there silently. Finally, I said, "You found somebody else?"

Alice nodded her head.

"Who?"

She told me that it was the attorney.

"Alice, I spent hours reading your letters. I believed you were somebody I could come back to. Was I wrong?"

She told me that most of the girls in her class had gotten married right out of high school if their boyfriends were still around. That she didn't know if I was ever coming back. That our worlds had grown just too far apart.

"But we can start over, Alice."

"No, we can't, Frank," she said resolutely.

"I'm willing to understand, to make adjustments."

Alice's face hardened. "No, you wouldn't. You don't get it, Frank. Look, I got involved with this lawyer I worked for. He was older and knew what he was doing. What I'm trying to say is that I had an abortion."

I gasped. "What?"

An abortion. That was why she was home, recuperating.

"Look, Alice. All during this war, I stayed with my beliefs. Abortion just isn't acceptable to me. Never was. I didn't get involved with anybody in that way. I'm sorry, but . . . but . . ."

"Look! Don't get righteous on me," she snapped. "I did what I did, and that's the end of the story."

I sank down in my chair. Alice jumped up and marched out of the room. I sat there for a moment and then got up slowly and started for the front door. I knew that I would never see her again.

The walk back to my mother's house was the longest journey of my life. Alice Anderson had been a dream that kept me going during a time when any minute I could have been killed. But no longer could I avoid the facts. She'd been my girlfriend through my school years, but school was over. Alice had become someone different from the person I'd once known. The matter was as simple as that. I had to pick myself up and go on. I had seen good men die. Their dreams and high hopes died with them. Somewhere back in the United States, life had to go on without them. Their families made the adjustment. I guess now it was my turn. While I had hoped for more, Alice ended those dreams.

That evening, the entire family gathered. I still had on my army uniform. Mother busted her budget with a fried chicken and dumplings supper for the whole gang that was as big as Thanksgiving. For hours, we laughed and shared stories from the past. I guess Mother had told them not to ask me about the war. Everyone steered around that subject, but I could tell they wanted to ask. The sisters kept hugging me, tickling me, and acting like Superman had landed. What an evening!

When it was all over, and everyone had gone home, I was still thinking about Alice. I could have seen the disaster coming, but I had ignored the obvious signs. I had probably been fighting homesickness and didn't want to admit it. That's what living in a foreign country under difficult conditions will do to you. I just had to wake up and live in the real world.

During the following days, I began to return to normal life. I put away my uniform and settled into dressing like everybody else. People didn't stop me on the streets. They wanted to forget about the struggle, the fighting, the killing, but not as much as I did. I wanted to forget, but couldn't. The faces of the Jewish prisoners in those concentration camps, especially, lingered. Mother said several times that I seemed to wake up in the middle of the night, yelling or pounding on the bed.

The years after the war were prosperous. The economy of Weleetka picked up, and a few new cars appeared. The automobiles looked different from what had been produced in the thirties. I needed a career. Of course, I could go back to being a welder. The oil field wasn't booming like it once did, but there was work out there. Or, the GI Bill promised I could go to college. Being a veteran had its benefits.

One day my brother Bob and I were walking down Weleetka's main street talking idly when I noticed a young woman crossing the street. With her raven black hair and striking face, she was a showstopper. For a second, my heart beat double time.

"Bob, who is that woman?"

"Where?"

"Across the street. The one in the red dress."

"Why, that's Donna Millard. Her family's new in town." Her father, Bob explained, was Guy Millard, our new Methodist preacher.

"Why, that's the most beautiful woman I ever saw. I'm going over there to get acquainted."

Bob frowned. "Why?"

"Because that's the woman I'm going to marry."

I did. We met in May and married in August. That was seventy-three years ago as of this writing. The decades that followed were filled with happiness. Our four children grew up, and they had eight children. Now we have sixteen grandchildren. Our life together couldn't have been better.

All those insights, perspectives, and disciplines I learned in the Third Army stuck with me, along with the promise and assurance from Psalm 91. Through the years, I often thought about what I had learned and seen during the war. While I didn't talk about most of the experiences, the memories of General Patton returned again and again. Although I hadn't seen him in person that many times, his persona still lingered. I tried to raise my children with those same ideals. I've tried to follow what I learned from George S. Patton. I hope General Patton might be proud of me.

Every now and then, a newspaper article, a television special, a conversation will bring up the past, and I will remember an incident as vividly as if it happened yesterday.

Yesterday. So far away and yet so close.

EPILOGUE

★ ★ ★

A NEW SIDE TO THE WAR

As the decades slipped by, Donna and I lived a prosperous and productive life. I finished college and got into the grocery business. Along the way came our children, Dee Dee, Cary, Tim, and Tina. Each child eventually left home, venturing off on a hundred other journeys of their own. Along the way, Dee Dee developed an interest in genealogy and began exploring where her original family migrated from. She was particularly interested in my side of the family, since no one seemed to have talked much about my heritage. I never spoke much about the war.

After interviewing my few remaining siblings, Dee Dee stumbled upon the name Emma Level, who was said to have been my grandmother. My mother, Myrtle Harris Sisson, was born in Oklahoma before statehood, and the family settled in Indian territory. Myrtle's memories of her mother's family were somewhat vague, and nobody seemed to know what had become of Emma. For seven years, Dee Dee searched the archives of the Oklahoma Historical Society, family records, old correspondence, and whatever memories of distant family members she could find. Eventually she turned up an aunt who remembered Emma.

"Yes," the old woman said. "It's been so long. But we all remembered that Emma had the strangest way of praying. We all talked about her peculiarity. None of us knew what she was doing."

"And what was that?" Dee Dee asked.

"Seems Grandmother Emma would always light two candles and then start making a circular motion with her hands over her face. Then she'd cover her face and pray."

Dee Dee couldn't believe her ears. She knew what such a ritual meant.

With this information in mind, she set out to discover Emma Level's origins. This important clue led my daughter down a new trail, where all the road signs pointed to . . . Germany. Emma's great-grandfather turned out to be Johann Jacob Hackman. Some of his family had immigrated through Virginia, where so many Jews entered America back in those long-gone days. At one time, the largest synagogue in America had been in Virginia. Dee Dee stared at her discovery almost in disbelief. The Hackman family was Jewish.

Johann Jacob Hackman certainly had a biblical middle name, which was typical of Jewish children. With this information in hand, Dee Dee soon discovered that he was born in Ibersheim, Worms, Rhineland-Pfalz, Germany. She immediately pulled out a map and started studying where this area might be located. Dee Dee was startled to realize that her ancestors had lived in the vicinity of the Dachau concentration camp.

For a long time, she stared at the map. Dee Dee knew well what this information meant. Nazis had struck this area first and rounded up all the Jews for the gas chambers. Picking up her car keys, she rushed to my home.

"Dad, sit down," Dee Dee said. "I've found some important information about who you are."

I laughed. "You found out that I am related to Pocahontas?" I laughed again. "I'm sure my mother, Myrtle, expected me to turn out to be a wild Indian."

Dee Dee didn't smile. "No, Dad. What I found is far more profound. I ran down Emma Level's personal history and where her family came from. They were all from Germany, in the area of the Nazi camp you helped liberate."

"What?" I leaned forward in my chair. "What are you suggesting?"

"Dad, your ancestors were Jewish, and their descendants were imprisoned in the camp you liberated."

I stared. My mouth dropped open slightly. I couldn't speak.

"Dad, by heritage, you are *Jewish*."

For months, I pondered what my daughter had learned. By this time, our daughter Tina and her husband, Sven, had moved to Germany, where he was a pilot. My head was still whirling from the realization that I might actually have helped liberate someone I was related to. I had to go back and visit that site again. In 2012 Donna and I traveled to Germany and found our way to the concentration camp. Tina and Sven came with us. After parking the car, we walked into the chambers of death.

Now that it had been cleaned up in such a pristine fashion, I almost didn't recognize the grizzly, cold death trap that my unit and I had walked through, with emasculated humans staring from behind barbed wire. Never in this life would I have imagined that I had something in common with Eli Cohen, whom I had met nearly seventy years earlier when both of us were preparing to fight the Nazis: me, as an American citizen; Eli, as an American citizen *and* a Jew fighting for his people.

I strolled alone silently, now seeing the camp through very different eyes. Recollections returned of starving men gulping down food but being so starved they couldn't keep it down. I might have been feeding one of my own. I felt a knot in my throat.

Soon I found a monument that was like a gravestone. The names of some of the victims had been chiseled into the black granite. Being raised a Christian, I'd stood before such headstones but had only looked. Although I had never done so before, I bent over and placed a small rock on the base of the monument, as any Jew would do.

For a long time, I stood there silently gazing at the monument.

Finally, I turned and joined Donna, Tina, and Sven on the walk back to their car. At the final gate, I stopped and placed another stone on the gateway. I kept staring behind my family at what they had walked through. Taking a deep breath, and with tears running down my cheeks, I prayed, "Let my people go."

Tina placed her hand gently on my shoulder. "Dad, for such a time as this was your generation born."

ACKNOWLEDGMENTS

Rikki Abrams has been a dear friend for a million years. A teacher to the disabled and mentally challenged, Rikki was the proofreader and offered responses to these pages. We thank Rikki for her tireless efforts and insights working on this project.

INDEX